0339342

W9-BLL-151

3

GREEK HISTORY

GREEK HISTORY

Advisory Editor:

W. R. CONNOR

CHAIRMAN, DEPARTMENT OF CLASSICS
PROFESSOR OF GREEK
PRINCETON UNIVERSITY

ASPECTS
OF THE
ANCIENT WORLD

Essays and Reviews

BY

VICTOR EHRENBERG

ARNO PRESS
A New York Times Company
New York / 1973

Reprint Edition 1973 by Arno Press Inc.

Reprinted by permission of
  Basil Blackwell & Mott Ltd.

Reprinted from a copy in
  The University of Illinois Library

Greek History
ISBN for complete set: 0-405-04775-4
See last pages of this volume for titles.

Manufactured in the United States of America

回归归

Library of Congress Cataloging in Publication Data

Ehrenberg, Victor, 1891-
  Aspects of the ancient world.

  (Greek history)
  CONTENTS: The beginnings of European history.--
The early history of the Etruscans.--The Greek country
and the Greek state. [etc.]
  1. History, Ancient--Addresses, essays, lectures.
I. Title.
D60.E5 1973   930   72-7889
ISBN 0-405-04785-1

ASPECTS OF THE ANCIENT WORLD

ASPECTS
OF THE
ANCIENT WORLD

Essays and Reviews

BY

VICTOR EHRENBERG

*Lecturer in Ancient History at Bedford College,
University of London, formerly Professor of
Ancient History at Prague University*

BASIL BLACKWELL · OXFORD
MCMXLVI

PRINTED IN GREAT BRITAIN IN THE CITY OF OXFORD
AT THE ALDEN PRESS

To my sons,
student of history and student of science,
to remind them that
history is not a science,
but the historian always the scientist's brother

CONTENTS

ILLUSTRATIONS   *facing*
                                                           page

PREFACE

THE articles collected in this volume were written between 1926 and 1945. In choosing them I deliberately took several suitable to be placed, not only before my fellow-scholars, but also before a more general public. A few of the papers, on the other hand, have the scholarly apparatus of notes and citations. I hope that each group of readers will find it possible to accept those articles which are less in their own line. My choice was also guided by the wish to print some unpublished material and to reprint some papers which had remained largely unknown because of the place of their original publication. Only one of the essays has been published in English before.

I have tried to arrange both essays and reviews in some sort of order, according to period or theme. But I did not wish to enforce upon any of the papers either the restrictions of a unifying scheme, or particular views which I hold now. If the attentive reader can trace repetition or some change of view, I do not think I need apologize for that. On the other hand, I could not see any advantages in clinging to every word as it had been written years ago. Thanks to the necessity of translating the text into English I have been able to make some alterations and additions, all intended to stress the points which I had tried to make. I have omitted a few passages which were simply connected with the occasion of the earlier publication. I have also corrected some mistakes and pointed out where anything of importance has been added.

Historical essays are a branch of literature for which the standards set in this country are very high. Writing in a language which is not my native tongue, I am aware of the difficulty, if not impossibility, of reaching those standards. Any success in that respect will be due to those friends of mine who have been good enough to give much of their time to revising various parts of my manuscript and to supplying valuable corrections and suggestions, foremost among them Professor G. B. A. Fletcher, Mr. Harold Mattingly, and Mr. B. S. Page. Mrs. McLean, the publisher's reader, contributed a number of last-minute improvements. So did my friend Raymond Preston, who read the proofs. I am deeply grateful to every one of them for their contributions, but I wish expressly to relieve them of the responsibility for anything that may be found lacking.

To Mr. Basil Blackwell I feel indebted for his willingness to publish another book of mine, despite all the restrictions of post-war-time, and to give it so pleasant an appearance. Finally, acknowledgments are due to the editors and publishers of the periodicals and books in which my articles first appeared in print. Under present circumstances, however, it has not been possible to get the formal permission to republish them except in the case of the *Durham University Journal* and *Die Antike*. Mr. C. T. Seltman and the Cambridge University Press, as well as The Oxford University Press of New York, have kindly sanctioned the reproduction of some coins from their respective books mentioned in the text.

V. E.

Bootham School, York
March 1946

I

THE BEGINNINGS OF EUROPEAN HISTORY [1]

ANY writer of Greek history, whatever the special features of his particular approach, can hardly avoid seeing that to the Greeks all life and all thought centred round the State. Art, theatre, religion, philosophy, economics, and so on, are to us matters independent of politics; in fact, we are anxious to preserve their independence — an idea which the ancient Greeks would never have understood. To them every one of these activities was essentially political, that is to say it was bound to the State, the *Polis*. To the Greeks politics as the life in and with the Polis was not a matter for professional specialists, but just life itself. It was similar, though at the same time different, in Rome where the *res publica* as an abstract power of immense strength absorbed, as it were, the individual citizen. For the Greeks, and nowhere in a more exemplary manner than in Athens, the word *politeia*, which means both citizenship and constitution, expressed the fact that the Polis was the community of the *politai*, the citizens.

The State had such importance in Greek life that this life cannot be understood without realizing the nature of the State and the part which it played in Greek history. This, however, is no isolated question. Greek history and the growth of the Polis must be seen in their relation to universal history. The Polis, not the only, though historically the most important, form of the Greek State, was the prevailing centre of history during that epoch which is usually called the classical period. But to cover the age of the Polis, the period must be extended backwards to the eighth and ninth centuries B.C., and forward to the age of Alexander. It is the period of Greek history in its narrower sense, the age dominated by Sparta and Athens. During the same period the mind has travelled the vast dis-

[1] Inaugural Lecture, given at the German University of Prague and published under the title *Vom Beginn der Geschichte Europas* (Prague, 1929). In the original lecture I spoke in more detail about my predecessor, H. Swoboda, and though this was more than the tribute of a passing moment, I do not think it would be appropriate to repeat it here.

tance between Homer and Aristotle. Here we are concerned only with Homer. That he should occur at the beginning of Greek history is sheer miracle; his poetry is perfect as a work of art, one of such great masterpieces as usually appear only at the very height of historical epochs. And indeed the contents of the Homeric poems belong to an earlier period of history, an age previous to that of the Polis. To the Homeric Greeks the State was not yet the centre of life, and no one will try to interpret Homer by means of political history and political institutions. On the other hand, Homer not only provided the foundation on which the Polis and the people of the Polis stood; he was their companion, always present to them, always alive with them, exacting a continuous and strong influence upon them. Thus he formed the eternal bridge linking the Greeks to their own past.

But Homer was more than that. While the Bible is the only book that belongs to mankind, Homer's poems are the truly European book, and neither Dante nor Shakespeare nor Goethe can contest their unique position. During the Middle Ages, it is true, Virgil, himself a genius but successor rather than originator, occupied the place which in fact belongs to the primary creator. It is Homer, the very fact of his existence, that makes the idea of Europe seem real. This European rôle of Homer cannot be explained by the contents of the stories he tells us — either by Achilles' wrath or by Odysseus' wanderings. Not even the perfection with which they are told, the greatness of the poetry, provides an adequate explanation. The essential factor, by which Homer has become both the eternal companion and teacher of the Greeks and the book of Europe, is his spiritual world, which represents something entirely new compared with the only preceding world of which we know, that of the Near East. We know nothing, and can guess only very little, of the foundations of Homer's spiritual world. The earliest period of the history of the Greek mind, the world of pre-Homeric Greece, is hidden in darkness. But it must have displayed the Greek genius in a most spectacular manner, for it ended in its greatest revelation. Still, there must have been general facts of history to which that spiritual world was bound, and it is a legitimate task for the historian to attempt an investigation of those dark times. Only then may it be possible to understand how a work of the ripest art and highest refinement can stand at the very beginning of the history of the European mind.

I am not going to describe what may be called the sociological soil and background of the Homeric poems, the world of Ionian aristocracy. Its picture has been drawn more than once. But this world, as well as the poems which grew out of it, was the result of a development of universal history. As a source from which to trace this development Homer is only of secondary importance. There are sources other than literary which enable us to say something about 'the Beginnings of European History'.

Our theme, however, needs a more precise definition. For the beginnings of European history are not identical with the beginnings of human life on the soil of Europe. Our theme will become meaningless and vanish into the fog of uncertainty, unless we recognize that the history of Europe is part of, and bound up with, the course of universal history. In speaking of the events and facts which led to a European history, we can and must leave outside our investigation all those achievements of early man which have been discovered as products of the palaeolithic and neolithic ages, or even of the bronze age, in Scandinavia and Germany, in France and Spain, in Hungary and by the Caspian Sea. I wish to emphasize that in my view prehistory is not history, although the border-line is never sharp and clear, and sometimes new discoveries have enabled us to date back the beginning of historical life. Thus, even the earliest written records do not necessarily coincide with the beginning of history; non-inscribed stones (or sherds of pottery, for that matter) can also 'speak'. But the history of the European peoples outside the Mediterranean did not begin before the time of the Romans, and the Western Mediterranean became part of history only through the peoples of the Eastern Mediterranean. For this reason we can neglect certain theories fostered, with much ingenuity and more fantasy, by prehistorians and geographers who speak of an early movement of civilization from West to East. These theories are founded on the fact that in the Mediterranean, between the East and the West very old relations of commerce existed, in which the Iberian peninsula played an important part as a goal for Eastern sailors and traders. But the importance of these relations has been very much exaggerated; they have, in fact, nothing to do with the course of universal history. The old-fashioned view still holds good that universal history first touched the soil of Europe in Greece, and that it came there from the countries and civilizations of the Near East. There was a first act of world history, not performed in Europe, although Europe determined to a large extent the later parts of the drama. The Near East, reaching from the shores of the Mediterranean to a line hardly farther East than the Western borders of India, was neither a world of its own which influenced Europe only from the outside, nor simply a field for colonial activities and cultural extension by the Europeans. During the period of antiquity the Near East belonged to the same geographical area to which the universal history of Western civilization belongs.

For this reason the Aegean Sea, Hellespont and Bosphorus, the region which nature has made the border district between Europe and Asia, became the earliest theatre of European history. The Aegean area, with its closely interwoven pattern of land and sea, with its bridge of islands from mainland to mainland, links two continents, and thus two epochs of the history of the world.

The darkness which for so many centuries obscures for us the early history of the Aegean area has been lightened, in an unexpected degree, by modern excavations. They started with the work of Heinrich Schliemann, an enthusiastic amateur, both in the good and in the bad sense, who discovered the sites of Homer's Troy and Mycenae. A historian who tries to draw a more or less complete historical picture from the results of archaeological excavations and of linguistic research, has to face the fact that he is to investigate an age which at least to us remains inarticulate, since either its peoples had no writing, or we cannot read what they wrote. A few documents from the East come to our support, chiefly by enabling us to fix the chronology of the Aegean civilizations. But, on the whole, there cannot be much doubt that any reconstruction will remain largely hypothetical, and that many questions cannot be answered. Thus we cannot help simplifying matters which probably were much more complex. I believe, however, that an attempt at a comprehensive synthesis will be useful and even necessary; it may serve as a working hypothesis, even though liable later to be refuted.

At the turn of the third to the second millennium the isolated histories of many States and nations of the Near East joined together in a common history and a common fate. Here, for the first time, we can talk of universal history. All along the Northern frontiers of the area between the Caspian Sea and the Adriatic, peoples and tribes began to move. The stage was set for the first great migration of world history, which shook and partly shattered the old powers from Troy to Babylon. New peoples appeared, new States came into existence, and eventually even the remote and almost inaccessible land of the Nile valley bowed under the yoke of foreign 'shepherd kings'. Tremendous storms, lasting for several centuries, were raging, varying in strength from place to place, but everywhere driven, as it were, by one impelling force. The North had sent out new peoples which demanded admission to the Southern world, in Iran and Armenia as well as at the Bosphorus and in Greece. The Indo-Europeans made their entry into history.

They were now the masters of the earlier inhabitants, but they remained below the level of those great civilizations which still flourished on the ancient sites of the river countries of Mesopotamia and Egypt, although these were no longer the only centres of high civilization. The empire of the Hittites made its first appearance in Asia Minor and Syria, but its ruling class, most likely of Indo-European stock, submitted almost completely to the cultural achievements of Babylon and Assur. And there was still another centre, Crete, the Southern cross-bar of the Aegean Sea. The miracle of the 'Minoan' world, as the Cretan civilization has been called, came again to light during the last generation, when Sir Arthur Evans began to dig on the site of Cnossus. Sea-power was here combined with the peaceful glamour of rich dynasts, religious fervour with frivolity and play, economic efficiency with easy-going luxury, busy town life with princely stateliness. A unique art grew up, an art of magnificent realism, of rich fantasy, of rococo-like charm. All this sprang up as from nowhere, at first confined to the narrow space of one island, but gradually radiating into the Aegean; it went through the ups and downs of a number of recognizable periods, but was nevertheless a unity from the beginning to the end, filling more than half a millennium with rare vitality and miraculous beauty. Youthfulness and ripe age seem united in this civilization, but many of its deeper and essential features remain to us an unsolved riddle — at least so long as we are not able to read what the Minoans wrote.

Crete, which is generally and rightly taken as a part of Europe, lived in this early age through the only great time of its whole history. This in itself is an astonishing fact, and it supports the view that the Minoan civilization was essentially non-European. There is a deep meaning in the story that on the back of the bull into which Zeus had changed, Europe came to Crete, and it is significant that this is a *Greek* myth. The shining light of the early Cretan civilization, bright and glorious as it is, was strange and foreign to the Aegean world. The people of Minoan Crete were connected, perhaps by race and probably by historical events, with the Philistines in Palestine. Whence these had come we do not know, though they certainly arrived from the sea. The Minoans were not Europeans, but we cannot say that they were part of the East. Seen against the other Eastern civilizations, Crete is just as unique as when compared with contemporary or later Europe. However, there were a few clear and even close bonds with Asia Minor, Syria and Egypt—bonds of trade, of religion, of social life. In particular the sultan-like life of the kings of Cnossus and Phaestus, their courts, their officials, their economy, displayed features which were similar to those of their opposite numbers in the Near East; they were equally unlike anything Western.

We are accustomed to speak of the Minoan and Mycenaean civilizations as a unity. Rightly understood, this indicates that in some sense Crete was continued in Mycenae, but it does not mean that there ever was a real unity, either political or ethnical or even cultural. What is called Mycenaean in its most general sense is represented by those numerous settlements, palaces and tombs of the second half of the second millennium which abounded in the Aegean area outside Crete, particularly on the Greek mainland. The Indo-European tribes, which in the beginning of the millennium appeared on the Northern frontier of Greece, had meanwhile entered the peninsula in several waves of invasion, everywhere subduing the original inhabitants. These men, rough warriors who still followed rather a primitive way of life, settled chiefly in the countries of Eastern Greece, but before long they crossed over to the Aegean islands and even to the Western shores of Asia Minor. In Asia the soil has not yet been sufficiently explored to enable us to come to a final verdict; odd discoveries of Mycenaean sites, especially near Miletus, do not prove a real colonization from the mainland. We must wait for further results of excavations, but it does not seem unlikely that some of the early Greeks reached Asia before the Dorian Migration forced larger groups to leave Greece and go eastwards.

The first wave of Greek immigrants probably consisted of the tribe (or combination of tribes) which later was called Ionian. In historical times they lived in the most Eastern districts of Greece proper, in Attica and Euboea, whither they had retreated as they gave way to the pressure of later immigrants. There are a few slight indications that Ionians also once lived in Central Greece and the North and East of the Peloponnesus. Ionians were afterwards the first to occupy the islands, the first also to found Greek cities on Asiatic soil. If it were certain that their name — originally *Iâvones* — appeared as early as about 1300 B.C. in an Egyptian inscription, as one of the peoples fighting with the Hittites against the Pharaoh Ramses II, this would make it almost completely certain that Ionians settled at a very early time in Asia Minor. Unfortunately the reading and interpretation of the name are much disputed. Other oriental sources do not speak of *Iâvan* before the eighth century B.C. The name appears in the list of peoples in *Genesis*, and it serves here and in other evidence as a name for the Greeks and for Greece as a whole — a clear sign of the pre-eminence of the Ionians over other Greeks at least in Asia Minor, the area nearest to the peoples of the East.

Meanwhile the Greek mainland had turned Achaean. In Thessaly, Boeotia, and above all the Argolis, we find the strongest Achaean powers. Here, the warlike chieftains of various small tribes erected their powerful citadels. Mighty ramparts, fittingly called 'Cyclopean' by the later Greeks, enclosed the palace of the chief, and, apart from it, usually sufficient space to receive and protect in case of war the people of the nearby settlement and the surrounding country. In the course of several centuries, the masters of some of these strongholds grew into powerful and wealthy dynasts — for example, in Orchomenus in Boeotia, where the stupendous

B

task of draining Lake Copais was accomplished, a task only renewed during the nineteenth century A.D. But the largest and strongest of all the citadels was situated on the hill of Mycenae, somewhat inland from the gulf of Argos. It is the town which Homer calls 'with broad streets' and 'rich of gold'. It provided the name by which we are used to call the Achaean Greeks and the age of their early greatness. Mycenae was the seat, it seems, of the most powerful of the Achaean dynasts; he was a real king. The discoveries of the archaeologists bear witness to the wealth and splendour of his royal position, and the roads radiating from Mycenae to Tiryns, to Epidaurus, to Corinth, indicate the wide area of his influence. Moreover it is the figure of Homer's 'sceptre-holding Agamemnon' which mirrors the greatness of the king of Mycenae. Undoubtedly the mightiest of the Greek kings before Troy, he is the 'lord of many peoples' who 'rules mightily over all Argives, he whom the Achaeans obey'. He represents an over-lordship as it was never known in historical Greece. And even through the transformation of Homer's poetry it is possible to trace signs in Agamemnon's position of a somewhat alien conception of divine grace; his was a kingdom by the grace of God, a form of monarchy that cannot have derived simply from that of a chieftain of Greek immigrants. Foreign, that is to say Eastern, influence had its share in creating and shaping this kingdom, and we need only look at the treasures that have been brought to light from the soil of Mycenae to realize what influence worked here, and whose position was the model of that of Agamemnon.

The Mycenaean civilization was a peculiar mixture, deriving from two widely different sources. The historical process which preceded it can easily be understood. The Greek conquerors, belonging to a primitive and prehistoric stage of civilization, were politically united only in loose communities of the sort which originate from warlike nomads. They now formed a ruling class of comparatively small numbers. There must have been much inter-marriage with the original inhabitants, and it is obvious that the people which by its genius was to found European civilization was far from being of pure race. Since the sixteenth century B.C. this ruling class had been influenced in an ever increasing degree by the magnificent civilization and art of Crete. The technique of

Cretan artists and craftsmen was accepted, and linguistic
evidence shows that various domestic utensils, which kept
their un-Greek or pre-Greek names, were taken over by the
Achaeans. Spiritual as well as material elements of alien
character intruded, gods and cults, mythological persons and
stories, sports and games. Even the words which in Greek
characterize the political position of the ruler were of foreign
origin. On the other hand, the goddesses were not so predominant over their• male partners as they were in Crete;
in fact, the highest god of the Indo-Europeans, the god of the
sky, came here into his own: Zeus, the father of gods and
men. On the whole, however, in spite of important differences,
a second and wider area of Cretan civilization was being
created. It reached its peak during the period between 1400
and 1200 b.c., the very period when the Mycenaeans over-
threw the rule of the Cretan overlords, destroyed their
beautiful palaces, and forced Crete into a decay which soon
ended in complete and lasting stagnation.

We can assume that some of the Cretan artists survived the
disaster. They came to the courts of the Mycenaean kings, and
there, in foreign surroundings, they were enabled to keep alive
their great traditions. This, however, cannot have been the
only, or even the chief, reason for the sudden and amazing rise
of Mycenaean art and culture. They culminated in an age that
in a very real sense was a 'golden' age, in which the Mycenaeans
most strikingly continued and even raised the standards of the
Cretan heritage. Here was more than mere maintaining and
copying. For the first time, the creative power of the Greeks
arose. It gave new and original life to the arts of Crete, before
it went on to express its own true genius.

The Mycenaeans lived a life widely different from that of
the Minoans. They waged war, hunted wild beasts, used
grave and serious forms of religious worship. All this became
the subject of art, as can be seen on Mycenaean frescoes, on
beautifully adorned swords, on many a gold or silver utensil.
The garments of the Cretans, products both of a Southern
climate and a strong sensuality, were not generally accepted,
neither the apron or loin-cloth of the men nor the crinoline and
open bodice of the women. Although the upper-class ladies
sometimes followed the smart fashion of Crete, we also find
both sexes wearing a simple long dress, possibly the original

of later Greek garments. The men often carried the arms and weapons of the warrior and hunter. In a fresco in Tiryns the graceful Cretan bull-game is depicted, but close to it a chariot can be seen, drawn by horses of stiff movement and measured pace. It is as if it comes from a different world, and we remember that chariot and horse were imported into the Mediterranean world by the Indo-European peoples as they pressed southwards during the second millennium. The content as well as the style of the works of art had become more virile. An aesthetic tendency towards the emphatic and monumental was revealed which formed a strong contrast to the playful grace of Minoan art and is most distinctly recognizable in architecture. Although details of decoration and sometimes even of construction followed the Cretan tradition, the manner of building on the whole was entirely different from Minoan architecture. In the large palaces of Crete a vast number of rooms of all kinds, with walls sometimes completely broken up by pillars and columns, with courts and upper floors and magazines, were united in a huge complex without any attempt at symmetry, though not without plan; all angles were right-angles, all walls parallel to the sides of the main court. It is significant of this kind of architecture that the fantastic ground-plan of the palace of Cnossus became in the memory of the later Greeks the labyrinth out of which nobody could find his way. The buildings of the Mycenaean palaces, on the other hand, display a clear ground-plan and a few clear-cut types. In contrast to the 'openness' of Cretan buildings we find everywhere a tendency towards seclusion and shutting out the world beyond the gates. The threatening ramparts, the long gorge-like ascents and narrow stairs which led from the strong outer gates to the second and third gates, the covered galleries which gave ample protection to the defenders, all the ingenious and elaborate fortifications turned a hostile face to the stranger. And the living-rooms were of similar character. There was not the variety of the airy rooms, opening one into another, that we find in Crete, where architecture was the framework of a peaceful and cultivated life. The Mycenaean palace consisted of a number of unconnected *megara*, one clumsily set beside the other. Each *megaron* was entered from a quadrangle of its own through a porch and an ante-room, beyond which lay the long and windowless interior with the warming hearth in the middle of the room. One common roof, probably gabled, covered the oblong building. This type of the *megaron* was undoubtedly a faithful copy of a type that originally belonged to the North; parallels have been found not only in Thessaly and Troy, but also in Hungary and Germany. It was imported to Greece; it is alien to Mediterranean climate, as it is a shelter against cold and rain rather than against the warm and sunny air of the South. When the invaders settled down, they kept their habitual building scheme in the new surroundings. But it changed its character. No longer an isolated and simple house, the *megaron* became an essential part of a new monumental and complex architecture. A style developed, entirely different from anything in the earlier architecture of the Mediterranean world. Facing a large and well-paved court-yard which was frequently surrounded by colonnades, strictly keeping to the principle of the middle axis in every detail of plan and structure, the *megaron* became the centre of a great architectural composition.

The same spirit which had been suggested in the lines of the ground-plan of the palace is revealed again in the imposing solemnity of the circle of vertical slabs surrounding the old royal tombs, in the noble and powerful Lion's Gate, and above all, in the imposing domes of the tholos tombs. The simple form of a beehive, native in the Mediterranean world and originally alien to the Northerners, had been accepted and shaped into a new and truly monumental form. The narrow passage of approach between high walls, the door that despite its rich decoration has good and simple lines, finally the miraculous dome the appearance of which seems comparable only with that of the Pantheon in Rome — everything combines to create the impression of monumental greatness.

It is essential to realize that the high civilization of Mycenae was based on military and political power. To confirm this, we need only look at the results of the excavations, or at the walls and ramparts still standing. But there is, it seems, other evidence too. Although evidence from contemporary Hittite sources remains scarce and doubtful, it is at least certain that a power called *Achijava* (Achaea) is mentioned in some Hittite documents; it is probable that, though it extended to Asia Minor, its centre lay farther to the West. In a treaty of the middle of the thirteenth century Achaea appears together with the great Eastern powers of Babylon, Assur, and Egypt, and more or less on equal level with these States. Some doubts remain as to whether Achaea can be taken as a 'great power' in the usual sense, as a realm of large territorial extent. It is hard to believe in an Achaean empire, for the multitude of Mycenaean castles and settlements seems the true predecessor of the multitude of the later Greek States. Moreover the almost complete lack of written records, which proves that the Mycenaean civilization was largely without the knowledge of writing, excludes the possibility that there existed a really organized empire. Agamemnon, on the other hand, the over-lord over many autonomous kings, had no equal or possible model in the period (tenth or ninth centuries) in which Homer wrote his poems. It seems obvious that Agamemnon's position reflects the real position of the king of Mycenae, the 'King of Achaea'. Particularly in war and in the relations with foreign powers, his predominance would become manifest, and the Great King in Asia might easily think of him as a 'brother', an equal of the other rulers with whom he concluded treaties.

Mycenaean Greece represents the first epoch of Greek history. In the achievements of its civilization something can be seen of the great and creative power which to us is insepar-ably connected with the idea of Hellas. At the same time, however, the prevailing dependency of Mycenaean civilization on that of Minoan Crete, with its unrivalled originality and amazing standards, reveals the grave problem which the early Greeks had to face. Was it possible that this vigorous and serious race would be able to ward off the predominant influence of the East, both past and contemporary? Could it learn from the East, without losing its own creativeness? Mycenae does not give a definite answer to these questions. Foreign influence and native character were here combined and mixed up to such an extent that both ways seemed yet to be open, that of assimilation to the East which would lead to deterioration and decline, or that of accepting the danger of temporary barbarization which would lead to a new, indepen-dent and creative civilization.

Fate, by dragging the Mycenaean Greeks into the larger conflicts of universal history, saved them from having to fight out the inner conflict between their original heritage and the

Cretan influence. An external and violent solution was forced
upon them. After the fall of Cretan sea-power only two great
powers were left in the Mediterranean area — Egypt and the
Hittite Empire. Neither stagnant Babylon, nor rising Assur,
nor any other power in Mesopotamia and Iran, was able at
that time to interfere in the West. But the Egyptians and
Hittites, after having measured their respective strengths on
the soil of Syria, concluded peace and an alliance which they
confirmed by a dynastic marriage. This coming to terms
between the two rival powers was caused by the fact that new
enemies had arisen, dangerous to both of them. Some of
these enemies came from the interior of Nearer Asia, particularly the Assyrians and Aramaeans who lived in the countries
of the upper Euphrates, in Mitanni, and threatened Northern
Syria. Others came from a different quarter. Mention has
been made of the treaty in which Achaea appears of apparently
equal rank with the powers of the East. And a few fragments
of other Hittite records seem to indicate that Hittite kings
were waging war against the rulers of Achaea. The Achaeans,
however, were only one of many peoples which in the second
half of the thirteenth century were on the move and, starting
from their homes in the Aegean area and in Asia Minor,
pushed forward towards the South and the South-East. The
'Peoples of the Sea', the 'Men from the North', against whom
Egypt had to defend herself then and later in the twelfth
century, bore names many of which have been recognized as
familiar in later periods. Among them are the Achaeans
(*Aqaivasha* in the Egyptian source) and the Danaans (*Dan-
auna*), both of them names which Homer used for the Greeks.
Possibly the various campaigns of Greeks against Hittites and
Egyptians were not more than raids to sack and plunder the
rich cities of the East. Perhaps it was only such a raid which
was to live eternally in song as the Trojan War. Seen as a
whole, however, these onslaughts were more than plunder and
piracy. The strong attacks on Egypt coincided with the sudden
and complete downfall of the Hittite Empire, and this coincidence shows that there was a common movement against both
the great powers. It is for this reason that the raids of the
'Peoples of the Sea' cannot be separated from new happenings
on the Northern frontiers of the Aegean area. A new Indo-
European invasion, the second great migration of history, had

begun to infiltrate the Mediterranean world. The peoples of
the North were on the move, once again, from the Caucasus to
the Alps. Phrygians and Mysians destroyed the Hittite
Empire in Asia Minor, the Dorian Greeks broke down the
power of the Mycenaean lords, and most of the Achaeans had
either to submit or to emigrate. It has been established that
the new immigrants did not bring iron to the Mediterranean for
the first time, as was the common view of modern scholars not
long ago. Nevertheless, a striking cultural upheaval replaced
bronze by iron. Hesiod's Heroic Age gave way to the Iron
Age, still in force in his own time four hundred years later.

The first period of history in which Greeks displayed their
power was at an end. Seen as a whole, this earliest period can
already be understood as a fight against the East. Crete had
been destroyed, the powers of Asia Minor perished through
peoples which were akin to the Greeks, Egypt kept off the
aggressors only with the greatest difficulty. But the early
Greeks, though they fought the East, never overcame it. On
the contrary, the Mycenaean civilization is the measure of the
debt which they owed to it. Now, however, a new era began.
In the East, out of the decline of earlier States, the Assyria of
Tiglatpilesar arose, carrying its terrifying power to the shores
of the Mediterranean. In Palestine the people of Israel opened
a new chapter of history. On the seas the Phoenicians tried to
cover the whole Mediterranean area with their commerce and
craftsmanship. It was too early then for this new activity of
the East to meet with resistance from the still infant West.
But it may be taken as a sort of answer, and certainly as a fact
which foreshadowed later events, that under the pressure of
the Dorian invasion of Greece the Aegean area became a
unity; it became Greek. It has recently been shown that the
artistic expression of the new age, the geometric style, was
something more than the outcome of the victory of primitive
barbarians over the dying Mycenaean civilization. But even
though the new style may have originated in the development
of the latest Mycenaean style, and though the gods and myths
of the Greeks were largely derived from Mycenaean religion
and had their sacred centres at the royal seats of Mycenaean
kings, the essence of the art and religion, and indeed of the
whole life and spirit, of the new epoch — little as is known
about it — can be understood only as an emancipation of the

later Greeks from the Mycenaean heritage. Forces broke into the open, Greek in their very character, which before had perhaps been only kept down; now, at any rate, they gathered new strength and life. This was a great and decisive moment. The events which the Greeks knew in legend as the Dorian Migration were in truth only part of an amazing transformation of the whole Mediterranean and the Near East; but they opened the way for what is called in a narrower sense Greek history, and thus indeed for the history of Europe.

Dark centuries followed, during which the Greeks slowly became what fate had destined them to be. In these centuries epic poetry grew to its prime. Its roots went back deep into the soil of the Mycenaean world; but though this connection cannot be denied, the main impression given by Iliad and Odyssey, irrefutable in spite of all analysis, is their poetical and spiritual unity, such as could be created by a single individual only. The poet whom we call Homer lived about the ninth century B.C. He was at once the exponent and the culmination of that Greek civilization which, while an heir of the Mycenaeans, had freed itself from their cultural hegemony. This is the place in history where Homer stands, and knowing this, we find the answer to the question with which we commenced. The road on which the Greeks had set foot is the road leading to man, man as a citizen *and* as an individual in his own right. Both these conceptions — if it is allowed to make a sweeping generalization — were alien to the East, which was and remained the domain of divine covenant and theocratic rule. The road on which the Greeks walked led away from everything for which the East stood. It was the road to the Polis and to political freedom, the road also of human pride instead of humility, the road leading to Heraclitus' 'I have searched myself', and Protagoras' sentence that 'Man is the measure of all things'. Thus the Greeks stood at the beginning of the history of the Western mind, forming its essential shape and initiating an eternal impulse, till the day dawned when the East came into its own once more. The same people which opened the history of Europe gave to it, from their untold wealth of creative genius, examples for all times to follow.

At this point, since we are talking about the awakening in Europe, we have to mention one other people, comparable of many ways to the Greeks, but — despite all exaggerations of their importance — much inferior in creative power. Among the 'Peoples of the Sea' which in the thirteenth century fought against the Pharaohs was one called *Tarsha* or *Tursha*, the Tyrsenians or Tyrrhenians. Later they went westwards to find a new home. The earliest date possible for their landings in Italy seems to be, according to recent research, the tenth century, although some scholars find no date trustworthy before the eighth century. Then the Tyrrhenians, apparently at first in small groups, began to invade Western Italy from the sea. They mixed with the native population, and a new people arose, the Etruscans, who up to the present day have been in many respects an enigmatic people, but were certainly of the greatest importance in the early development of Rome. We do not yet know how to fill the large gap between the thirteenth and the tenth (or even the eighth) centuries. Possibly the *Tarsha* and *Shardana* (Sardinians?) who raided Egypt were small sections only of their tribes, and the bulk of the peoples remained for several centuries in their old seats in the Aegean or in Asia Minor. We actually know of Tyrrhenian pirates who as late as the sixth century were still active on the Aegean Sea, dwelling probably in the islands of Lemnos and Imbros. At any rate, these peoples who went westwards at an early time are, apart from the Greeks, the most striking proof of the creative power that radiated from the Aegean. In the West, too, we must ring up the curtain on the great drama of European history, now to be performed. The Etruscan civilization, which marks, on Italian soil, the separation of history from prehistory, displayed features which seem strongly to support the view that its origins lay in the East. Some scholars, it is true, many of them acting unconsciously under political or scientific bias, firmly believe that the Etruscans are an indigenous Italian people. If we reject this theory, as in fact most scholars do, the history of the Etruscans provides one of the most impressive examples of Eastern influences in the West, thus teaching us how to judge the similar phenomenon in Greece or, in fact, the whole situation and history of Europe. Relations with the East, whether welcomed or declined, are indeed the greatest issue of European history from its very beginnings till the present day.

I should like to conclude this attempt at historical synthesis with a few more general remarks.

The previous discussion has, I hope, made it clear that no historian can be satisfied to use only those sources which in a narrow sense are called historical. He needs equally the results of archaeological and linguistic research. In other cases he will gratefully accept the help of the jurist, the economist, the philosopher or the theologian. By this, of course, I do not mean that those other disciplines are merely *ancillae historiae*. If I can read the signs of our own time, almost the opposite is true. We find that many people are, in fact, turning away, not without good reasons, from an over-estimate of history, at least from the claim that history can lay the foundations for a true philosophy of life. This claim is nowadays expressed by the half derogatory term of *Historismus*. But there is another claim which all historical scholarship, worthy of the name, must maintain with determination. History as a branch of scholarship deals with the whole of the past as far as it is human. This total can and must not be restricted to questions of politics and economics. We acknowledge only one subject, the history of man, and it is alive in every possible and particular form and expression of human life.

The ancient historian is, in this respect, in a special position. For ancient history is not only part of universal history, it is also part of another unity, divided into sections but nevertheless a total, the unity which we call 'the Classics'. The methods of history, philology, literary criticism, archaeology, and so on, are different, but each, as far as it is concerned with the ancient world, is part of a whole from which it is entirely inseparable and which it serves. Thus the student of the Classics may claim that he, in an important section of general scholarship, clings to, and to some extent revives, the old *universitas litterarum*, which in modern times has largely become an empty form. Perhaps the Classics, which for a considerable time in the past led the way within the 'Arts', may still be useful to other disciplines, especially for the methods they apply. This, however, will only happen if the mechanization of modern life is permeated, and to some extent at least conquered, by some sort of humanism.

A second point which I should like to stress is the following. I have several times used the expression 'synthesis', in order to describe the aims of this exposition. Many people — not only empirical scientists — dislike both the word and the idea. In this special case synthesis may fairly be called premature. But every synthesis must be premature in some sense — otherwise scholarship would cease; on the other hand, synthesis is necessary — otherwise scholarship would become meaningless and empty. A historian ought to be to some extent sceptical. He will not share the easy optimism of positivist scholars who think that a particular question can be settled finally and for ever. But he will believe that essential results are only gained from a combination of exact research and intuitional insight. To the historian this is the only possible means of distinguishing what in history is unique and particular from what belongs to mankind as a whole. Three questions must be asked for every historical fact: First, what roots has it in the past? Secondly, what is its unique and essential nature? And thirdly, what does it contain of permanent and universal value? Only by answering all three questions shall we be able to avoid Mommsen's reproach to those historians who neglect 'what happened nowhere and never'. 'This alone never grows old.'[1]

A final point. The history of Greece is inseparably bound up with the whole of ancient history. It is connected with the history of the East, it is even more closely connected with that of Rome. There is a unity of ancient history. At the same time ancient history represents the first great period of universal history. The theme that governed the beginnings of the history of Europe was maintained and continued in Hellas and Rome. Predominant always was the importance of the relations between the West and the East. Thus the foundations were laid upon which, during the Middle Ages and modern times, the civilization of Europe was gradually built. Anyone therefore who has an interest in history (and I am thinking especially of those who study mediaeval and modern history) has a kind of obligation never to forget the inseparable connection between all later times and the ancient world.

This exhortation sounds commonplace enough, but it is, I believe, necessary. A further conclusion can be added. The

---

[1] Mommsen quoted Schiller's words:
> 'Was sich nie und nirgends hat begeben,
> Das allein veraltet nie.'

It is more surprising to find such a view expressed by Mommsen than, for example, by Mr. T. S. Eliot: 'Here, the intersection of the timeless moment
is England and nowhere. Never and always.'
And: 'history is a pattern of timeless moments' (*Little Gidding*).

history of Europe as the life-story of European civilization is both a heritage from, and a contradiction to, the Near East. If we consider the way that Europe has gone we can easily find out to what extent she has all the time been influenced by the East. We need only think of the great religions to realize that the East has a share, certainly equal to that of the West, in creating the civilization and shaping the mind of Europe. We can describe the spiritual position of Europe as lying *between* East and West. This indeed gives European history its true meaning. European history is, at least to us Europeans, universal history. It is only at the present time (and we are living under the immediate impact of this fact) that Europe has become a part, admittedly a leading part, of the world. Our globe has begun to become 'Americanized' and 'Asianized'. Europe, once the only bearer of history, has entered a larger scheme of universal history. But standing as she does between Edison and Dostoevsky, between Jazz and Buddha, between America and Asia, Europe faces, in a new sense, the old and eternal problem which has determined her beginnings and her history.

II

THE EARLY HISTORY OF THE
ETRUSCANS

THE title given to this article is a translation of the title of a
book[1] which is the result of extraordinary thoroughness and
careful scholarship and has a strong claim to the attention of
ancient historians. It is full of ideas, if also of hypotheses not
ultimately proved, providing, certainly for the present writer,
abundant instruction and yet greater stimulus. The chief
question considered is the much disputed problem of the
origin and nature of the Etruscans. Dr. Schachermeyr has
collected and discussed all the scattered archaeological, linguistic and historical evidence. Moreover he has made an attempt
to explain within the framework of universal history this
particular Etruscan question, which is usually treated in complete isolation. By investigating the forms of tombs and the
customs of burial as well as the many shapes of *fibulae*, the
author has found confirmation of the view that the Etruscans
originated from the area of the Aegean and Asia Minor. He
proposes to set these results of archaeological evidence into the
framework of general history. The whole Etruscan question in
its intricate complexity had become a subject rather of divergent
beliefs than of exact research. Particularly for this reason a
universal outlook is of the greatest value. The outlook of the
writer of universal history has sometimes led to distorting
generalizations, and has therefore recently met with sharp
criticism: the critics have even attacked its basic principles. It
is, however, as dangerous in historical research to draw
analogies between various historical periods — a danger which
is sometimes apparent in this book — as it is to put on scientific
blinkers, however plausible the reasons given for them.

The outstanding conclusion reached in this book is that the
Etruscans came from Asia Minor and were not autochthonous

---

[1] *Etruskische Frühgeschichte.* By F. Schachermeyr. Berlin, 1929. This review was
published in the *Historische Zeitschrift*, vol. 146 (1932).

in Italy. We accept this result and we appreciate the imposing amount of labour which the author has put into his work. But there remains room enough for criticism; we are frequently inclined to question details, even important details, and also have some doubts about his methods. 'The Balance of the Near East', for instance, which forms the title of the first chapter, is rather questionable and contrasts strongly with Eduard Meyer's 'Period of Egypt as the Great Power'. Surprisingly enough Schachermeyr does not try to give exact dates for this epoch, but seems to refer to the age of the Ramessides (fourteenth and thirteenth centuries B.C.), which is the last great phase of the period between the two migrations. During this period the countries of the Near East and the Aegean area were interconnected in the historical unit of a real system of States. But the right formula to characterize the period seems rather that of a political dualism between Egypt and the Hittites; the balance, at any rate, was very precarious. The author's comparison with the Holy Alliance of Napoleonic days is not illuminating.

Dr. Schachermeyr contrasts the 'Balance of the Near East' with the Aegean Civilization, unfortunately called once more 'Creto Mycenaean', and thus seen too much as a unit. This probably follows, at least in part, from the assumption, which is too readily made, that there were Indo-European elements in Minoan Crete. On the whole, the treatment of the Minoan civilization is not adequate. 'Love of sports', for instance, which is called 'specifically Indo-European', is an entirely inappropriate expression in reference to the Cretan bull-game; and phrases like 'active trade-balance' or export to the 'consumer-countries' hardly agree with the political and economic conditions of the age. On the other hand, I am glad that Schachermeyr definitely applies the name of Achaeans to the Mycenaean Greeks, whose earliest wave of immigrants, probably the later Ionians, did not enter Greece before the early centuries of the second millennium. I also think it is right to make cautious, though not unduly sceptical, use of the Hittite sources for forming a picture of the rule and civilization of the Achaeans.

All this refers to events preceding and accompanying the one event which alone gave the 'Etruscans' (which was not yet their name at that time) the opportunity of emigration from Asia

Minor to the West. This event was the great movements and migrations of about 1200 B.C., called by Schachermeyr — and he is not the first to call it so — the 'Aegean Migration'. This is not a completely adequate name, since the destruction of the Hittite Empire in Asia Minor was no Aegean affair, and the direct effects of the migration actually reached far to the East. The traditional name of the 'Dorian Migration' is even less suitable, but for want of a really adequate name for this second Indo-European migration it seems better to keep the traditional name just because it is traditional.

In outlining the historical facts of the migration, the author lays particular stress on what he calls the 'phase of greatest strength', an epoch which is to be assumed in the history of every group of wandering tribes before their final settlement. Thus he sees, for instance, the Celtic, Germanic or Slavonic group in a sort of internal concentration from which it was freed by its own explosive power towards migration and dispersion. But even if we accept this general and somewhat mystical statement, it should not be pressed too far. This is certainly done when Schachermeyr talks about an entirely hypothetical and nameless 'Indo-European mother-people' somewhere in Europe as having gone through that phase of strength and thus caused the whole migration which, in fact, was a movement chiefly of the North-Western Greeks and the Dorians in the West, and of the Phrygians and Mysians in the East. We can approve the general statement about the geographical origin and direction of the migration, but Schachermeyr overestimates its power of destruction, although he tries to anticipate this criticism. In the valuable list of places of excavation (p. 32ff.) he overlooks the fact that the destruction of many of the Mycenaean settlements was neither so complete, nor so certain in date (for instance, the destruction of Tiryns), as he assumes. There is a kind of pottery which shows the decay of the Mycenaean style, and its transition to the geometric style without any sudden break. Schachermeyr knows this, but takes too little account of it historically. Moreover he connects in a categoric manner the Philistines with the Aegean Migration, declares them to be Indo-Europeans (partly because Goliath was so tall), and makes them masters of an ephemeral Cretan sea empire. It is regrettable that a critical examination which is sound in its fundamentals is so largely spoiled by exaggerations and unfounded hypotheses. The story ends by becoming completely fantastic when Schachermeyr considers the supposed savage destruction of the Mycenaean cities to be the work not of the Greeks who were already 'close to civilization' (*kulturnah*), but of barbarian tribes, among them again the Philistines who are said to have wandered through Greece before the last wave of Greek immigration. No evidence can be cited for this assumption, nor can the author explain the silence of Greek tradition by distinguishing between epic and historical memory. The way in which he describes the development of epic poetry in Greece does not carry conviction.

It is not possible to review the whole book in the same circumstantial manner, especially because nobody can make any investigation into the Etruscan problem itself without knowing and using the immense and partly unpublished archaeological material. It is, however, hardly necessary to do this because in this matter Schachermeyr provides not only subjective views, but the results of accurate and comprehensive research, although some of the suppositions in the chapters on the *necropoleis* of Asia Minor and Etruria, and on Italian pre-history, remain disputable and seem to be set forth too confidently. Were there, for instance, really Ionian tholos tombs between the twelfth and the tenth centuries, and again in the seventh? Is it an essential point that the *Iliad* ends with the burial of 'an Asiatic'? Is Schachermeyr right in opposing von Duhn (p. 153) on the method of distinguishing between Etruscan and Italic tombs? And other questions present themselves. But I firmly believe that even numerous objections to details will not upset the whole argument. A magnificent and striking story is related, full of facts and carrying conviction. If anyone still wants to deny the Asiatic origin of the Etruscans, at least he can no longer maintain that the only evidence for this view, apart from Herodotus, consists of a few linguistic parallels.

Whether the chronological results are final I cannot say; but compared with the attempts to date the Etruscan invasion of Italy, on account of the excavations, as late as the eighth century, the time-table given by Schachermeyr with its two waves of immigration provides a far more probable story. These are his dates (p. 200):

c

1000-950 First immigration: occupation of Corneto, Populonia, probably also of Caere.

950-820 Advance as far as Lake Bolsena.

about 810-800 Second immigration.

after 750 Occupation of Vulci.

In the chapter 'The Etruscans in the Mediterranean' the writer returns to the questions already treated. To explain how the Etruscans or Tyrrhenians came to migrate to Italy, the attempt had to be made to see them as part of the history of the Eastern Mediterranean. Thus it was necessary to find out whether there is evidence for their existence outside Italy. I do not propose to speak of the Hittite sources, the interpretation of which is still entirely uncertain. But the Egyptian evidence is of primary importance. An Egyptian official as early as the thirteenth century was called Juntursha; but to conclude from this name that he was of Etruscan origin is perhaps not safe and, even if true, not sufficient to justify the further conclusion that there was then in Egypt 'a fairly large colony of Etruscan foreigners'. But the well-known record of the Pharaoh Mernephta (about 1220), in which the *Tursha* or Tyrrhenians are mentioned among the enemies of Egypt, has hitherto been considered as one of the strongest documentary proofs for the 'Dorian Migration'. However, Schachermeyr — and independently von Bissing — regards the foreign troops of the Libyan dynast (whom he surprisingly and anachronistically calls the king of Cyrene) as mercenaries, and not as independent allies. If this is correct, the 'Men from the North', such as the *Akaivasha, Tursha, Luka, Sherdana* and *Shakalsha*, were not whole peoples in migration. As a further proof we can take the fact that the losses of these men, compared with those of the Libyans, are small; thus their contingents, too, can hardly have been very large. Perhaps it is even possible to explain by the assumption that these peoples were only mercenaries the peculiar fact that Achaeans and Etruscans are depicted as circumcised. This would then be less a characteristic of the peoples concerned than of mercenaries in general. Thus only the second large attack on Egypt, the one under the Pharaoh Ramses III about 1190 B.C., would derive from a real coalition between the Libyans and the 'Peoples of the Sea'. This alliance was most certainly a direct consequence of the great migration.

But I must admit that I do not feel quite satisfied with an interpretation which deals in an entirely different way with two reports which are fundamentally so much alike. We must not exclude the possibility that the small groups of the first event were small sections of peoples which in fact had been expelled from their former homes by the migration. The *Tursha* are not mentioned among the peoples of Ramses' record, and Schachermeyr (p. 229) explains convincingly why the *Tursha* chieftain, depicted here among six other captive leaders, does not prove their presence. Other reasons confirm his suggestion that the *Tursha* were not a nomad people, but had settled down before they were attacked, and perhaps overcome, by the migrants.

Following a chapter on the Etruscan language, which I must confess myself entirely incompetent to judge, Schachermeyr deals with the much disputed question of the Pelasgians. He is rightly cautious in avoiding a final judgment, but does not shrink from expressing his opinion. The Pelasgians were pre-Greeks and possibly had some connection with the Tyrrhenians who during the tenth and ninth centuries, jointly with the Phoenicians, ruled the sea as so-called pirates. The Greeks only gradually began to compete with them, while in Mycenaean times it was the Tyrrhenians who had not been able to prevail against the Achaeans; they may then still have lived in the interior of Asia Minor. At any rate, it is understandable that they are never mentioned in Greek epic.

The books ends with three more chapters, in the first of which the rather hypothetical attempt is made to place the town of Tyrsa in Mysia and thus to assume that the area of Mysia and Lydia was the original home of the Etruscans. The next chapter deals ingeniously with the relations between Asia Minor and Etruscan civilization and in particular Etruscan religion. It is important that combinations and conclusions which are commonly looked upon as the prime reason for accepting the Eastern origin of the Etruscans, are used here only to support previous arguments, and not to provide the real proofs.

Dr. Schachermeyr's book, interesting, though disputable in much of its contents, deserves praise, particularly as a proof of courage. It was courageous to attack such an immense subject: it was more than that for a historian to trespass into the domain of archaeologists and linguists, and, most dangerous of all, to intrude into the wasps' nest of Etruscology. Courageous, too, are some of the new hypotheses which enable the author to reconstruct the whole of early Etruscan history. It is the courage of genuine scholarship which is displayed in his learning and acumen as well as in his bold interpretation of historical facts.

III

THE GREEK COUNTRY AND THE GREEK STATE [1]

Books and pictures tell us of the miracle of the Greek country. Yet it reveals itself only to those who are allowed to tread its sacred soil. Poets have sung of the amazing beauty and grandeur of Greek scenery, though very few painters have attempted to reproduce it. To anyone who is alive to its wonders this landscape can tell more, perhaps even about the ancient Greeks, than many large volumes. '*Das Land der Griechen mit der Seele suchend* . . .' I venture to repeat the often quoted words of Goethe's Iphigenia because they disclose a deep knowledge of something that is more than mere nostalgia. The poet realized a fundamental and dominating fact — the degree to which the Greeks were tied to their soil and country. We who belong to a different age and different environment may reach a deeper understanding of Pindar at Olympia, of Sophocles on the Acropolis, of Homer when we look at the breakers of the blue Mediterranean Sea. We ought equally to gain from Greek geography a clearer impression of the Greeks as political beings — and political they essentially were, at least during those centuries which we call classical. The young science of political geography speaks of the State as 'a synthesis between a section of mankind and a section of the soil'. This definition makes it abundantly clear what a large part the knowledge of the natural conditions can play and ought to play in every attempt at explaining any type of State. To achieve this we are compelled to dispense with the praise of beauty, and come down to sober facts. We must approach the picture of the Greek country by means of scientific research and reasoning. It is the purpose of the following pages to describe the important political effects of the geographical position and character of the area in which the Greeks dwelt.

[1] This essay was published in *Die Antike*, vol. III (1927). There I added a map and a number of photographs of Greek scenery; but they were not closely related to any special passage of the text.

GEOGRAPHICAL POSITION

Europe is geographically nothing but a small appendix of the immense bulk of Asia. But Europe has had a history of her own which lasted for several thousand years, and she has gradually 'Europeanized' the world. The Mediterranean created truly independent geographical units when, by its bifurcation into two large valleys stretching towards the North-East and South-East, it divided the continental mass of the 'Old World' into three parts. Africa, in whose territory the torrid zone has such a dominating share, remained as a whole almost outside history; Carthage was Mediterranean rather than African, and Egypt, the exception which confirms the rule, belongs historically as well as geographically almost as much to Asia as to Africa. It was different with Europe. She is the only continent which lies completely within the temperate zone. She is, at the same time, more distinctly divided in herself than any other continent. By this double gift of nature she gained not only independence but leadership. Europe became the heart of the world.

A glance at a map will show that Europe lies open in three directions, towards the North, the West, and the South; only in the East there is no way out. Behind the immense extent of the Russian plains, which for many centuries of European history remained in silent seclusion, the boundary is formed by the towering walls of Ural and Caucasus. The steppes of the South, on the other hand, and the inhospitable shores of the sea which only the Greek colonization of the seventh century chose to call 'Hospitable Sea', the *Pontus Euxinus*, formed no gateway but for the migrations of prehistoric tribes and the brief inroads of bellicose hordes. And yet, human history took its start from the immense reservoir of the East. The hundreds of miles where continent borders on continent remained inert and dark. All the light of history was to be concentrated on that area which nature itself had made the path from Asia to Europe. There are, on the one side, the shores of Asia Minor, pushing forward to the West with their many bays and harbours, and, on the other side, the much-divided country which forms the most eastern peninsula of Europe. Innumerable islands, large and small, have preserved the coherence and configuration of the two continents, which up to a comparatively recent age of the history of the earth formed one mass of land. The islands have built a number of bridges across the narrow space of the Aegean Sea. In the South, Crete is situated 'on the cross-roads of three continents', while in the North, between the Aegean and the Black Sea, only two narrow channels separate the continents. It was at all these places that East and West met. It was by this route that men as well as gods, merchandise and new inventions as well as religious and philosophical ideas, crossed over from Asia to Europe. The position which nature and fate gave to the Greeks was indeed of outstanding historical significance. Greece was the most advanced outpost of Europe: it was open to invasion, and its victorious defence was of vital importance for Europe. Viewed, on the other hand, from Asia, Greece lay on the Western verge of the civilized world, and she was directly exposed to the impact of this world. The Greek mainland, though not rigidly separated from Europe by Alps or Pyrenees, is open only to the South and East. It was like a hand of Europe's stretched out towards Asia. It was not a fortress which by its protecting walls could ward off a hostile world, but rather a market-place throbbing with a life of the greatest vividness and variety.

Nothing seems to be less changeable than geographical position. For real changes occur only within cosmic periods and revolutions, and they cover ages compared with which the few millennia of human history shrink to nothing. Yet it is possible to say that Greece within historical times did change her position, inasmuch as the geographical conceptions changed. The position as the outpost of Europe, which has been outlined, is only seen from what we know to-day about our earth. Geographers in ancient times were bound to regard the position of Greece in a different light, because they had a different idea of the world. The names, it is true, of our continents, whatever their linguistic explanation, were coined by early Greek geographers. But to them Europe was not the continent between the Arctic, the Atlantic and the Mediterranean; it was merely formed by the Northern shores of the Mediterranean and the Black Sea, that is to say essentially by the three peninsulas of Greece, Italy and Spain, interconnected in the rear by countries which were almost unknown. Ancient

Asia was not the gigantic continent of to-day. It was chiefly the Western part of the peninsula which we call Asia Minor, the Syrian and Phoenician coastlines, and a 'hinterland' which to the knowledge or even the imagination of the ancient world hardly stretched beyond Mesopotamia, which was still within fairly easy reach of the Mediterranean. India remained a fairy-land at the end of the world. Lastly, Africa, called by the Greeks Libya like the central district of its Northern shore, was never anything but this shore, the Southern fringe of the Mediterranean — and this in spite of early and partially suc-cessful attempts by Egyptians and Carthaginians to sail round the continent.

All ancient conceptions, therefore, of geography started from the sea in the centre. The separation of the two continents of Asia and Europe was originally an artificial division into two of the continental mass which surrounded the Mediterranean Sea. 'I cannot but laugh when I see numbers of persons draw-ing maps of the world, and yet nobody having any sense to guide them. They draw the ocean as flowing all round the earth, which is an exact circle as if described by a pair of com-passes, and they make Europe and Asia of the same size.' Thus Herodotus (IV, .36), who in this passage just as in others makes fun of his predecessor Hecataeus of Miletus. Hecataeus believed that the earth was a circular disc with the centre at Delphi, and he divided it in two equal parts, a Northern half, Europe, and a Southern half, which included Asia and Libya. Thus he boldly violated the geographical facts for the sake of a theory which originated in the conception that the earth was arranged round a centre. This conception, however, shaped also the geographical ideas of Herodotus and even later writers. Greeks and Romans alike regarded the inhabited earth, the *oecumene*, as an area round the Mediterranean. This was so from the early beginnings till the *oecumene* became the universal Roman Empire. There was only one exception, Alexander's empire, which, following the outlines of the Persian Empire, was an essentially continental power. Over and over again the idea of *mare nostrum* occurred in ancient times — the same idea which governed the policy of Rome against Carthage. Its ideal goal was always the creation of a closed ring of surrounding shores, not to be broken by any foreign power. It seems justifiable to a large extent to see in this conception something typical of and fundamental for the ancient world. Classical antiquity, based on the sea, stands apart both from the early East, based on the river, and our modern world with its new continents, based on the ocean.

It is therefore inadequate to describe ancient Greece as a peninsula in the South-Eastern part of Europe. It was, in fact, the area of shores and islands which roughly forms the periphery of the Aegean Sea and the Propontis, and which modern geographers have rightly conceived as a unity under the name of the Aegean area. A small hinterland only belonged to this area, while other shores of the Mediterranean joined later and gradually. By identifying Greece as a geographical unit with the Aegean area we reduce the peninsula, which from its historical position bears the name of the Greek motherland, to only a section of this unit. The Greek world had its share in Europe as well as in Asia. Thus the separation of the two continents, in a way, becomes arbitrary. It is significant that the Greeks never succeeded in finally agreeing on a definite land frontier between Europe and Asia.

The area of the Aegean was, to a much greater extent than could be said of Greece proper, a brisk market in which all sorts of material and spiritual goods were exchanged. From our knowledge to-day we may assume that the unity of the Aegean world was almost as old as the residence of Greeks within the boundaries of the Mediterranean world. It is by this unity that the Greeks were enabled to fulfil their historical task. An area of the ordinary continental type would never have become a link between two worlds to the same extent as this fringe of open shores round a sea full of islands. The Greeks did not simply receive the gifts of the ancient civilizations of the East in order to transfer them to the European hinterland. They assimilated what they received, and in their own world it was re-born to a new and different life. We can say that, in a sense, the Aegean area was responsible for the opposition of the Greeks to the East which brought about the first revelation of the creative civilization of the West, and equally for the unique independence and greatness of Greek civilization, which often tend to disguise the Eastern influences which the Greeks actually underwent. There are two vital factors — the Aegean area as an ethnical and cultural unity with a share in both continents, and the separation of the coasts with only a bridge of islands to connect them. The two factors, though apparently contradictory, belong together; a third must be added: the Greek genius.

The unity of the Aegean area is the basis from which the world of the ancient Greeks must be explained. This unity never became a political unity; the multitude of independent States was never overcome. Their individual position within the Aegean area had its influence on their history, according to a law which follows of necessity from the geography of the whole area. Those districts which, in agreement with the general trend of the Aegean area, turned their faces towards the interior, that is to say towards the sea, were the protagonists of a strong and creative civilization. To them the sea was the centre of their life, though not of their territory. The districts of Western Greece and certain more or less continental districts like Arcadia and Thessaly, that is to say the States without a really Aegean position, either were second-rate powers or made a very late appearance in the course of Greek history. Western Greece did not even awake when, through the colonization of Sicily and Southern Italy, the Ionian Sea was included in the Greek area.

It has become usual to lay stress on this kind of differentiation, which is based on the geographical position of each individual State. But it must not be overlooked that every Greek State, even the most remote, had some share in the unity of the Aegean area, and therefore also in the position which the area as a whole held within the known world. This share was not only based on commerce and traffic, on colonies and cleruchies, and on schemes of political leadership. Its firmest foundation was the psychological fact that the citizens of every Greek State knew that they were part of a whole. The pride of being Greek and belonging to a Greek world in the midst of barbarians, went beyond all political frontiers. All Greeks had this in common that they knew of their ethnical and cultural bonds, and this went back ultimately to the fact that the Aegean area turned towards the common centre of the sea. Small wonder that the Greek State differed from the political forms of both East and West.

MOUNTAINS AND SEA

Mountains were once formed by geological folds of the earth, some big plateaux sinking, while others rose. The sea deeply invaded the land, or flooded earlier valleys. Some rivers dug deep ravines, others filled wide bays of the sea. Volcanic eruptions created mountains and islands. By a number of such events in the long history of the earth, the coherent mass that once connected Europe and Asia was changed into a country distinguished by a restless variety. In the Greek landscape, in its mountains and plains and valleys, its islands and peninsulas, a writing can be read, perhaps more clearly than in most other parts of our earth, that tells of the gigantic revolutions which occurred long before all human history. The result of these revolutions is that land and sea have each entered the other's sphere, and now form one common area.

Greece proper, emerging from the continental mass of the Illyro-Thracian area, becomes more and more divided and dissolved, the further it extends to the South. The whole is called the Balkan *peninsula* on account of its situation between the Adriatic and the Black Sea; but this situation had almost no influence on its nature. The Balkans are a continental country. Only in its Southern part, in Greece, through a process of ever growing intensity, does the mainland become a peninsula, while peninsulas become islands. This is Greece seen horizontally. Seen vertically it is equally varied. The mountain system which fills the Western Balkans is continued in a magnificent curve which stretches through Greece over the Aegean islands into Western Asia Minor. This is the spine from which individual mountain chains keep emerging eastwards like ribs, encompassing the area of Eastern Greece. These diverging mountain ranges determine the structure of the country. But there are also the results of geological destruction — zones of disruption and mighty upthrusts, both of which occurred in comparatively recent periods of the history of the earth. As a result, the whole area became a crisscross of mountains, hilly lands, and plains. Wherever the sea entered this land of many contours, a coast-line was created, as varied and fantastically divided as can be imagined. The zone of the Gulfs of Patras and Corinth, continued to the East in the Saronian Gulf, is of particular importance. It separates the Peloponnesus from the mainland, and it is in this zone that we find the economically outstanding cities of Greece. Moreover, the Corinthian Gulf was finally responsible for the dualism of Greek history — the division between Sparta and Athens. And since the same gulf made the Peloponnesus almost safe from military invasion, it was at least one of the reasons why national unity against Persia was never fully accomplished.

No place in the Peloponnesus or in Central Greece was farther away from the sea in ancient times than a two days' journey, and Arcadia was the only district, apart from the small Doris, which did not border on the sea. In many places between islands and peninsulas, the sea was the common, if not the only, way of communication between one human settlement and the next. Thus, the mainland was and is everywhere strangely and decisively broken up, but the same is true of the sea. Nowhere did the sailor lose sight of land, and in early times sea-traffic cautiously groped its way from island to island and from shore to shore. The sea, to us Northerners a symbol of infinity, is something essentially different in the Aegean; it hardly ever passes the narrow limits of sight to disappear into the sky of the horizon. The high cliffs of the shores appear to the eye even nearer than they are because of the transparent visibility of the Greek air and the bright rays of the Greek sun. It is indeed the sea which, by interpenetration with the land, created the unity of the Aegean world from the Thracian coast to Crete and from Byzantium to Corcyra. Every island and every district of the mainland was but a section of that whole. It was the sea that created a widespread economic unity in which a people originally purely agrarian learned to go forth in ships and to found colonies. It was the sea that was essential in the creation of a civilization which was to be neither Milesian nor Athenian, but Greek; a civilization overriding the boundaries of the States, and thus keeping alive the Greek people as the people of one area, the 'people of Greece'.

The statement, however, that water does not separate but binds together, is valid only to a limited extent. First, man must conquer the sea. It becomes a bridge only when it serves. Although that stage was reached at a comparatively early period, there was never more than a small section of the Greeks which ventured to follow the sea. Hesiod, who regarded his

short crossing from Aulis to Euboea as an important event and
almost a heroic deed, was not unique in cautioning men against
the sea. Even when their trade and traffic reached a peak, the
vast majority of the Greeks were still peasants, and this was
true not only of more or less continental districts such as
Boeotia or Arcadia but also of Attica and even of most of the
islands. Where man is bound to the soil by the work of his
hands, where all his wealth consists in his own piece of land
and in what it yields, he does not think of going to sea.
Although the sea was a link and a means towards unity as
far as the exchange of goods both material and spiritual was
concerned, to the formation of political units it set up almost
insurmountable barriers.

Mountains combined with seas to check any but casual
advances. Sending a cargo across a channel or a few loads along
a mountain mule-track is very different from extending the
political power of a State beyond the natural boundaries of sea
and mountains. In those areas which had no outstanding
political centres and therefore no real means of expressing
common political aims, growth over and beyond the natural
space was obviously impossible. But even where political life
had been shaped more firmly, it had usually to stop in face of
the natural frontiers. How long it took Athens to gain a
firm hold on Salamis or Euboea! The same sea bound together
the innumerable parts and particles of the Greek world, and
yet made each single one survive as an independent unit.

The sea, however, could not have separated and isolated the
political units as it did, had the land offered the chance of
creating a really great power. Such a power, and it alone,
could overcome the obstacles which the sea provided. As it
was, the country was divided into many small areas which were
separated by mountains, and the Greek tribes, differing among
themselves in character and history, were in addition split into
innumerable political communities, all of which were bound
to be rather weak. Not only were the natural regions severed
from one another by nature, but also each one was again
subdivided into mountains and plains, which in their continual
alternation created many opportunities both for settlement and
traffic and made possible many varieties of political growth.
Thessaly was the only Greek district which contained plains so
large that they might possibly lead to a considerable area being

united as one political unit. But in Thessaly, half-way between the real Hellas and the half-Greeks of Illyricum and Macedon, conditions were different from the ordinary, and especially affected the social structure which was based upon the feudalism of great landowners. In the other parts of Greece there were no large plains. Even the valleys of the larger rivers are either ravines in which the water breaks through the mountains, or are interrupted and divided by various mountain ranges. Only the basin of the Eurotas, although it, too, is interrupted by hills, displayed a unity which enabled it to form the centre of that State which alone among all Greek States was essentially based on an extensive and coherent territory. But even Sparta's power, although it included Taygetos, remained restricted by the Argive and Arcadian mountains. In a similar way, every settlement found in its mountain barriers a surrounding belt to form its frontier and provide protection. On such a natural foundation a number of political units could grow and consolidate in isolation from each other. It is one of the most obvious and almost elementary factors which shaped Greek history that the natural formation of the country made political particularism a necessity. But it is equally true that this particularism frequently went farther than the natural conditions demanded. Its effects could be overcome by a single ruling power only temporarily, if at all.

There is a further point. Greece was never a rich country. The character of the landscape is largely determined by the preponderance of mountains, which mainly consist of fissured and porous limestone. That is the reason why the larger part of the country has no springs and cannot be cultivated. At some places things may have been slightly better in ancient times; the mountains then were not yet deforested to quite the same fatal extent as to-day, and there was therefore sometimes cultivable soil where now nothing is left but bare rock. But the general picture was not very different from that of to-day. No large forests now exist except in the mountains of the North-West. More frequently, in particular on the rounded summits of medium height, there are stretches of high, evergreen bushes. But wide and waterless areas either show the bare rock, or are covered like a steppe with low, dry shrubs. Cultivated plants such as vine and olive grow only in the fertile plains. Significant for the whole vegetation of Greece

are the sudden changes from one kind to another, caused by the
geological conditions. Subtropical abundance and desert-like
barrenness often lie side by side almost without any transition.
The differences in height are responsible for great differences
in climate, which is no less influenced by the strong contrasts
between Eastern and Western Greece and between summer
and winter. They lead to a great variety of winds, tempera-
tures, and intensities of rainfall. All these factors have collabor-
ated in saving man from becoming soft and weak. Even in the
plains, where alone an intense life is possible, men remained
for a long time a hardy race. Here the long summer with its
dry and rarely oppressive heat brought human life into close
and continuous contact with nature. Even the townsman lived
very largely an outdoor life, and there was little social activity
inside the house. The nature of man and State alike was
strongly influenced by these facts. It is notable, at the same
time, that owing to the variety of climate and vegetation a
uniform way of life was possible only within small areas. Since
natural conditions varied from place to place, the ways of life
differed even among neighbours. The soil was at the bottom
of the lack of political unity.

It is a matter of course that the economic and social conditions equally depended on these natural conditions. Even to-
day, when the methods of commerce and communication
have, after all, made progress since ancient times, the difference
between the townsfolk and — to a smaller extent — the farmers
on the plain on the one hand, the shepherds in the mountains on
the other, is probably larger than any class difference in the
capitalistic Western world. There was another factor which
enhanced the general disunion. Each single settlement was
driven on by the desire to be independent. Village became
town, and town became State — that State which was essentially characterized by the facts of political and religious autonomy, and the ideals of economic and spiritual autarky. In the
process from which the Greek States emerged, a violent
individualism was at work. Thus the *Polis*, the State centred
on a single urban community, the city-State, became the
typical form of the Greek State. But the Polis, while still in its
cradle, suffered a tragic fate. The close union of town and
countryside led to an accumulation, both social and political,
of dangerously explosive material. There was a process of

breaking-up, which did not stop at the State, but eventually extended to society and the individual. The individualism of the States, which prevented a Greek nation from coming into being, developed into the individualism of men, which at last destroyed the State.

NARROWNESS OF SPACE

Space is the necessary frame for every political community. There can be no State without the area which it covers — its territory. Aristotle's first definition of the State is 'to live in a common locality' (κοινωνία τόπου). By this expression he does not merely indicate the close connection between community and soil as contrasted with nomadism. He thinks also and above all of the firm unity which compels every political community to fill up all the available space and to extend its territory to its natural boundaries. It is almost a historical law that the political frontiers tend to coincide with the natural frontiers. This law is carried out most swiftly and completely where, as in Greece, a larger area is divided into numerous small parts and particles. Apart from Sparta, which in all its aspects remains unique in the Greek world, Athens was the only State the territory of which was identical with the whole district, however much it was divided by mountains and hills. The territory of Athens was Attica, and it was not larger than Luxembourg. The territories of most of the other Greek States can be compared with those of the Free Cities in Germany or the smaller cantons of Switzerland. The Aegean area as a whole, though not so very small, is divided into sections which were small even before the age of railways and steamships. There is, in fact, no large expanse, either of land or sea, which is not interrupted, no plain nor any part of the sea that can be called spacious. 'On my return from Asia, when I sailed from Aegina to Megara, I began to look round. Behind me was Aegina, in front of me Megara, to my right the Piraeus, to my left Corinth.' The man who wrote this was a friend of Cicero, a Roman of the late Republic which ruled almost the whole world. He found it remarkable that at the same time he could look upon four States which once had been independent. No Greek would have wondered at that.

The Greeks found the fulfilment of their political aims within small, even tiny, areas. As it was easy to know and exploit all the natural resources and possibilities of such areas their political form was stabilized at an early date and their political individuality strongly developed. Starting from urban settlements, which were built within narrow boundaries and set in the many small plains of the Greek world, the States soon expanded into such narrow spaces as were open to them. Wherever the basis formed by the fertile plain was too narrow or in too unfavourable a position, the desire and the strength necessary to build a State usually weakened and came to nothing. Peasants and shepherds who had to wage a bitter, endless fight with the waterless sterility of the soil never outgrew a form of settlement which consisted of scattered villages and farms. There was no urban centre, and the tribe was held together, if at all, only by the adherence to a common place of religious worship. If, on the other hand, a city, though situated in a small plain, was lacking in sufficient hinterland, the State was cut off from its main source of population. In such a case — as is shown by the example of Corinth compared, for instance, with Athens — the State, despite all its economic prosperity and a geographical position of unique advantage, did not become one of the great powers.

The chief factor that determined the character of all the Greek regions and States was the smallness of their territories. Thus it often happened that quite a small section of a tribe would found and maintain a State of its own. The population of such a small area, which could contain only restricted numbers of men, quickly became a firm political community, a State, in which most men would know each other personally. The individual citizen was made to realize at every moment and in everything that the community was indeed a common interest. All who had a share in the same State lived under essentially the same conditions, and, in spite of all natural and inevitable differences, their beliefs, thoughts and desires were largely the same. Every individual saw that the same boundaries confined his own existence and that of the other citizens. The will of the individual was dominated by the will of the community, that is to say by the fact that there was a State. A type of man was created which was uniform in one respect; it was characterized by that close union between

D

every citizen and the State, which prevented the individual from being no more than an individual. Hence arose the strong patriotism of the Greeks which was the expression of an almost complete unity between political life and life as a whole. To sum up we can say that in the small area of the Greek State man became a 'political animal'. If that happened in large territories at all, it did so much more slowly and with far less intensity.

With this is connected another fact, which leads us a step further. The political, economic and cultural possibilities of a small territory could be easily perceived and fully developed. No spot of fertile soil remained untilled, no habitable region empty. The same was true of the political and intellectual soil. Everything was close together, and therefore every part, whether material or spiritual, had a share in the whole. The life of such a community, with its dense population, pulsated strongly and soon reached its prime. The development of each community took its own line, in accordance with the conditions of its special piece of territory and the nature of the men living there. Thus every State gained a strong individuality of its own. The unity within the narrow space created a conscious political will of remarkable strength, and this again unleashed powerful instincts which caused mutual competition and restless rivalry. The history of the Greeks as well as the life of every individual citizen was largely shaped and determined by these instincts. The citizen found his highest aim in gaining the olive-branch of gymnastic victory at a Panhellenic festival for the glory of his own State. The States, on the other hand, lived in such a close proximity to one another, that no natural and political boundaries could exclude strife and struggle, while at the same time every State was fully aware of the resources and the power of its neighbour. In this, Sparta was again the exception; she was notorious for keeping secret all her institutions and domestic affairs. The general rivalry caused countless wars and, on the other hand, attempts at creating some sort of balance — a fatal combination which in turn led to the dualism of the Greek world in the Peloponnesian War.

We have seen that each State had its own strong individuality, that its area was swiftly and completely filled, that strong tension was the normal state of affairs on most of the inner-Hellenic frontiers, that man became wholly political. All this combined to give each of these small communities an important history of its own. Moreover, to these small States it was given once at least to play a decisive part in universal history — in fact, to become for a time the exponents of history. That can teach us something more. In speaking of small and large States we ought not to be satisfied with stating the absolute extent of the various areas. There is a relativity of space even in the world of history and politics. The Athenian State covered a territory as large or as small as that of Luxembourg. But the two territories are different in their very natures, not only because Attica was a country in a different situation, inhabited by a different kind of people at a different historical period, but above all because the thousand square miles of Attica in the historical conditions of time and space formed a 'great power', which Luxembourg never has been and never will be. The impact of space on men and times changes, and the narrowness of Greek conditions could give the character and the importance of a large area to a territory which, by the standards of every other period of history, was small.

Narrow space, on the other hand, always remains narrow. The Greeks realized this for the first time when they found that narrow space could become too narrow, when the area no longer provided either sufficient food or sufficient room for a population which through natural increase grew steadily. The territory of the State could no longer hold and digest the surplus. That happened at different times and in varying degrees in the various Greek States, but the problem was always there as a necessary consequence of the natural conditions. The philosophers, when they outlined their ideal States, came to the conclusion that the numbers of the population ought to be constant. That, of course, was no solution, although we find the explanation of this impracticable idea in the smallness of the State's territory. For centuries, the only possible solution was pressed almost everywhere upon the Greeks. The narrowness of space was mitigated by a natural complement of far-reaching effects — the permeation of the whole Greek area by the sea. The State, confined within a narrow space but with access to the sea, gave a powerful impulse to commerce and colonization. The Greek colonists set out across a sea which was everywhere interrupted by islands and shores. Thus by a gradual process new places of settlement were seized, although the nearest places were not always the first to be colonized. The colonization was not the work of the common will of a whole people; it grew out of the temporary conditions of many individual States. This is an example of a fundamental fact of history. Seafare, sea-trade, piracy, and colonization — as distinct from conquest abroad — rarely originate from large continental countries which have sufficient opportunities for internal economy, internal trade and internal settlement. They rather derive from the limitations and the insularity, the exhaustion and the overcrowding, of small areas.

We have realized that small areas necessarily lead to a high density of population as well as a high intensity of life, both economic and spiritual. But the concentration in space is bound to be also a concentration in time. In narrow areas the life of man and the life of the State run out at greater speed. A swift rise, a short and brilliant prime, an early old age — that was the fate of the Greeks. The moment came when the limited strength of the area was exhausted, when the isolation brought inbreeding both of men and minds, when natural progress was hampered and checked by boundaries which had become too narrow, when life therefore grew petty and futile, institutions lost their meaning, and the rivalry of the States was nothing more than senseless quarrelling. At that moment the State was destroyed by the narrowness of its living space.

To avoid this end, the only salvation was the extension of the territory, and for the Greeks there was only one way out, the sea. In almost every Greek State there was a strong tendency to get down to the sea, although everywhere it had to fight against the natural opposition of the farmer population. Trade tried to go by sea, wherever it was practicable. Seldom was a road built in the interior, and the people who lived near the shore usually took the lead in politics. The moment had come when every State tried to overcome its isolation and insularity. Trade and colonization paved the way, and politics followed. Miletus, Ephesus, Corinth, Aegina, Athens, are examples — none of them more consistent or successful than Athens. In early times she had extended her political frontiers to the natural frontiers of Attica. Later, under the guidance of a great statesman, Themistocles, she became a sea-power. The voluntary offer of her fighting allies gave her the chance of leadership, first against Persia and then within the Aegean world. It is no real contradiction that Athens soon, in a kind of inevitable aggressiveness, began to monopolize the sea and to make it part of her territory. But even Athens never attained more than a temporary and tyrannical hegemony. The Athenian Confederacy was the rule of Athens over a wide area, but it never became a true empire, because it never became one State. The most spectacular attempt of any Greek State to go beyond its narrow frontiers by extension oversea did not achieve its aims. Greece perished because of the smallness of her political formations.

But there is something more to be said. An area such as the Aegean, which owes its name and its nature to the fact that its centre is the Aegean Sea, is of necessity lacking in any wide geographical horizon. Narrowness then was a typical feature not only of the individual Greek State, but also of the whole Greek part of the Mediterranean. This situation changed only very slowly through the colonization from the ninth to the seventh century when the Greeks found outlets from the Aegean into a larger world. Even when the Greek view came to take in Black Sea and Mediterranean as a whole, the sea was still at the centre of their lives and thoughts. To the Greeks the *Periplus*, or circumnavigation, meant something completely different from what it meant, say, to Vasco da Gama. He tried to discover the boundaries of the earth, they those of the sea. It was a vital fact that the Greeks, at least those on the mainland and the islands, knew of no other political neighbours but Greeks. In Asia Minor alone they came to realize the immediate neighbourhood of large empires. The experience of the Persian Wars made most of the Greeks aware of the contrast between themselves and a large continental power. But even then the Greeks did not see in Persia anything but the despised despotism of the barbarian East; that is to say, they judged the great empire entirely and only from the standards of their own cultural self-reliance and political narrowness. The Macedonian Alexander was the first who, though an heir to Greek culture, learnt how 'to think in continents'. This is one reason among others why he actually brought about the great *peripeteia* of the Greek world, by which the Polis lost all its significance and importance.

THE PEOPLE

A glance at a political map of ancient Greece (if there were one of sufficient accuracy) would disclose that there were many more political than natural frontiers, more States than geographical districts. This fact clearly confirms the view that politics and history can never be explained merely by the geographical conditions. The 'natural environment' (*Naturlandschaft*) is the material which is used by man, who is the creator of every political and cultural development. Every group of men has a complex character of its own, formed during the pre-State period and displayed in race, language, religion, politics and economics. Thus, man creates the 'cultural environment' (*Kulturlandschaft*) as the fertile soil on which the State is to grow and live. It is this kind of 'landscape' that we are trying to describe in ancient Greece, and our interpretation of the geographical facts has throughout taken into consideration the work done by man. The aim is to show what man has made out of what nature had given him. It would be of little use in this connection systematically to separate natural and cultural environment. For the only point in question is to find out the historical effects of their combined impact. Still, after having laid the whole stress on the natural and geographical factors, we ought to outline in brief what other factors were essential in the formation of the Greek State.

The first of these was the people, its 'race' and ethnical composition. The Greeks were immigrants to their country. Before they came, the Aegean area was inhabited by a pre-Indo-European population which in itself varied in origin and cultural level. On one occasion the pre-Greeks reached an epoch in which man's genius displayed itself at its greatest — in the realm and civilization of Minoan Crete. The same island of Crete did not play any important part in the politics or the civilization of the Greek centuries, either during the mainly Aegean period of Greek history, the time of the Polis, or during the Hellenistic Age when Rhodes and Delos gained the position which one might have thought was due to Crete. The most likely explanation of this strange development is the ethnical factor. In the second great inroad of Greek

tribes Crete became Dorian, and then sank into a state of
stagnation with very little evidence of cultural achievements
during many centuries to follow. But it was through Dorians,
men of the same stock, that Corinth became a rich centre of
trade and traffic, that Sparta was to grow into a State of
warriors and the strongest political power of Greece, that in
Southern Italy some of the most prosperous and most luxurious
colonies were to be founded. Nobody then will think of taking
the ethnical factor alone as being decisive, but its relevance
cannot be denied.

The first wave of Greek invaders, the Achaeans, made the
Aegean a Greek sea. The second wave followed, the Dorian
Migration, which was reflected in the heroic legend of the
return of the Heraclidae. When the last immediate effect of
the migration had quieted down, the peculiar distribution of
tribes and dialects had taken place which is the basis of our
knowledge of Greek history during the dark centuries. It is
impossible to explain by the nature of geographical conditions
alone why, for example, Thessalians and Boeotians used an
Aeolian dialect which belonged to the Achaean stratum and
showed only a slight infiltration of Dorian, while several districts between them were purely Dorian. These found their
continuation in Megara and the Peloponnesus, while Attica,
though situated between Boeotia and Megara, preserved its
pure Ionian dialect to such a degree that Athens was regarded
as the metropolis or mother-city of the Ionians, and the
Athenians firmly believed that they were indigenous. Sometimes, the frontiers formed by sea and mountains coincided
with the linguistic frontiers; but it is more important to
realize that to some extent the general variety of the Greek
world was derived from the differences in ethnical origin and in
language. The variety of dialects worked with the political
independence of each of the many States against any possible
unification of the whole of Greece.

During the period of immigration it was the tribe that
counted politically. The States derived from the tribes, and
the subdivisions of the tribe became those of the State. The
phylae and *phratriae* into which, as far as is known, every Greek
State was divided, had their origin in the period of migration
when life was largely ruled by military organization and family
law. Thus they had no connection with the act of settling nor

with the soil of the new State. Only after a period during which men settled down and the State was consolidated, could a regional division emerge to give full effect to the 'law of the soil'. This process, however, was complicated by the changes of social structure. As early as the time of the migration a class of nobles separated from the community of all free men and found a new form of common life in a fellowship, later called *hetaeria*, which was a group of men bound together by military comradeship and erotic ties. This community was from the beginning opposed to any general system of society, whether political or regional. From the society of the noblemen, which dominates the social picture of Homer, arose the *genos* or clan, as a product of the forces of family law which had gained strength in the settled community of the growing State. The clan was the form in which the nobility entered the State as an integral part. It had a local centre in the residence of the patriarch, the leader of the clan, and thus, for the first time, elements of kinship and elements of local ties grew together. Out of the class of noble families, though in opposition to it, the new political and social structure developed, the State, which was a fellowship of all its citizens.

The process of settling down involved a close connection between each individual and the soil. This was achieved, among the Greeks no less than among most peoples of early times which conquered or colonized new territory, by the division of the area into more or less equal 'lots'. Private property in land, although at first without the right of free disposal, was the foundation on which the Greek State was built. Even where the principle of assigning allotments of land was not carried out immediately and completely, the stage of collective property in land was passed at an early date, if it ever existed at all. The individualism of the Greeks, nourished as it was by the formation of their country and their own national character, soon completely removed the tribe and the clan from the ownership of land, whether the settlers lived in villages on a loose regional basis, or round the urban centre of the Polis.

Among the landowners to whom a share — in fact, a large and special share — was granted from the beginning were the kings and the gods. The latter migrated to their new homes with the people, tribe, phyle, or phratry, to which they traditionally belonged. These gods came as invaders to take their place beside the indigenous deities who as gods of agrarian labour or 'chthonic' darkness were closely bound to the soil. The religion of the Greek State was decisively shaped by the fact that its gods, though of different origin, were included in one Pantheon. It was no simple and straightforward process, and it seems worth while to point out its two most remarkable aspects. One was that after the Greeks had settled, the gods of the migrating people were worshipped at certain fixed places, were frequently identified with the ancient lords of the country, and thus received the surnames by which one Zeus was distinguished from another Zeus, one Apollo from another Apollo. The second was that only in the divine hierarchy of Homer's Olympus did the gods emerge, free from their attachment to the soil, as those great unfettered figures who lived in mythology and art and who so largely determined what was typical in Greek religion. Both aspects were united when the various and heterogeneous elements from which the whole community arose coalesced in the unity of the Polis.

VARIETY AND UNITY

We have tried to discuss the most important historical aspects of the rise of the Greek State. It appears that the influence of the geographical surroundings was to some extent balanced by the influence of other factors. But it is most remarkable that the two fundamental and contrasting features of Greek geography, its variety and its unity, were reflected in the historical process itself. Even apart from the effects of geographical conditions, variety and unity seem to have shaped everything. That is the reason why in the general picture of the Greek mind as well as in the course of Greek history a twofold character and a twofold trend can be noticed. The most striking expression of this dualism is found in the two great epochs of Greek history, the Age of the Polis and the Hellenistic Age. But the same phenomenon can be detected within each of the two epochs and, in fact, within all divisions of the life and the mind of the Greeks.

The unique position of Sparta within the world of the Greek States was not caused, as is sometimes assumed, by the fact

that the Spartans conquered their country. It was based on a
peculiar and unique relation between the State and its territory.
There were a few Greek States which never went overseas.
But in Sparta alone was this the fundamental principle of a
vigorous policy. Sparta was driven to seafaring only by the
ambition of a few great men among her leaders, and even then
only temporarily. Sparta tried to fight the narrowness of
space on land. She was the only Greek State which consciously
and exclusively pursued a territorial policy — a policy, in fact,
beyond her strength. While everywhere else the smallness
of the territory led to over-population, an intensified way of
life, and finally to expansion, Sparta's comparatively large
territory was ruled by a dangerously small number of citizens.
This explains, at least partially, why Sparta, despite its mili-
taristic spirit, pursued a fundamentally peaceful foreign policy
from about the middle of the sixth century. At that time the
State, within its extended frontiers, had reached the stage of
saturation. The extension of the territory did not, however,
influence the essential character of the ruling citizens, the
Spartiates. While the enslaved masses of the helots tilled the
soil, in Sparta itself a new form of narrow concentration of life
was created, that rigid and complete system of militarized
in-breeding which eventually destroyed both the numbers and
the spirit of the Spartiates.

The slow-moving mechanism of Sparta was the result of a
sublime quixotry, derived from the warlike and primitive
conquerors, but later shaped by the will of statesmanlike
rulers. It had a second chance when the attempt of Athens
to extend her power overseas had failed. Political discipline
might restore the forces which had been destroyed, and were
still being destroyed, by the effects of the small area. Political
theory took Sparta's system as a model and turned it into an
ideal. One point now emphasized was that the ideal State
must be removed from the sea. 'It is agreeable enough to
have the sea at one's door in daily life; but, for all that, it is, in
very truth, a "briny" and bitter "neighbour".'[1] Thus, with
words borrowed from the Spartan poet Alcman, Plato, in his
comparatively realistic picture of an ideal State in the *Laws*,
cautions the founders of a new State against the sea. Land and
sea had joined to create the Greek State, its variety as well as

[1] *Legg.* 705a. Translation by A. E. Taylor.

its narrowness. The philosopher, in ruling out the sea, was trying to get back to that narrowness which was one main aspect of the real State; but he was excluding its other aspect, as vital as the first one — its variety.

It is, however, open to question whether the elimination of variety for the sake of an ideal unity contradicted reality to such an extent as it seems at first sight. Plato and Aristotle were *politai* themselves, citizens of a Polis; but their theory — a word which meant 'beholding' rather than abstract thought — went beyond the limits of their own city and deeper than a mere knowledge of the variety of States. Not only Plato's intuition, but also the empiricism of Aristotle, who had studied an immense number of individual States, discovered the real truth, the unity behind the variety.

The multitude of Greek districts as well as the larger multitude of Greek States was an outcome of the nature of the land and its inhabitants. Between the loose community of a tribe settled in villages and the closely built-up area of a large city, between a purely agrarian State and an emporium as a centre of trade and commerce, between the rule of a class of noble landowners and the sovereignty of an urban mob — every possible form between these extremes existed within the Greek world at some place and at some time. We see a picture of inexhaustible variety, the wealth of which was equally responsible for the striking vitality of a unique civilization and the tragedy of a history which ran to its unhappy end with amazing speed. And yet, the face which looks at us through all the troubles of history has the features of quiet majesty. Behind the variety there was always the unity of Greek life and the unity of Greek man. The Greek, by nature as well as by tradition and history, was, above all, a 'political animal', and the unity of which we are speaking grew out of the political community. The State was the framework of that unity and therefore itself an expression of unity. Among all the variety of political forms and political aims the searching mind will find the Polis as *the* Greek State. All the individual States were, in a sense, only antecedents or variations of the Polis.

To find out what was the essence of the unity of the Polis, we need other guides than the philosophers. For this essence is not something ideal; it is a reality as it was shaped by life and history. Philosophical thought at a time when democracy had degenerated could take Sparta with its mixture of primitive and artificial features as the perfect form of the Polis. And an aristocrat like Jacob Burckhardt could repeat this judgment, although coloured by his own liberal point of view. In truth it was Athens which came nearest to perfection. Here Greek art and thought reached their peak because it was here that man and State, more closely than anywhere else, approached the goal that fate had set.

This is the picture of the Polis in its essentials: a community, free and autonomous, self-contained and self-reliant, centred locally round the city, spiritually round the god of the city, a unity in small space. The picture seems almost a repetition of that picture which we have in mind when we think of the Aegean world as the geographical basis of Greek life and history. The Aegean area, too, can be called free and autonomous, self-contained and full of pride and self-reliance before the foreigner, centred round the sea, a unity in small space. The individual Greek State was in general the more alive and important the more closely it was connected with the Aegean. But there was more than mere connection; there was a sort of identity between the Polis and the Aegean world which gave identical features to all Greek States, even to the colonies on foreign shores. It makes no difference in principle that the common legacy revealed itself in different degrees. We can be sure that it was because of that common legacy that behind the multitude and variety of Greek States there is firmly set up the unity of *the* Greek State.

The whole movement of Greece was from variety to unity. But it is a symbol of the Greek destiny that the Polis never reached the final goal, the complete unity between the individual and the community, between man and life. Yet the ideal rose out of the chaos of early disruption. Utopia, the State that is 'nowhere', is derived from the State that was bound into narrow space. Plato seized the torch as it fell from the hand of the *polites*, the citizen of the Polis. Thus its light was not extinguished, but burns for all time.

IV

GREEK CIVILIZATION AND GREEK MAN

THE Swiss historian Jacob Burckhardt, famous and honoured as the author of the *Cicerone* and the *Kultur der Renaissance*, died in 1897. When shortly after his death some books of his were published from copies of lectures and manuscripts, there were only very few who welcomed these volumes with reverence and enthusiasm; and neither were they men of professional scholarship nor did they represent the large educated public. To-day[1] it has become possible for almost all the chief works of Burckhardt to be republished in a collection intended for a wide public. And it looks as though the far-seeing publisher will find his courage rewarded. Here I wish particularly to draw attention to the new edition of the *Griechische Kulturgeschichte* (History of Greek Civilization), edited with an interesting epilogue and a comprehensive index by R. Marx.[2] The four volumes of the original have been reduced to three, and 'repetitions, enlargements, notes, and addenda' have been left out, a procedure which must be considered justifiable, since the work was never finally prepared for publication by the author himself. In general, it seems, the editor has done his work well. Like the first editor, Jacob Oeri, a generation ago, the new editor has not dreamed of modernizing a book which in its criticism and many of its details was obsolete before it appeared, and when Mr. Marx sometimes adds notes of his own (clearly indicated as additions), they are largely only explanatory. When he records results of more recent research, his notes are arbitrary and superfluous.

Naturally no one will expect to find in Burckhardt's book up-to-date evidence of our knowledge of Greek civilization. It is true that no comprehensive work is available giving this evidence, and therefore Burckhardt's work is in a way unique;

---

[1] This review was written in 1929 and published in the Sudeten-German periodical *Hochschulwissen*, VII (1930).
[2] *Griechische Kulturgeschichte.* By Jacob Burckhardt. (*Kröner's Taschenausgabe*, vol. 58-60.) Leipsic, 1929.

but it is not this uniqueness which is truly remarkable. We must not judge this book by inadequate standards. Its singularity is indeed not to be found in the choice of the subject, although we may think it significant that in this too Burckhardt has found no successor. But truly unique is the way in which he treats the subject. Vast and infinitely complex material is given, by deep thought and clear shaping, an imposing unity. This is a supreme achievement, both intellectual and artistic, and it is this which has given the signature of unique greatness to the work.

We pass over the general question whether it is still worth while to-day to occupy ourselves with the questions asked and answered by the civilization of ancient Greece. We are speaking only to those who by inner compulsion or desire try to keep in touch with the eternal sources of our own civilization, and firmly believe that the Classics — by their own re-birth, continually repeated though each time in a new way — keep alive and creative our own civilization, whether national or European. There were Renaissances before the period particularly so called: there have been and there will be others afterwards. It is the belief and hope of some to-day that we are once again about to enter some new kind of humanism, and there are witnesses in increasing number who testify that Burckhardt may well be one of the most important leaders in such a humanism, even though we shall have to differ from him in many fundamental positions. Mention may be made here of a book on Burckhardt by Carl Neumann, professor of the history of art at Heidelberg, who deals in great detail especially with the *Griechische Kulturgeschichte*, and whose remarks on several points will be found akin to what follows.

When Burckhardt, in the seventies of the last century, delivered his course of lectures on the history of Greek culture and civilization at the university of Basle (and he gave it during several sessions), the predominant view of the Greeks, among both scholars and laymen, was that of an idealizing classicism and aestheticism, largely shaped by the impressive work of Ernst Curtius. Burckhardt opposed this view with his own particular brand of realism. This is not the realism of the critical school of historians, the greatest of whom was Eduard Meyer; Burckhardt differed from its positivism in a fundamentally philosophical approach to history which did not renounce a belief in values, both absolute and historical. Burckhardt too, and perhaps more strongly than any other historian, opposed and helped to destroy the picture of the 'gay' Greeks. People had believed in those happy and serene gods and men of Greece; now they were suddenly faced by a picture in which the dark colours were plainly predominant. Burckhardt's realism, that 'sober genius' of his which has been duly praised, went hand in hand with an enthusiastic belief in the uniqueness of the Greeks, a belief perhaps not quite free from romanticism. It was just this combination of realism and romanticism which enabled Burckhardt to reveal the deeper values and to distinguish between things time-bound and things eternal.

Thus it can easily be understood why Burckhardt exerted a very strong influence upon his young colleague Friedrich Nietzsche, an influence undoubtedly reflected in some of the latter's early books. But their relations also resulted in some reciprocal effect of the younger on the older man, and it is certain that the picture of Greek pessimism, which arose in the two men, completely new though it was, would never have been shaped without the philosophy of Schopenhauer. The genius of Nietzsche in particular was struck by its lightning. Burckhardt's incorruptible and realistic sense of historical truth did not allow him to follow Nietzsche's ingenious, though extravagant, utterances and theories, and he never shared entirely the one-sided preference for the Dionysian over the Apollonian Greek. In fact, he fully acknowledged the sublimity and singularity of the works of Greek intellect and Greek art, characterized by clarity and beauty. The picture he draws in his book is composed in bright as well as dark colours.

I have said that Burckhardt recognized values in history. This does not mean that he described historical phenomena as good or bad. Indeed, he once made his position clear, with all the outspokenness that could be desired, when he condemned those historians who indulged in 'giving marks'. Burckhardt's own attitude towards the Greeks, and his idea of man as reflected in this attitude, can perhaps be best shown by three characteristics — his method of historical writing, the way he selects his material, and his fundamental position when confronted with the 'three potentials' (*Potenzen*), or powers, which he distinguishes as State, religion and civilization. Something may be said on these three points.

About his method Burckhardt makes some illuminating remarks in his Introduction. What is essential is his intention to deal with the lasting and constant factors instead of events of the moment, with quality instead of action, with conditions and institutions instead of wars and political struggles. It is consistent with these aims that he refuses to write according to chronology. Thus he almost entirely eliminates the idea of evolution, which during his lifetime was the very core of general thought. He fails to see the characteristic features of Greek civilization in their development and succession. He does see them essentially in the shape and power given to them as units once and for all.

The second point is the 'subjective and arbitrary selection', which Burckhardt, as he unhesitatingly admits, has made from the extant evidence. In one of his letters he writes: 'In my books I am dealing only and exclusively with such things as are of interest to myself.' A method based on such a principle, if accepted generally, would undoubtedly be dangerous. But it must be realized that the 'interest' of a great man can be a safer guide than the aim of covering the whole ground, adopted by many so-called 'objective' historians. For, in fact, the craving for completeness may sometimes lead further astray than a sensible and honest method of selection. In the case of the *Griechische Kulturgeschichte* there was even less danger of narrowness and one-sidedness, because Burckhardt never tires of admiring and describing the inexhaustible wealth of appearances, the whole multi-shaped nature, of Greek civilization.

But he ignored economic questions, and this ignoring was conscious and deliberate. It was due not to an unrealistic aestheticism, but to the right and true understanding which is often not possessed by present-day scholars, that economics played only an inferior and subordinate part in the Greek mind. It goes without saying that the eternal values which mankind owes to Greece belong to an entirely different sphere; but there is more than this. To the ancient Greeks themselves, despite all their love of wealth and money, economics were not of primary importance. The type of the *homo oeconomicus* was unknown to them, at least before the fourth century B.C. and probably even then. It is simply not true, as is asserted to-day by scholars of a particular type, that at all times economics have played an equally important part, still less that they have played the decisive part, in determining the way and nature of history. Among the Greeks many a man who knew quite well how to look after his own advantage cannot be taken as a specimen of 'Economic Man', neither the greedy squire nor the State's pensioner in democracy, neither Peisistratus the mine-owner, nor Agesilaus, mercenary soldier and king in one. Something similar to this is true of law, its practice and its science, which, like economics, has recently become a subject of intense interest to scholars. Although the idea of justice and law was one of the great moving factors in Greek politics and civilization, it remained largely in the sphere of philosophical, and not of legal, thought. However interesting it is to study Greek economics and Greek law as early phases of the general history of economics and law, they tell us very little about the true nature of the Greeks. By applying Roman or modern standards and ideas we may, in fact, entirely misunderstand them. It is different with another aspect of human and social life — *Eros*. The problems of love in its very different forms are only occasionally touched on by Burckhardt; he never treats them with recognition of their full importance. Whatever the reason — and it may be thought that the characteristics of the Victorian age were not confined to England — something really essential has been left out.

In taking the three potentials which have been mentioned as the most important and powerful factors in Greek civilization, Burckhardt proclaims a tripartition which he has elaborated in its fundamental aspects in his *Weltgeschichtliche Betrachtungen*.[1] I cannot agree with this division for the simple reason that in my view civilization (or *Kultur*) represents the total of all the phenomena of human existence, and therefore includes State and religion. When Burckhardt gave to his lectures the title of *Kulturgeschichte* he actually outstepped his own scheme and expressed the same view as our own. Thus it seems superfluous and ridiculous to bring big guns against that tripartition which has perhaps not even grown in Burck-

---

[1] Now translated into English under the title *Reflections on History* (London, 1943). I wonder whether publisher and translator will show even greater courage in undertaking the heavy task of an English version of the *Griechische Kulturgeschichte*.

E*

hardt's own garden. On the other hand, it is just this tripartition into State, religion, and civilization which is of particular importance for our understanding of Burckhardt's position. Volumes 1-3 of the original edition (1-2 in the new edition) contain a description of Greek civilization, divided into various chapters under the three main headings of State, religion, civilization. What was the intellectual and psychological background which may, or may not, explain Burckhardt's intentions?

He was a son of the city-State of Basle, and so closely bound to this community that he refused to succeed the greatest German historian, Friedrich Ranke, at Berlin university. Burckhardt himself lived, as it were, the life of a Greek citizen. Basle even to-day is still a Polis, and Burckhardt had all his roots in the soil of the petty city-State. Thus, as Friedrich Meinecke once put it, 'he never went through the school of fighting for State and nation'. This was said by way of criticism, and it is justified. But for the same reason Burckhardt was able to see beyond the horizon of the political historians, and thus he coined a phrase which breaks forth like thunder from a style that on the whole is sober and restrained: the phrase 'Might is evil in itself' (*Die Macht ist böse an sich*), a significant parallel to Lord Acton's famous utterance. The sentence became the *Leitmotif* in Burckhardt's judgment of State and politics. It is strange that the very idea expressed in these words was turned into the exact opposite by Nietzsche. We shall not really understand the meaning of this sentence for Burckhardt, unless we realize that this citizen of the Polis Basle was at the same time an absolute aristocrat and individualist, a man who fervently believed in freedom as the foundation of all civilized life. It is for this reason that in his inmost heart he was equally remote from, and therefore equally unjust about, State and religion, both of which he visualized as the great powers of compulsion and force. He was not simply a rationalist, but some part of his soul, and not the worst, belonged to the eighteenth century. He was both historically-minded and a child of the period of enlightenment, both citizen of a small city-State and a European.

To understand the personal position of Burckhardt will enable us better to understand his striking picture of the Polis as a State based on brutal coercion. Love and aversion are

mixed in this picture, very much as were the feelings in Burckhardt's soul for his small and homely, but all too narrow,
community of Basle. The Polis is to him *la città dolente*, and its
typical example is the rigid shape into which State and society
were formed in Sparta. Sparta was a unique phenomenon in
the Greek world. But it is clear why Burckhardt took it as
typical for the Polis as a whole. His picture of the Polis is
painted in the darkest colours because the artist's brush was
directed by the hostility of the proudest individualism to the
demands of the State. The account is very impressive in its
grandeur and its single-mindedness. Of the bias with which it
is written the author was perhaps conscious himself. But
although we must recognize the general bias, all the particular
features are described with such accuracy of observation and
such intensity of imagination that, once again, we realize the
influence of the author's own experiences. Burckhardt has
clearly seen — and in this he is perhaps the disciple of Hegel
with whom otherwise he has so very little in common — that
the ruling idea of the Polis is the rule of the Law (*Nomos*).
Thus he paved the way, which up to now has been little followed, to the knowledge of the true nature of the Greek State
behind and beyond its outward constitutional forms of monarchy, aristocracy and democracy. It is a mistake to claim
Burckhardt as a witness for the view that the Polis was nothing
but a deterring, repulsive and barren specimen of a State.
Although he fully realized the senselessness of the many violent wars between the Greek States, and although he believed
that the citizen of the Polis lived under unrestricted force, he
never doubted that — to quote the words of Charles Andler,
the French biographer of Nietzsche — 'we learn best from the
Greeks what it costs to become a reasonable and law-abiding
people'. We may add that Burckhardt's style, his sober
pathos, is of a monumental greatness, so that we must listen
to him, as people will do at all times, however their opinions
may differ from his even in important and fundamental
matters.

It is not possible to speak in quite the same tone of Burckhardt's treatment of Greek religion, a section of the book which
appears to be in a way antiquated. Burckhardt's realism prevented him from following certain theories and fantasies concerning the history and nature of religion which were very

common in his lifetime. But ten years before the *Griechische Kulturgeschichte* was first produced, Erwin Rohde's *Psyche* was published, and it is surprising that Burckhardt did not add a single note to his manuscript referring to this outstanding book which very soon became famous. The position which thus arose is odd. Burckhardt's genius went right down to the roots when in the first chapter of the whole work he revealed the importance of myth as the fundamental fact in all the thought and belief of the Greeks. To an extent unheard of at the time when he delivered these lectures, he does justice also to the peculiar and significant part which cult and rites played in Greek religion. At the same time he emphasizes the singularity and uniqueness of Greek religion, thus anticipating and refuting later exaggerations of the comparative method in the history of religion. In spite of all this I do not think that he realized those deepest and strongest forces in Greek religion which *Psyche* had so strikingly revealed. Burckhardt's approach was much closer to the strictly moral powers in the life and mind of the Greeks, and the chapter in which, under the striking and hardly translatable heading *Zur Gesamtbilanz des griechischen Lebens*, he reviews these powers, is one of the most beautiful things he wrote, and, even with its over-emphasis on the negative side, one of the most profound passages ever written on the Greek character.

The pessimistic view of Greek politics and religion is clearly and consciously contrasted with the picture of art, poetry, music, philosophy and science. When Burckhardt deals with these subjects his intense sensitivity to aesthetic values makes itself felt, and so does the enthusiastic conviction that it is in the artistic and intellectual activities that the truly great and indeed the typical creations of the Greeks are to be found. Hence it can be seen that Burckhardt's general pessimism in regard to the Greeks, though it derived from his own philosophy and is perfectly sincere and genuine, could not mislead him. The realistic historian knew that the eternal works of Greek art and thought bore witness to the most powerful optimism, an optimism which was never shallow and was in fact based on optimistic forces in the general character of the Greek people. Burckhardt himself once said that 'the whole phenomenon of Greek pessimism derives its full peculiarity from the emphatic optimism of the Greek temper which is fundamentally creative, plastic, turned towards reality, and at the same time — on the surface — loves to use and enjoy every moment'.[1] Naturally enough Burckhardt did not say that such a statement as this undermines his own pessimistic views on Greek politics and religion. But he knew very well that, especially with the Greeks, his three potentials of State, religion and civilization were most closely interconnected. He lays stress more than once on the fact that the works of art, whether statue and temple or epic and tragedy, were not merely spontaneous achievements of a freely creative genius, but also deeply set in the political and religious traditions of the people, from which they drew their undying power.

In the last volume the whole immense subject, which had been systematically investigated in the previous volumes, is once again comprehensively dealt with, but now in a purely historical scheme. 'Greek Man in his Development' is the title of this imposing attempt to give, as it were, the history of the mind and soul of the Greeks in several chapters according to the generations and centuries of their history. Once again Burckhardt draws from the stupendous riches of his knowledge and insight to place before us the equally striking pictures of 'Heroic Man' who belongs to an age essentially mythical, of 'Colonial and Agonal Man' representing the archaic period in which fundamental features of Greek humanity received their decisive shape, and further the pictures of Man in the fifth century, in the fourth century, and finally in the Hellenistic Age. This sequence has never been presented in a similar way, neither before nor after Burckhardt. It impresses us like the acts of a sublime tragedy. Burckhardt has here accepted in a specific form the chronological principle, which previously, and in fact in all his other books, he had denied and opposed. He has done so with the intention not of showing historical development but of displaying the unique phenomenon of Greek man, as he appears in the historical moment of each period, as a rounded and complete figure, truly in accordance with the outstandingly sculptural character of the Greek mind. It is always the totality of Greek humanity that is reflected in

---

[1] 'Die ganze Erscheinung des griechischen Pessimismus erhält ihre volle Merkwürdigkeit durch den entschiedenen Optimismus des griechischen Temperaments, welches vom tiefsten Grunde aus ein schaffendes, plastisches, der Welt zugewandtes ist und ausserdem – an der Oberfläche – die Verwertung und den Genuss des Augenblicks sehr zu schätzen weiss.'

each historical epoch. A historical psychology is displayed such as has been applied to hardly any other people.

If we ask ourselves why we believe that this great book will always be read, the first answer must be because it is a very great work of literature which is of more than purely scientific importance and has a value and a purpose in itself. Furthermore we find here a clear and striking expression, such as exists nowhere else, of the belief that the Greeks were the first to live through the whole cycle of human civilization, and not merely to live through it, but to suffer by it, and also — despite all pessimism — to enjoy it. Burckhardt once wrote to Nietzsche: 'As is well known I never entered the temple of real thought, but was pleased to dwell in the court and halls of the enclosure [peribolos is the word he uses], in the domain of the pictorial in the widest sense of the word.' Burckhardt, no doubt, is too modest here. He was not only 'pleased' with the beauty of the 'enclosure', he not only received it fully and with joyful appreciation, he also reproduced it with adequate power of expression for the sake of all of us who are so much less able to see and to understand.

There is a third and last answer to the question why we ought to, and shall, read Burckhardt. The final goal he sought and searched for, in practically all his books, is Man. To Man in one of his purest and greatest embodiments the *Griechische Kulturgeschichte*, and particularly its last volume, is dedicated. Burckhardt was an explorer of man, and he knew man, although in his quiet retreat at Basle he became shy and remote. He was a humanist in the deepest sense of the word, and it is for the sake of man that again and again men have found, and will find, their way to Burckhardt.

V

ESSAYS IN HISTORICAL CRITICISM

A CONSIDERABLE number of articles, some published before, some not, is here collected in an impressive volume to reveal the work of a scholar who is outstanding in constructive criticism, and at the same time writes exceedingly well.[1] The volume deals with a great variety of subjects, bearing witness to Mr. Gomme's versatility and the wide scope of his scholarship, both on historical and literary subjects. The chapters vary widely in size and contents, but they are connected by a common and characteristic method which is displayed both in the selection of problems and the choice of solutions.

Mr. Gomme's method of research is, naturally enough, not a fundamentally new method. It is, however, the expression of a very determined impulse, making use of the normal means and methods of historical scholarship. Mr. Gomme brings out his points by reconsidering a number of views and con-clusions which are either the *opinio communis* of modern scholarship, or at least upheld on account of the authority of some great scholars. These views are carefully and severely examined. Questions are raised and some essential points opposed, but all this is done without any attempt on the author's part to show his own originality or to pose as a revolutionary. Mr. Gomme relies entirely on an unprejudiced and, in fact, consciously conservative interpretation of our sources. Thus it is indeed a critical impulse, though it is never carried too far, which leads him to deal with a number of inter-esting questions and the answers given by other scholars. In doing so, he makes full use of his wit and sharp sarcasm, and in many cases at least he presses his attacks home to a con-vincing conclusion. The methodical and intellectual attitude which gives the book its character and its unity shows that the

---

[1] *Essays in Greek History and Literature.* By A. W. Gomme. Oxford, 1937. This review was written in 1938, and actually set up in print, for the periodical *Eunomia,* which began its life in Prague early in 1939. I do not know whether it ever reached more than one number; my collaboration, at any rate, ended then, and the review was never published. The original had to be fairly short; I have therefore added a few passages to make some points clearer.

learned author has a strong individuality of his own. Although some of the essays are rather specialized, any student of antiquity, whether British or non-British, will find it well worth his while to read through the whole volume.

The introductory chapter deals with a fundamental question. Mr. Gomme is concerned with investigating the very nature of historical writing by examining the Greek historians. He tries to show, perhaps to the surprise of some readers, that the Greeks knew of no patriotic history-writing, and he thus touches on a question which has its modern implications. Even though, as I believe, he over-emphasizes his idea, its core is sound. The Greek historians were clearly lacking in a 'Polis nationalism' that could be compared with the 'State national-ism' of modern historians. Mr. Gomme does not, however, put the question whether the part played by the ancient historians in shaping and expressing public opinion is compar-able to that of the historians of the nineteenth and twentieth centuries. What about the patriotism of Athenian tragedians, comedians, and orators?

The second chapter, written some thirty years ago and enlarged by a short appendix, criticizes sharply, though with full justification, V. Bérard's hypothesis of an early and far-reaching 'thalassocracy' of the Phoenicians, at least in so far as he tried to prove it by the early history of Boeotia and the famous story of Cadmus, the legendary founder of Thebes. In a careful description of Boeotian topography, based on personal knowledge of the area, Gomme shows why Boeotia, though called 'of three seas' (τριθάλαττος), was not an 'Isthmic' country, but a remote agrarian district which was virtually cut off from the sea. He rightly denies that trade was of any major importance here: but he is well aware of its im-portance as far as Greece in general is concerned. This be-comes evident in the next chapter 'Traders and Manufacturers in Greece', in which the author opposes the one-sided and exaggerated views of Hasebroek, although he agrees with him in stressing the smallness and narrowness of all individual economic activities in Greece. It is illuminating to find these activities based on the element of property, such as field, shop, workshop, ship, rather than of capital. Although the economic activities of the individual always remained on a small scale, this by no means prevented Greek trade as a whole from extending into a very large area and becoming a decisive factor in shaping public as well as private life. Like other modern scholars, though in a particularly convincing manner, Mr. Gomme seeks and finds a middle way between the extremes, say, of Beloch who measures Greek trade by modern standards, and Hasebroek who considers it completely unimportant. This will undoubtedly be the line of future scholarship in the economic history of ancient Greece.

Chapter IV is of a more specialized character. It too had been published before, but a note has been added to refute some later criticism. The chapter deals with questions of Athenian citizenship, the decree of Demophilus (346-345 B.C.), and Pericles' notorious law of 451-450. The latter is treated in a very short and somewhat unsatisfactory way. I do not think that the 'xenophoby' of this law was mainly an expression of the wish to restore the idea of kinship as the basis for citizenship. The aim was to keep the number of citizens low, and it may be true that this was done, not only to prevent too many from sharing in their privileges, but also for the purpose of keeping in working order the constitution, which might be endangered by too large a number of citizens. Nevertheless, the narrow policy of Athens in granting citizenship was one of the chief reasons for her decline. It was at variance with Pericles' imperialistic policy, but it was, as I would maintain against Gomme, democratic in the ancient sense of the term. For democracy was not the rule of as many human beings as possible, nor that of the 'Common Man', but the rule of the people — that is to say the citizen body. The exclusion of foreigners and half-foreigners was the result of the natural, if unwise, egotism of the people. Was this law therefore a symbol of Athens 'remaining true to her past'? I doubt it, the more so since the law was not made retrospective.

Both amusing and instructive is the chapter on 'The Position of Women' in classical Athens. Mr. Gomme is fully justified in emphasizing that women played an important part in Attic literature even before Euripides, who is generally considered to be the mouthpiece of female emancipation. Gomme is even more right in opposing the method of describing the position of women by selecting a number of scattered phrases on the subject of 'Woman's place is the home'. He quotes a few passages from modern English literature, and very wittily reveals the absurdity of such a method. But he knows that, although the view commonly held on this matter is one-sided and not well founded, the opposite is not necessarily true. He wished to put a question, and that he has done; but he has not yet given a full and definite answer.

Four chapters deal with Thucydides, who time and again is defended against his critics. The particular subjects are 'The Greatest War in Greek History', Sphacteria, Mantinea, and — the most important item — 'The Speeches'. All these articles are full of clever and interesting remarks, and there is much to learn whether one agrees or not. But I shall confine myself to the last and most extensive section. Here Gomme launches a bold and brilliant attack on the opinion, widely held, that Thucydides' speeches are to a very large extent 'free inventions'. He attacks in particular the radical views of E. Schwartz, expressed, for instance, in his review of Taeger's somewhat nebulous, but by no means negligible, book on Thucydides. Gomme very ably discloses the essential weaknesses of the arguments of Schwartz. He knows, of course, that, apart perhaps from a few literary quotations, the *form* of the speeches is wholly Thucydidean. 'Before he wrote them down, they did not exist.' It is for this reason that Thucydides lets none of the orators speak τάδε or ταῦτα, but τοιάδε and τοιαῦτα. As to the famous words in the chapter on his method (I, 22) (ἐγγύτατα τῆς ξυμπάσης γνώμης τῶν ἀληθῶς λεχθέντων), it is Gomme's firm belief that, if they are interpreted without prejudice, there is only one, 'the natural, and therefore the proper, translation', and only one possible meaning. Thucydides says that he is 'keeping as close as possible to the general sense of what was actually said', and that means, according to Gomme, that the contents of the speeches are not Thucydidean. He is right in pointing out that the interpretation of the phrase by ancient critics must not be used in modern discussions; for it was concerned with the literary form alone and not with the historical contents of the speeches. The strict distinction, on the other hand, of form and content, of manner and matter, is easily made. But does it go deep enough? The contents of a speech, frequently pushed to a fundamental issue and brilliantly phrased, cannot really be separated from its form. And the recent attempts of some German scholars (Schadewaldt, Grosskinsky, Patzer) to reach a more subtle understanding of

Thucydides' words on his method, although they are inclined to become over-subtle and hair-splitting, suggest that the question is not quite so simple as Gomme assumes; there is, in fact, more than one possible translation of γνώμη. Gomme examines in detail the possible ways in which Thucydides may have got his knowledge of the speeches as they were actually delivered. This kind of approach is very much to the point, and has not always been sufficiently adopted. The position varies for the different speeches. But although it must have been extremely difficult sometimes for Thucydides to collect his material, we need not, and, according to Gomme, must not draw the conclusion that this or that speech was freely invented. The fact that the eighth book of Thucydides does not contain any speeches is as usual explained by the fact that the whole work was left unfinished. But Gomme does not only think that death prevented Thucydides from giving the last book its final literary shape; he also argues that, when Thucydides had to stop writing, he had not yet sufficient material for the last part of his work. The chapters of the eighth book in which the contents of speeches are given in indirect speech are, in Gomme's view, only notes about the material as far as it then was known to the writer, and not drafts which had only to receive their final literary treatment. This particular view will provoke strong doubts and opposition. But even if we do not agree, everything this critic says about the whole important Thucydidean question is noteworthy, the more so as, in dealing with the historian Thucydides, he never overlooks the artistic point of view of the writer Thucydides. This is most relevant, for there can be no doubt that artistic aims had a strong influence on the composition and arrangement of the speeches. Can Gomme's view be applied even to the Funeral Speech? He answers: 'Even if there is more of Thucydides' own thought in the Epitaphios than I would allow, it is still certainly meant as an objective picture of Periclean policy, not a vehicle for the expression of his own views, whether in 430 or 415 or 403." I feel this answer is not quite satisfactory, for the will to give 'an objective picture' can be traced in every one of Thucydides' speeches, and will be largely admitted even by those who take them as pure inventions. On the whole, I believe that Gomme's arguments are somewhat lacking in depth; his presentation of a very intricate matter, lucid as it is, simplifies too much. But he fights for something that it is in itself justifiable and even necessary to fight for, namely the rehabilitation of the prestige of the historian Thucydides, who is frequently too much neglected for the sake of the writer and thinker Thucydides.

In the tenth chapter a factor of naval strategy is discussed, the relevance of the very limited range of action to which Greek warships were confined. Again, we find many interesting observations, in particular about the double battle of Artemisium and Thermopylae. I am less in agreement with the next long chapter on 'The End of the City-State'. In defending the thesis that the battle of Chaeronea did not really put an end to the Polis, Gomme says the obvious thing and fights an opinion which, I believe, cannot really be upheld. But I must admit that the *Cambridge Ancient History* has rather surprisingly accepted Beloch's strange and misleading view of Philip as having created 'Greek unity'. Gomme makes the year 262 B.C., the end of the Chremonidean war, instead of 338, the date of the final fall of Athenian independence. But this new date remains equally unconvincing. A few lines later Gomme himself writes: 'The form of the πόλις remained, so that it was easy for an apparent autonomy to be restored in 229.' The truth, as I see it, is that in 338 the gradual decline of the power of the Polis reached a decisive point. If Alexander had lived on and continued the policy of his last years, the Polis under his reign would have almost completely lost its independence in foreign policy. After his early death, however, the ups and downs of the policy of Athens as well as of other small States went on, but they were completely dependent on the struggles between the great powers. Nominally, the autonomy and structure of the Polis did not perish, even when some of the city-States were merged in the confederations of the Achaeans and Aetolians, even when Rome ruled Greece. The Polis still survived, though as a mere shadow of itself. Events as late as the revolt during the First Mithridatic War confirm this view of the history of the Polis. It was not before the reorganization by Augustus that the Greek Polis definitely became a mere provincial town. While disagreeing with Gomme on this subject, I share to a large extent his view on the 'blindness' of Demosthenes and Aristotle to the political developments after 338. The small space which Gomme gives to this question does not supply more than a few hints. As far as Aristotle is concerned, I have tried elsewhere to reveal his complete neglect of Alexander's monarchy and the deeper reasons for his attitude.[1] Gomme is right in maintaining that the fourth century B.C. was for the Greeks not merely a period of degeneration. But perhaps he does not take sufficiently into consideration to what extent during this period the political strength of the Greek States dwindled away, and the old political forms, when faced in an increasing degree with the power politics of territorial monarchies, lost their meaning.

A last chapter is dedicated to Menander. It is the only section of purely aesthetic and literary criticism in the book. With great ability and sympathy Gomme draws the picture of a poet who, according to what he says, has not yet been acknowledged in Britain as the great artist he actually was. Gomme does not mention the last chapter of Gilbert Murray's book on Aristophanes, in which some important things are said about Menander. His own essay is full of sensitive insight and thoughtful argument; it has great merits and should be read also by other than British readers.

The whole volume, with its many different aspects, ends with the reprint of two *Letters to the Editor* which *The Times* had not published. The one of more general interest is the second, in which the writer proposes that England should pay off some of the debt she owes to Greece for Lord Elgin's 'enlightened vandalism'. At least the Caryatid from the Erechtheum ought to be returned, so that she may stand again among her sisters, in Attic air and sun. It is to be assumed that this courageous proposal will meet with little response. And however much we may sympathize with it, we should not forget that Lord Elgin, albeit unwittingly, saved most of the Parthenon sculptures from final destruction.

---

[1] See *Alexander and the Greeks* (1938), ch. III.

VI

EUNOMIA [1]

THE THREE SISTERS

It is right to start our investigation from the lines of Hesiod's *Theogony* (901ff.) in which Zeus is said to have had as his second wife 'shining Themis, who bore the Horae, Eunomia, Dike and thriving Eirene, who mind the works of mortal men'.[2] We are not concerned with the original significance of 'shining' or 'rich' Themis, nor with the question whether the Horae are taken collectively as usual to mean the Hours or Seasons, or not.[3] The relationship of the three goddesses as daughters and sisters is indeed relevant to the following discussion, but the explanation must be sought in their individual names, not in the collective name of the Horae. There is a definite ethical and political meaning in that family of four. Hesiod's lines have rightly been called the first expression of a commonplace conception of later days, the blessings of justice and peace.[4] Perhaps they can teach us something more.

Besides the Horae, the Moirae are mentioned as daughters of Zeus and Themis (904ff.).[5] This double set of daughters probably originated from the confusion of two different versions. The Moirae, in another passage (217), are also called the daughters of Night, while no other genealogy than ours is given for the Horae. The three individual goddesses are what is often, though not quite appropriately, called 'personifications'; they certainly enjoyed very little real religious worship or cult. They represent, I believe, a later stage of religious development than the Horae as a unit; in fact, they derive from

[1] First published in *Charisteria, Alois Rzach zum achtzigsten Geburtstag dargebracht* (1930). I have made a few alterations and added some notes.
[2] δεύτερον ἠγάγετο λιπαρὴν Θέμιν ἣ τέκεν Ὥρας,
Εὐνομίην τε Δίκην τε καὶ Εἰρήνην τεθαλυῖαν,
αἵ τ' ἔργ' ὠρεύουσι καταθνητοῖσι βροτοῖσι.
[3] Cf. U. v. Wilamowitz-Moellendorff, *Hesiodos Erga*, on v. 228.
[4] Cf. B. Keil, *Eirene* (*Berichte d. Sächs. Gesellsch. d. Wissensch. Phil. – hist. Klasse.* 1916), 37.
[5] Cf. my *Rechtsidee im frühen Griechentum* (1921), 39, 3.

the kind of religious speculation or theology known to us in
particular from Hesiod. It is likely, although it cannot be
proved, that the three persons with their individual names
actually owe their divine existence to Hesiod. When people
began to speak of Eunomia and Dike they did not think of
them as merely abstract conceptions. Yet before they could
enter Hesiod's Pantheon as goddesses, they must have been
alive as expressions of hope, desire and imagination — as
'ideas'. Before they were united in a triad they must have lived
in a world which was not that of Hesiod's *Theogony* and its
intricate genealogies, indeed not that of any kind of purely
religious thought. There is only a step from this world to that
of the same poet's *Erga*, the external side of his life, his
political surroundings. Here we enter the world of the early
Polis. We must not think only of his native Ascra, where the
process of the growth of the Polis had only just begun. Hesiod's
Erga goes beyond his personal fate. He wants to teach a lesson
which is typical and general; the poet is eager and able to look
beyond the narrow world of Boeotia.[1] When he puts forward
moral demands which are closely bound up with the Polis, this
only shows that the forces and ideas that shaped the general
development of society and State were fully alive in his thoughts.
Dike means the right claimed by the weak and oppressed.
Opposed to force (βία) and wantonness (ὕβρις), it is the
expression of the spirit of the Polis, a community the inner
coherence of which was steadily growing stronger.[2] Eirene,
as far as we can see from very scanty evidence, indicates the
state of peace, both as a period and as the blessings provided
in this period.[3] There can be no life of the community without
Eirene. The origin and meaning of the third name, Eunomia,
have been much discussed; but, however it is explained, the
world to which it belongs is again the world of the Polis. It is
this same world in which the union and collaboration of the
three 'ideas' attain their full meaning. The family connection
of mother and daughters, on the other hand, can be partly
explained by the exigencies of the *Theogony*. In the form and
the spirit of this poem the genealogical scheme was the only

[1] Cf. A. Rzach, *Pauly-Wissowa*, VIII, 1180. Wilamowitz, *l.c.*, on vv. 504, 568,
640, 643, and elsewhere.
[2] Cf. *Rechtsidee*, 62ff.
[3] Cf. Keil, *l.c.*, 33ff.

possible way to express the union of various moral conceptions or their divine counterparts. Moreover, the 'family group' expressed the pious belief of the poet that all peaceful community life owed its existence to the wisdom of Zeus. It also reflected the fact — and this was a historical fact, not a mere belief on the poet's part — that Themis, the sacred norm of life in an earlier aristocratic society, had been or was being replaced, as the leading political force, by Dike and her sisters.

Before we approach the special questions connected with Eunomia it may be worth while to take a brief look at the part played in later authors by that combination which was formed for all future time by Hesiod. The lines in which Pindar praises Corinth (*O.* XIII, 6ff.) are hardly more than a paraphrase of Hesiod: 'For there Eunomia and her sisters are living, Dike, and Eirene who grew up with her, safe foundations of cities, guardians of wealth, the golden children of well-counselling Themis.' What is new in this description, as compared with that of Hesiod, is due to the endeavour to expound in greater detail what is merely indicated in the earlier version by the words 'who mind the works of mortal men'. The success of man's work and life, and still more, his general prosperity, depend on the peaceful and secure life of the community as it is described by the combination of the three sisters. Similarly, in an anonymous lyrical fragment (II, 159, frg. 5 Diehl), the Moirae, here again the daughters of Night, are invoked to send our three goddesses to make the city forget its distress. We do not know what city in distress is meant. But Eunomia, Dike and Eirene appear as the means by which Fate may relieve the misery of the State. It is natural to assume that the city had formerly been ruled by injustice, strife and war. Pindar (*P.* 5, 67), in a similar vein, calls Eunomia 'alien to war' (ἀπόλεμος). Other variations on the theme of Hesiod occur,[1] but they do not teach us anything new. The only remarkable point is that from the fifth century Eunomia was often replaced by Plutus. That has rightly been explained by the change of meaning which Eunomia underwent as a conception of pure politics.[2]

It is interesting to realize the influence of Hesiod's genealogy

[1] Cf. in particular Pindar *O.* 9, 16; Bacchylides 12, 183ff., and the last part of Timotheos' *Persae.* For other evidence see Waser, *Pauly-Wissowa*, VI, 1129ff.
[2] Keil, 39ff. Cf. below, p. 86ff.

on Orphism. The Hymn to the Horae (XLIII) accepts the three names, but only the names. It praises the Horae as the goddesses of nature and the natural seasons; the individual names seem meaningless. But beyond what looks like a merely mechanical tradition some deeper meaning was applied, for example, in Proclus' commentary to Plato's *Timaeus* (III, 118, 30D.=frg. 181 Kern). He sees the Horae as a symbol of the course of nature, but at the same time as the individual figures of Eunomia, Dike and Eirene — in other words, as the principle of law and order ruling the cosmic world. But the original, in a narrow sense political, meaning of the three names has been lost. This is not surprising in such a half-mystical and sectarian group as the Orphics, who had no real contact with the life of the Polis.[1]

The double nature of Hesiod's three goddesses was retained at an even later period. They remained, on the one hand, a political conception; on the other, they were worshipped as deities. This worship,[2] as far as one of them individually was concerned, appears, however, comparatively late. We tend to speak of 'deification' as the Greek equivalent to our 'abstraction'. But this is a far too mechanical way of putting it. To the Greeks an abstract idea was a divine power, conceived of as a divine person. The worship of gods such as Eunomia or Eirene can be understood as the religious sanction of a theological speculation produced in terms of *theogony*. Even this sounds rather rationalistic, and it is probably a mistake to draw too strict a line between cult and theology. In our case the worship of each of the three goddesses may have followed the old and widespread worship of the Horae. Eunomia was even taken into the *entourage* of Aphrodite, perhaps as one of the Graces. One form of worship is particularly notable; that is the common worship of Eucleia and Eunomia in Athens, which is known from late inscriptions. A temple of Eucleia, mentioned by Pausanias (I, 14, 5), stood near the Pnyx; it was supposed to have been founded after Marathon. If this is true, the union between Eucleia and Eunomia (though mentioned by Bacchylides) must here have occurred later; for, as we shall

---

[1] Cf. also the Hymn to Zeus, found in Pergamum (I. v.Perg. 324, 13ff.). The inscription belongs to the second century A.D., but the hymn is much older.
[2] Cf. O. Gruppe, *Griech. Mythologie u. Religionsgeschichte*, W. Roscher, *Mytholog. Lexikon*, and *Pauly-Wissowa*, s.vv.

F

see, it is impossible for some time after 490 B.C. that Eunomia
should have been given a new cult in Athens. A way of meeting
this difficulty will be suggested later in this essay.

THE CONCEPTION OF EUNOMIA

From Hesiod onwards there is evidence to an ever increasing extent that justice was the fundamental principle that ruled
the Polis, a fact first expressed by *dike*, later by *nomos* or 'Law'.
The divine triad of the daughters of Themis tells the same tale
in richer detail. The connection of Eunomia with Dike,
whether set forth by Hesiod for the first time or not, had
become traditional at an early date. It expressed the conception
of the good and happy conditions which were to be achieved in
the Polis. Thus, *eunomia* became a symbol for the life of the
Polis, ruled by justice. But was it then just an anticipation of
nomos?[1] To answer this question it will be necessary to discuss,
once more, the early history of the word *eunomia*.

Since ancient times the views of scholars have differed on
this point. Is the word derived from νόμος or from νέμω (or
νέμεσθαι)?[2] To most of the ancient grammarians and, even more,
to the popular mind as early as the fifth century B.C., the first
derivation was natural. If Aristarchus favoured the other one,
he did so only because he denied that Homer ever used the
word *nomos*; in *Od*. 1,3 he read νόον against Zenodotus' νόμον.
The word *eunomia*, which occurs in Homer once (*Od*. 17, 487),
was by no means, in Aristarchus' opinion, to be connected with
the un-Homeric conception of *nomos*. The method of this
argument may be faulty, but that does not necessarily mean
that the result is erroneous. Aristarchus' view may still be the
right one. In a way both explanations are mistaken, for the
abstract noun *eunomia* is based on the adjective *eunomos*. Its
origin, however, does not seem any more definite than that of
the noun. From the fifth century it had only one meaning:
'with good laws'. But that does not prove anything as to
its earlier or original meaning, because of the change which
the conception of *nomos* underwent; of that we shall speak later.

[1] This seems the view of Wilamowitz, *Staat u. Gesellschaft d. Griechen*[2], 63, when he
translates Hesiod's Dike and Eunomia by 'Gerechtigkeit und Gesetzlichkeit'.

[2] H. O. Stier, ΝΟΜΟΣ ΒΑΣΙΛΕΥΣ (1927), 11f., discusses most of the literature relevant
to this question.

In looking for analogies to *eunomos*, we find ευ- much more often combined with a noun than with a verbal stem;[1] but examples of the latter do exist. The combination with *nomos* may be more likely, but the last word has not yet been said on this question.

A different problem arises from the fact·that νέμω has no simple and clear meaning. Both in the active and in the middle voice the word is so ambiguous that no translation of *eunomia* which is based on the verb can be taken for granted. It is possible to think of a community being well governed, or of things being well distributed or well arranged, or even of the same ideas in the active. It is very much simpler to adhere to the root νόμος; but then we have to take into consideration the history of that word. It is beyond doubt that *nomos* did not gain the meaning of 'law' before the end of the sixth century.[2] For its original meaning Hesiod provides the earliest, and also very ample, evidence. 'Traditional order', 'custom', 'usage' — that is what the evidence points to. *Nomos* has no central position in Hesiod's thought, yet it has a clear and significant meaning. It belongs to the world of religion and custom, the order created by tradition, not by law. In the life of the Polis it was to play an important part,[3] but for political thought in its narrower sense it did not yet count. *Eunomia*, if it is derived from this *nomos*, could mean something like 'good order' or the existence of good and sensible customs. Obviously, there was no anticipation of the later *nomos*, and it is clearly a mistake to translate *eunomia* by something like 'conditions of good laws' (*Wohlgesetzlichkeit*). If we discard the sense of 'good distribution' (*Wohlverteiltheit*) there is not much difference between the possible meanings of *eunomia*, whatever origin we prefer. In general, it will be neither possible nor necessary for our discussion, to find out from its meaning what were the original components of the word.

As already mentioned, it is in the Odyssey (17, 487) that *eunomia* (εὐνομίη) occurs for the first time. When Antinous is

---

[1] It is well known that ευ- in Homer is still the adjective ἐΰς, not merely the adverb which alone is used in later times.

[2] Cf. my *Rechtsidee*, 122ff., Stier, *l.c.*, 7ff., also Wilamowitz, *l.c.*, on v. 276. W. Jaeger, *Solon's Eunomia* (*Sitzungsber. Preuss. Akad.*, 1926), 82, neglects this fact.

[3] In *Rechtsidee*, 116, I have tried to show the spiritual reasons why Homer does not use the word *nomos*. But it must also be taken into account that the language of Homer's poetry does not contain such words as *logos*, *tropos* and *nomos*.

about to injure the beggar, somebody tells him: 'Be careful lest this be a god. For the gods wander through the cities in various disguises, to behold and mark the wantonness and the *eunomia* of men.[1] The point in question is chiefly whether men are hospitable to strangers. Although this is not a political question, it had the greatest importance for the life of men in early ages. Homer speaks of the two contrasting conceptions of *hybris* and *eunomia*; to that there is an analogy in the contrast between the 'savages' (*hybristai, agrioi*) and the 'just' (*dikaioi*) (*Od.* 6, 120, and elsewhere). The latter are the civilized men who have a share in *dike* because they are hospitable and pious.[2] Thus, the meaning of *eunomia* in that single passage of Homer seems clear; hospitality was probably the most important part of custom and tradition, essential in the ancient order under which men lived in early times. Yet the word *eunomia*, which occurs in Homer nowhere else, was probably strange to epic usage, both as an expression and as a conception. The same conclusion may possibly be drawn from the idea that the gods walk on earth in disguise and visit mortal men in order to test their hospitality. This is a well-known motif from fairy-tales, but little in conformity with the common conceptions of Homer.[3] The same is also true of *eunomia*, and the earliest evidence of the word does not therefore exclude the possibility that it is derived from the equally un-Homeric word *nomos*.

The connection between *eunomia* and *dike*, as revealed in Homer by their common contrast to *hybris*, was probably the reason why Hesiod made Eunomia the sister of Dike. By then, *dike* had become the idea round which political thought centred, and it was only natural for *eunomia* to follow suit. This, in fact, might happen without any essential change of meaning. Just as it was applied earlier to individual men, the word was now used to describe good order and sound traditions in a community. I do not think that it has any significance that in

[1] . . . εἰ δή πού τις ἐπουράνιος θεός ἐστι.
καί τε θεοὶ ξένοισιν ἐοικότες ἀλλοδαποῖσι,
παντοῖοι τελέθοντες, ἐπιστρωφῶσι πόληας,
ἀνθρώπων ὕβριν τε καὶ εὐνομίην ἐφορῶντες.
[2] Cf. *Rechtsidee*, 60.
[3] The objections to this argument by E. Römisch, *Studien zur älteren griechischen Elegie* (1933), 41, 2, are not to the point. Gods in human appearance are, of course, frequent in epic poetry; but the Harûn-al-Rashid part which they play in this passage seems quite unique.

Hesiod's verse Eunomia is the first mentioned of the three sisters; Dike, at any rate, had to be in the middle for metrical reasons. In general *eunomia* as well as *eirene* played a far less important part than *dike*, which alone was a sort of war-cry of the new and rising forces, and at the same time the expression of Hesiod's passionate moral demands. The human ideal of *dike* became a goddess and as such the divine representative of justice, of that justice which was created and protected by Zeus. *Eunomia* stood at her side as the exponent of the forces of tradition, representing the conception of a human order, 'willed by Zeus'.

EUNOMIA IN EARLY SPARTA

Hesiod's genealogy naturally was not yet generally known or accepted during the seventh century. A different, though perhaps not an independent, genealogy comes from Sparta, and for this reason it has particular interest for us. In one of Alcman's poems[1] the poet invokes Tyche as the sister of Eunomia and Peitho and the daughter of Prometheia (foresight or clever forethought). The fragment does not tell us anything but the mere names of mother and daughters. Its explanation is difficult, and no interpretation can be guaranteed to be correct. Still, the names do tell us something, particularly if we try to combine them with what we know of early Sparta.[2]

Prometheia, or Forethought, is significant for Spartan methods of government. One can say with some justification that at all times Spartan policy, both domestic and foreign, was mainly ruled by a cautious reluctance which might be called forethought. If we find Prometheia combined with Tyche, it is possible to understand this as the success that originates in prudence. Both conceptions refer, as we should expect in

---

[1] frg. 44 Diehl:

⟨Τύχα⟩,

Εὐνομίας καὶ Πειθῶς ἀδελφά

καὶ Προμαθείας θυγατήρ.

[2] The following attempt differs to some extent from the interpretation which I suggested before. But, now as then, I cannot agree with the explanation given by Wilamowitz (*Hermes*, 64, 487), who speaks of Eunomia as the 'basis of lawfulness' and of Peitho as the art of handling men. Both interpretations are, I believe, at variance with the spirit of archaic Sparta. Wilamowitz thinks that Alcman 'must have spoken of his State or of the rulers of the State'. I should prefer to say that the poet wished to express certain fundamental ideas of the political wisdom of Sparta.

Sparta, to political and communal life, and not to the life of the private individual. But forethought is a quality of the individual, and we may well expect it to be the most desirable quality in those men who ruled Sparta. It is also a quality of older men rather than of the young, and it seems justifiable to think here of the Spartan Gerusia, that Council which included the kings and was the real leader of Spartan policy during the seventh century.

It is perhaps more difficult to understand the part played by Peitho. Her name is well known from ample evidence in Greek literature as the embodiment of Persuasion, whether as the orator's clever art or as the loving companion of Aphrodite. I cannot think of any section of the social or political world of Sparta, even of the Sparta of the seventh century which had not yet the rigidity of the post-Chilonian State, that could be governed by Persuasion. The argument in Plato's *Laws* (718ff.), contrasting persuasion with 'Right and Might', is definitely un-Spartan, and, indeed, Plato (722B) finds all Greek laws working by compulsion only, and not by persuasion. 'Authority is never tempered in their law-making with persuasion'[1] Even understood in a wider sense as the generally accepted form which determined the relations between the rulers and those who were ruled, it would not be typical of Sparta. Sparta rested on the obedience of her citizens, and obedience would follow a command, not mere persuasion. Obedience is a second, legitimate translation of Peitho; it must have been the meaning of Alcman's goddess.[2] In his 'family' the chief guiding principles are put side by side, one for the leaders of the State, the other for the Spartiates in general. Both conceptions were to dominate the relations between the individual citizens, whether *gerontes* or ordinary Spartiates, and the State.

---

[1] οὐ γὰρ πειθοῖ κεραννύντες τὴν μάχην νομοθετοῦσιν. Translation by A. E. Taylor, who reads (with Badham and others) ἀρχὴν for the corrupt μάχην of the manuscripts. Ast's correction ἀνάγκην would mean essentially the same – that 'compulsion is not mixed with persuasion'.

[2] Peitho as obedience appears, for instance, in Xenophon (*Cyrop.* 2, 3, 19; 3, 3, 8; cf. *resp. Lac.* 8, 2f.), who is so strongly influenced by Spartan thought. Plutarch, to whom we owe the knowledge of Alcman's fragment (*de fort. Rom.*, 318a), speaks of Tyche coming to Rome from the East. He contrasts the Roman Tyche with Pindar's ἀπειθὴς Τύχα, and compares her with Alcman's. But just as his Tyche is that of the second and first centuries B.C., so he takes Peitho as Persuasion, which then had been the normal interpretation for several centuries.

Eunomia had to serve the same State and the same political ideal. The word did not yet indicate the Spartan constitution itself as it did later (as, for instance, in Herodotus I, 65f.). We expect Eunomia to conform in general to the character of Peitho and Prometheia, and it is no daring conclusion to think of her, too, as a principle determining the attitude of every citizen towards the State. Like the sister of Dike in Hesiod, the sister of Peitho and daughter of Prometheia is the 'good order' that was to prevail in the individual as well as in the State, and particularly in the relations between them. If 'Nomos the Master' (δεσπότης νόμος) ruled Sparta then as it did later, Eunomia was the conformity with, and the obedience to, this Nomos in which the will of the State was embodied. And this Nomos was not 'Law'. The Spartan word for law was *rhetra*, and Nomos represented the force of tradition which was so particularly strong in Sparta. It might include law, but that does not make Eunomia an expression of mere lawfulness. She covered every aspect of life and State.

The combination of Prometheia, Peitho, and Eunomia is the ideal of which Alcman speaks. He invokes Tyche, and we can perhaps assume that he saw in her the outcome of that ideal collaboration. She was, it seems, a 'good' Tyche, success and good fortune. For Plutarch contrasts her with Pindar's 'relentless Tyche, turning the double rudder' of fate (frg. 20, Bowra), although Pindar describes Tyche also as φερέπολις, upholding the State (frg. 19) — a description which seems to be very appropriate to the sister of Eunomia.[1] The logical meaning in Alcman's genealogy remains elusive. But he was not a didactic poet like Hesiod, but a lyric poet.[2] We must not try to press the meaning of his genealogical scheme too far. Even though we may think that the three sisters are not of the same kind, and cannot be derived from Prometheia, we must acknowledge that the poet could not speak of three mothers and one daughter! It may even be that Alcman saw in Tyche not so much the result of the activities of the three others, but the luck of chance which could be regarded as their necessary

[1] Both Tyche and Eunomia appear in Pindar as Σώτειρα (*O.* 12, 2; 9, 16); so does Themis (*O.* 8, 21).

[2] Tyche and Peitho are sisters in Hesiod, *Theog.* 349, 360, but there they are only two out of a large and rather mixed crowd, the daughters of Oceanus. There is no reason to connect Alcman's genealogy with this section of Hesiod's poem.

companion.[1] He wished, at any rate, to describe something
rather complicated, the desirable co-operation of certain leading forces of political life. To do this, he could only use the
scheme of family genealogy, and this led unavoidably to simplification. Yet, Alcman's goddesses were practically the same
in the world of Sparta as were Hesiod's daughters of Themis
in the wider world of the Polis in general. They were the
exponents of the political and social community.

It is well known, and clearly attested by Alcman himself,[2]
that during the seventh century Sparta had moved away from
the 'Lycurgan' State, which had its roots in the primitive
community of earlier times. It was probably the ephors who
were responsible for the creative reaction of the following
century, by which what was alleged to be the Sparta of Lycurgus was restored in a new and more rigid form. The work of
the ephors crowned a policy that had been influential for some
time past in its opposition to the growing decline of Spartan
standards. The ideal, expressed in those lines of Alcman,
found its parallel, although one of a much more vigorous type,
in the protests and exhortations of Tyrtaeus, who lived at
about the same time but was not, as Alcman probably was, a
foreigner. Scholars seem now to agree that Tyrtaeus was a true
Spartiate. He appealed to a generation that had lost much of
that martial spirit and the will to sacrifice itself for the State,
which were supposed to be typical of Spartan tradition. In
some of his poetry, Tyrtaeus contrasts the youth of his time
with earlier, harder and more warlike, generations. In other
verses he speaks more generally of Sparta's glorious past
(frg. 2, 4, 5). He praises the ancient traditions and the old
order of Sparta. Although writing in Ionian style and metre,
which had already become fixed for this kind of poetry,
Tyrtaeus was the protagonist of those who fought against the
Ionian spirit and the dissolution, threatening and already
partially achieved, of the traditional Spartan standards.

One of Tyrtaeus' poems bears the title *Eunomia*. The name
was probably given by some later editor who saw that in that
poem not only the origin of the Lacedaemonian State was

---

[1] That is the way in which Pelasgus in Aeschylus' *Suppliants* (523) expresses his
hope that he will win his people for the suppliants with the support of Peitho (Persuasion) and 'effectual Tyche'.
[2] Cf., e.g., his fragments 49, 55, 71, 108. On 49 see *Hermes* 68, 288ff.

mentioned as going back to Zeus (frg. 2) but also, as we may
assume, the Great Rhetra given to Lycurgus. This Rhetra,
according to the lines added to the old oracle (Diod. VII, 12, 1,
as compared with Herod. 1, 65), created the *eunomia* of the
Spartan State. The man who gave the poem its name probably
thought of the meaning of *eunomia* which was prevalent during
the fifth century and later, indicating that constitution which
was opposed to *isonomia*. But even so, the name was actually
justifiable, and it is likely that the word *eunomia* appeared somewhere in that poem of Tyrtaeus. It is even not impossible that
Alcman, whose exact time we do not know, but who undoubtedly
lived in a peaceful age, wrote after the Messenian War. If so,
he knew of Tyrtaeus' *Eunomia* when he wrote those lines
which we have discussed, and Tyrtaeus may have been the first
who applied the word to the Spartan *kosmos*. He, however, did
not think of an 'ideal constitution', and the original meaning
of *eunomia* was perhaps not so much expressed in the one
particular poem about the origin of the State as in the whole
poetry of Tyrtaeus. The *eunomia* of earlier times, the 'good
order' of an idealized past, that same *eunomia* of which Thucydides (I, 18, 1) declared that it had ruled Sparta for most of her
earlier history — that was the goal which Tyrtaeus set before
the minds of the Spartan youth. Eunomia inspired his poetry,
and his poetry breathed new life into Sparta's Eunomia.[1]

SOLON'S EUNOMIA

The title that an ancient editor gave to the poem of Tyrtaeus
was given again by a modern scholar to Solon's elegy *Our City*
(frg. 3).[2] The last part of this poem is expressly dedicated to
the praise of *eunomia*. It was a justifiable and happy idea of
Professor Jaeger's, and he made use of it in the attempt to
reach a deeper understanding of Solon's thought. According
to Jaeger, Solon's *Eunomia* reflects 'the spirit of Athens as a
State based on justice and law. Eunomia is an absolute ideal

[1] Sparta's Eunomia is the main subject of two valuable articles of more recent date
which I can only mention here: A. Andrewes, *Cl. Q.* XXXII (1938), 89ff., and H. T.
Wade-Gery, *Cl. Q.* XXXVIII (1944), 1ff.
[2] W. Jaeger in the paper mentioned above, p. 75, note 2. A hint to the same
effect was given by Wilamowitz, *Textgeschichte d. griech. Lyriker* (*Abh. Gött. Gesellsch.
d. Wiss.* IV, 1901), 107.

which Solon wanted to realize on the foundations provided by the prevailing conditions' (p.82). We shall try to find out how far this view[1] agrees with the general results of our discussion of *eunomia*. Solon — even with such predecessors as Hesiod and Archilochus — is the first Greek who is really comprehensible to us both in his historical position and in his individuality. It will be therefore the more important to analyse his conception of Eunomia.

A question which has first to be answered is what *nomos* meant to Solon. In the only passage of his extant poems in which the word occurs, the text is ambiguous (frg. 24, 15ff.):

ταῦτα μὲν κράτει
νόμου βίην τε καὶ δίκην συναρμόσας
ἔρεξα καὶ διῆλθον ὡς ὑπεσχόμην.

This is the reading of the London Papyrus of Aristotle's *Constitution of Athens*, while the Papyrus fragment in Berlin and the literary tradition (Aristides and Plutarch) have ὁμοῦ instead of νόμου.[2] The latter has been more or less generally accepted.[3] I must explain in some detail why I believe that ὁμοῦ is the right version. Neither of the two versions can be called the *lectio difficilior*; for it seems just as possible that ὁμοῦ was written for νόμου as the other way round. A decision can be reached only on the basis of the logic of the context. Essential for it is the combination of two opposite conceptions of force or might (βία) and justice or right (δίκη). They had been contrasted before, but the contrast became stronger and more fundamental when *dike* grew in importance by outgrowing the world of the merely human court of justice. No word was superfluous that might stress the fact that two actually incompatible conceptions were here considered to be consistent with one another. When Solon put ὁμοῦ at the beginning of the verse, he found a very satisfactory introduction to a statement which was rounded off by the last word συναρμόσας. The

---

[1] Cf. also K. Reinhardt, *Rh. Mus.* 71 (1916), 133f., and my *Rechtsidee*, 86.

[2] The translation is either: 'By fitting together Right and Might through the power of *nomos* I did these things and accomplished them as I had promised' or: 'By fitting close together Right and Might I did these things through my power and . . .'

[3] For example, by E. Diehl in the first edition of his *Anthologia Lyrica* and by H. Oppermann in the most recent edition of the 'Αθην. πολ. Cf. also Stier, *l.c.*, 8ff., and Jaeger, *Hermes* 64 (1927), 32. Mr. J. M. Edmonds, on the other hand, in *Elegy and Jambus* (*Loeb Libr.*) has ὁμοῦ.

'harmony' which is contained in the verb must not be taken as very emphatic, as is proved by the following lines: 'And laws I wrote that made straight justice, *fitting* for everybody, upper and lower classes alike.'[1] A word to emphasize the 'fitness', the 'harmony', was, if not necessary, certainly desirable. We realize that ὁμοῦ is not a superfluous addition as it has been called. Solon was able to combine 'Right and Might' on account of his position and power, his κράτος, which he held by the election of his fellow-citizens, due to the ability which he had shown before and which the people expected him to display in his difficult task.[2] Every word in those lines of Solon's has its appropriate and necessary meaning.

If Solon had said that he combined force and justice 'through the power of *nomos*' (νόμου κράτει), it would first prove that the idea of *nomos* — which could only have had the meaning of custom, tradition, ancient order, not that of law[3] — was of particular importance in Solon's thought. For this there is not the slightest evidence. Another consequence would be that *nomos* provided the means to bridge the gulf between force and justice. It is the *Seisachtheia*, Solon's revolutionary measure of a 'disburdening ordinance', which is described in the lines with which we are dealing. Its method was force, its meaning and goal justice. How can the *Seisachtheia* be understood as the result of *nomos*, of custom and tradition? The means necessary to achieve the union of force and justice were to be found nowhere else but in the heart and brain of the law-giver. How could a *nomos* provide for that union? Such an interpretation would come dangerously near to the possible meaning of Pindar's famous phrase, which was coined one and a half centuries later, of the 'King Nomos who makes just the most violent force' (δικαιῶν τὸ βιαιότατον). I am convinced that ὁμοῦ is the only possible reading for our passage.[4]

All this naturally does not disprove Solon's knowledge of *nomos* in its old meaning. But since he never mentions it we can

---

[1] Θεσμοὺς δ' ὁμοίως τῷ κακῷ τε κἀγαθῷ
εὐθεῖαν εἰς ἕκαστον ἁρμόσας δίκην
ἔγραψα.

[2] Stier is splitting hairs when he objects to this interpretation because it would mean that Solon shifted the responsibility from himself on to the citizens.

[3] This was seen by Stier who in that respect is right against Kaibel's defence of ὁμοῦ.

[4] It was accepted by Diehl in the second edition of the *Anthologia Lyrica*. Cf. also Römisch, *l.c.*, 46.

at least conclude (without pressing the *argumentum ex silentio* too far) that it was of no particular interest to him. Solon, with all the conscious discipline of his own individuality, his sincere piety, his idea of a middle line in political and general human affairs, had nevertheless the natural pride of a man with a creative brain.[1] When he defended his work in his poetry and showed his pride, it was natural for him to lay emphasis on what he himself had thought, wished, and achieved, although he always saw himself at the same time carrying out the higher will of the State and of the gods. Even after his reforms there was much left which belonged to *nomos*, to custom and tradition, in both the social and the political field. Much of this had to be, and was, overcome during the sixth century. To him this *nomos* probably meant little. Solon issued his laws in the spirit of *dike* which was to him the ideal expression of the will of the Polis; thus he created 'straight justice'.

The 'political man', who acted with the clear foresight of the true statesman, realized 'the wisdom of an immanent law which permeates the social life of men' (Jaeger, 80). This law he saw in Dike, the power that could reward and retaliate. Influenced by earlier traditions of ethical and political thought, such as are seen in Hesiod, Solon pursued his aim of building up a possible future for his Polis by serving Dike through his own lawgiving, his *thesmoi*. There was therefore no room in his thought for a Nomos of similar importance.

That being so, it becomes at least unlikely that Solon thought of *nomos* when he praised *eunomia*. In his elegy he draws a picture of the inner disintegration of the Polis, caused by the fault of the citizens. This picture of 'bad order' or *dysnomia* is the warning which he offers to his fellow-citizens: 'This it is that my heart orders me to teach the Athenians' (frg. 3, 30). In contrast to the bad order of the actual State he then depicts the effects of *eunomia*. It makes all things orderly and perfect, puts the unjust in chains, stops insolence, destroys *hybris*, and 'withers the growing flowers of ruin'. Crooked judgment becomes straight, the struggle of factions ceases, everything is perfect and wise. It is obvious: *eunomia* is an ideal state of affairs. It is not a definite constitution, nor is it a State with good laws. It is a human community which is ruled by

---

[1] Cf. the picture of Solon, drawn by R. Pfeiffer, *Philologus* 84 (1929), 147, although it is seen from a different point of view.

moderation, unity and order. We hear nothing of custom and tradition, nothing of the good old times. They were, in fact, anything but good. Solon was not a romantic, but an idealist who traced his picture of *eunomia* in an ideal future.

There is, on the other hand, no mention of an ideal or natural law. *Eunomia* was for Solon a goal of his personal policy, the sort of thing he had promised to Athens before-hand for the time when he might be given full power. There is something new in this, although here again, in contrasting *eunomia* and *dysnomia*, Solon followed Hesiod who knows Dysnomia as one of the children of Eris (*Theog.* 230).[1] It was Solon whose political thought first centred round that contrast, and it is possible and important to find out from his poems what meaning he actually attributed to the two contrasting conceptions.[2] The essential point of the whole elegy is the guilt of men. That is why he contrasts with much emphasis the gods who protect the Polis, and the men (αὐτοί) who destroy it. Just as *dysnomia* is the result of the guilt of the citizens and therefore embodies the political and moral chaos of the Polis, *eunomia* is the result of the 'guilt', that is to say the merit, of those who maintain moderation and good sense. The *nomos* contained in the two words was to Solon no more than a general expression for the 'order' of the Polis, its state of affairs, which might be good or bad. But *eunomia* and *dysnomia* expressed a moral attitude, or a state of mind, on the part of the citizens. Solon used conceptions which had been known before to political thought, and he also followed earlier thought in that he did not yet really distinguish between subjective feelings and objective facts. To him the good order of the State was identical with the willingness of its citizens to maintain this order. Moreover, by the great task which Solon set him-self he learnt the causes of the illness of the State and the remedies needed to restore it to health. This implies that he found himself compelled to form a definite 'view' of the State, a *theoria*, an ideal picture as the final goal. This ideal naturally

[1] Cf. also K. Ziegler, *Neue Jahrbücher* 49 (1922), 196, who however speaks of 'quotations' from Hesiod; this does not do justice to the relations between the minds of the two men.

[2] Stier, 13, rightly rejects Jaeger's assertion that it was only on metrical grounds that δυσνομία was used instead of ἀνομία. The latter appears first in Herodotus (I, 96f.), that is to say at a period in which for a long time past εὐνομία had had no other meaning than 'conditions under good laws'.

grew from the vital forces of the Polis,[1] but to the rational and active mind of Solon — and in this he is quite different from Hesiod or Tyrtaeus — the ideal of *eunomia* became a piece of practical work which it was possible eventually to bring to life. Thus Solon, out of his own mind and heart, gave new contents to traditional forms and conceptions. We can see something of the working of the political mind of the Greeks. Its tools were political ideas, and they were gradually being shaped and developed, one way in Athens, another way in Sparta.

OTHER EVIDENCE

It is common knowledge that early Greek ethics were in general distinguished by a kind of naive eudaemonism. In the most definite sense of the word, they were no ethics at all. We can perhaps say that the essence of their aims was to give the real life of the community an ideal background. Hesiod's moral demands are undoubtedly forceful and had passion behind them, but he did not aim at morality for morality's sake. The community which was to be preserved by those ethical demands is seen in all its real and material setting, although the poet insists on its ideal features. The ideal community, supported as it is by the pure and determined will for *dike*, is set up as a goal to be aimed at for the sake of happiness — general as well as individual — which is mainly displayed in glory and wealth (πλοῦτος, ὄλβος, κῦδος).[2] Thus the later unions of Eirene and Plutus (who frequently took the place of Eunomia[3]) and Eucleia and Eunomia were foreshadowed in earlier thought as expressed by Hesiod and Pindar. It is easily understandable that it is just *eunomia* or 'good order' (the shortest and most suitable translation of the word in its earlier meaning) that was regarded as the cause of wealth and prosperity.

Xenophanes expresses a similar view in a passage (frg. 2) in which he praises what he calls his wisdom (σοφία), denouncing

---

[1] As to these, cf. my paper 'When did the Polis rise?' in *Journ. Hell. Stud.* 57 (1937), 147ff., esp. 153ff.

[2] As is well known, ὄλβος is often, and as early as in Homer, said to lead to κόρος, and is then linked with ὕβρις – the very opposite to its connection with δίκη. Cf. also D. H. Abel, *T.A.P.A.* 84 (1943), 95.

[3] Cf. Keil, *l.c.*, 46ff.

the general overestimate of physical competitions. Even though there may be an excellent wrestler or boxer or runner among the citizens, 'the Polis for that reason would not have more *eunomia*'.[1] Even a victory at Olympia brings only 'little joy'. 'For thus the stores of the city are not filled.' It is typical that even this rebellious opponent of all athletic contests had plenty of the spirit that inspired them. He tilted not only against his poetical rivals, but also against the whole conventional order of his day. It is equally typical that he does not connect *eunomia* with that way of life. He speaks of his wisdom, his art and poetical power, as being capable of strengthening *eunomia*; for, in contrast to the 'power of man or horse', his wisdom contributes to the material prosperity of the Polis. However vague Xenophanes' conception of his wisdom may be, it illustrates, in a new and intensified manner, the fact that rational pride and consciousness now played their part in the political field. The vagrant rhapsode was not a man of the Polis. After 67 years of wandering through the whole Greek world he had no home. Moreover, relying on the power and acumen of his reasoning and being at the same time a passionate fighter for truth, he dared to oppose popular beliefs and the general ideal of life — that is to say the very spirit of the Polis. But just because he was so aggressive, he was compelled to adapt himself to the intellectual and emotional level of his audience. He could only hope to overcome his opponents by beating them with their own weapons. Thus he claimed to be the man who, better than the idolized victors at the Olympian games, could provide for the *eunomia* and the well-being of the Polis.

In the Homeric Hymn to Mother Earth (XXX, 11f.) we find again the combination of *eunomia* with the wealth of the Polis. Of the men who are blessed by Gaia it is said that 'they rule with *eunomia* in their cities of fair women; bliss and wealth follow them'.[2] The word *eunomia* is used here in the plural.

---

[1] Keil, 40, is completely mistaken in assuming that εὐνομία has here the meaning of oligarchic party-politics.

[2] αὐτοὶ δ' εὐνομίῃσι πόλιν κατὰ καλλιγύναικα
κοιρανέουσ'; ὄλβος δὲ πολὺς καὶ πλοῦτος ὀπηδεῖ.
It is something similar when Pindar (*N*. 9, 29) expresses the wish that Aetna, Hiero's new foundation, may have μοῖραν εὔνομον. In *I*. 5, 27 Aegina is called εὔνομος πόλις. This may be the same, but it is also possible to think here of the oligarchic character of the city (cf. Wilamowitz, *Pindaros*, 63).

This might be a mere consequence of epic style; the hymn is written in traditional language, and it would be a mistake to look for any great subtlety of expression. Yet, it seems reasonable to assume that the writer of this hymn did not know of the old meaning of *eunomia*, which excluded the use of the plural. The hymn was certainly composed at a comparatively late date, and it is likely that the poet understood *nomos* as 'law' and therefore used the plural of *eunomia* as a mere equivalent to 'good laws' — εὐνομίαι are καλοὶ νόμοι. This may be a clumsy way of expression, but it conformed to the epic style and metre.

EUNOMIA AND ISONOMIA

We have passed beyond the most important change which *eunomia* underwent. Before we try to explore its meaning we ought to remember that there were other expressions of a similar kind which have to be taken into account. I have already mentioned *dysnomia* as the natural opposite to *eunomia*. But of special importance were *isonomia* and later *autonomia*. It is by no means certain that all these words are to be explained in the same way. For each of them came into use at a different period, and the formation of a compound word from *nomos* may have a completely different meaning, according as it happened in 600 or 450 B.C. *Autonomos* and *autonomia* are probably creations of the fifth century.[1] We do not know whether the words were used as early as the sixth century to describe the position of the members of the Peloponnesian League, but it is very unlikely. We know of the word *autonomia* in no other meaning than 'to have and to use one's own laws',[2] and that meaning could occur only after the development of the conception of *nomos* which I shall presently describe.[3]

Isonomia, on the other hand, occurs first, though as an adjective, in the famous Athenian drinking-song on the tyrannicides:

---

[1] Earliest evidence: Herod. I, 96; VIII, 140a. Soph. *Ant.* 821. Hippocr. *de aere*, 16.
[2] τοῖς αὐτῶν νόμοις χρῆσθαι. Cf. U. Kahrstedt, *Griech. Staatsrecht* I, 86.
[3] It is perhaps worth noticing that the earliest inscription which has the word comes from Dorian Crete (fifth cent.): [αυτ]ονομ[ο]ι καυτοδικοι (Dareste, 31 = Schwyzer, 177).

'I'll carry my sword in a myrtle-branch
like Harmodius and Aristogeiton,
when they slew the tyrant
and made Athens free and equal.'[1]

The song, like others of the kind — as, for instance, that on
the dead of Leipsydrion (24 Diehl), where the nobles suffered
bloody defeat at the hands of Hippias — was a product of the
aristocratic upper class. Harmodius and Aristogeiton are
praised in these lines as the foes of the tyrants; they were not
yet as in later legend the founders of democracy. Actually
their revolt had brought no freedom, but rather an intensifica-
tion of tyranny. *Isonomia*, the claim of Athens to be 'free and
equal', is in this poem the opposite to monarchy. As far as I
know, it has never been noticed that *isonomia* was at first an
aristocratic conception,[2] the conception of those members of
the nobility who expelled Hippias with the help of Sparta and
felt themselves as successors of 'dearest Harmodius and
Aristogeiton' who had killed Hipparchus. *Isonomia* was the
equality of noblemen, as contrasted with the lack of equality
expressed in the rule of one man. The idea of equality, after
all, had strong roots in the aristocratic forms of communal life
such as the life of the Spartan 'peers', the *Homoioi*.[3]

The opposition of *isonomia* to monarchy rests on more than
the interpretation of that poem. That the contrast was well-
known appears from a more or less contemporary source, a
fragment of Alcmaeon the Pythagorean (frg. 4 Diels) — that is
to say, of a man who, as a Pythagorean, must have held aristocratic views in politics. We find the contrast here transferred
to the field of medicine, *isonomia* being a state of good health,
'monarchy' one of bad health. In the late résumé which we
have of Alcmaeon's theory, *isonomia* is explained as 'equal mixture of qualities' (σύμμετρος τῶν ποιῶν κρᾶσις). The fact that
the language of philosophical medicine could usurp for its own
purposes the conceptions of politics makes it clear that both

---

[1] 10, Diehl II¹, 184 (cf. 13): ἐν μύρτου κλαδὶ τὸ ξίφος φορήσω
ὥσπερ Ἁρμόδιος καὶ Ἀριστογείτων,
ὅτε τὸν τύραννον κτανέτην
ἰσονόμους τ' Ἀθήνας ἐποιησάτην.

[2] Though B. Keil, *Griech. Staatsaltertümer*, 364f., has stated that ἰσονομία existed
before democracy. See further on the subject of ἰσονομία my article in *Pauly-Wissowa*,
Suppl. VII, 293ff.

[3] Cf. already *Iliad* 16, 53.

G

Alcmaeon and his readers knew of these contrasting conceptions.[1] Whether we are also justified in accepting the meaning of 'mixture' as inherent in *isonomia* is questionable. The common ground of politics and medicine is not provided by the conception of 'mixture'. Essential is the contrast which existed between equal distribution of power on the one hand, and excess of power on the other. We may try to explain Alcmaeon's *isonomia* as 'equal distribution', but an 'equal *nomos*', that is to say a balanced order, is just as good an interpretation. Thucydides naturally knows of political *isonomia* as the programme of mass democracy, opposed to a 'sensible aristocracy' (III, 82, 8; cf. IV, 78, 3; VI, 38, 5); but when he speaks of a somewhat remote time and place, the period of the Persian Wars in Boeotia, he can oppose an aristocracy called *isonomos*, or a democracy, to the 'rule of a few men' (δυναστεία ὀλίγων ἀνδρῶν) which is 'the nearest thing to tyranny' (ἐγγυτάτω δὲ τυράννου) (III, 62, 3).

The idea of equality was naturally less strong in an aristocratic society — in which it often arose only after opposition to a tyrant — than in the development of democracy. An obvious sign of the impact of equality on the growing democratic forces was the popular demand for the distribution of land (γῆς ἀναδασμός) or, as Solon once put it in a more general way (frg. 23, 21), the demand for *isomoiria* — that is to say for equal share in property and power.[2] This was the most extreme and therefore most fundamental demand of the poor and powerless. It is well known that Solon rejected their request with the utmost determination, and he mentions this refusal in the same context as his refusal to become a tyrant. The passage reveals the close bond that existed between tyranny and democracy, and foreshadows the historical development from Solon to Peisistratus and from Peisistratus to Cleisthenes.

During the sixth century the *thesmoi* were replaced by the

---

[1] W. Jaeger in an earlier paper has spoken of *isonomia* with regard to the famous fragment 9 of Anaximander (*Staatsethik im Zeitalter des Platon*, 5). But in the article on Solon, to which I have frequently referred, he rightly emphasizes that the leading principle of Anaximander was *dike*. Cf. also *Rechtsidee*, 89ff. It would be almost justifiable to take *eunomia*, expressing as it does the order of the political *kosmos*, as an adequate description of Anaximander's philosophical *kosmos*; but then the ideas of justice and the punishment for injustice would not be clearly expressed, and therefore Anaximander followed Dike and not her sister Eunomia.

[2] Ἰσόμορος is already used in *Iliad* 15, 209 for Poseidon's claims against Zeus.

nomoi. In other words, the individual enactments became parts of a new 'Nomos', covering the whole of political life. From meaning 'custom' and 'order' Nomos came to mean that unity of traditional and enacted standards which is inaccurately translated as 'the Law'. The process can best be traced in Athenian history; but it must have been similar in other States, even though the individual law was not everywhere called *nomos.* Sparta, in her great political change of the sixth century, followed an order, whether real or ideal, of the past; thus even here it was the conception of Nomos that became political. The *rhetrai* were to Sparta something like what the *thesmoi* were to Athens. But the well-known proclamation of the ephors when they entered office probably originated in the sixth century,[1] and it contained (apart from the interdiction of wearing a moustache) the command 'to keep to the *nomoi*'.[2] These *nomoi* were parts of the Nomos just as in other States. Nomos became everywhere an expression of a truly political order, thus superseding an earlier order that, essentially, was dominated by non-political forces.

Eunomia changed its meaning together with *nomos.* It now indicated a State with good laws — that is to say with a good constitution; for the Aristotelian discrimination between *nomoi* and *politeia* had not yet been discovered. *Eunomia*, at the same time, kept the meaning which was so strong in Sparta but was never quite lost anywhere, that of long-established customs and habits, in brief — tradition.[3] Democracy broke with these traditions to an ever-growing extent. It was the idea of equality that dominated the opposition of the demos to oligarchy. *Eunomia* was no longer an adequate expression for the aims of new political forces and ideas, as it had been in the time of Solon. A surprising change took place on both sides.

[1] Cf. *Epitymbion f. H. Swoboda* (1927), 24.

[2] προσέχειν τοῖς νόμοις. Aristotle, frg. 539. Cf. below, p. 101.

[3] Thuc. I, 18, 1 uses the word εὐνομεῖσθαι for Sparta which was always ἀτυράννευτος. Here the political meaning clearly prevails. Cf. now A. W. Gomme, *A Historical Commentary on Thucydides* I, 128f. I largely agree, except that I cannot share Gomme's doubts with regard to Her. I, 65. If we assume, as we must, that the Spartan reformers of the sixth century largely restored, or pretended to restore, the conditions of an earlier past, Herodotus' 'carefree chronology' becomes less of a puzzle, while it is more than doubtful that he 'seems to preserve so clearly the tradition that εὐνομία was unknown in Sparta before the beginning of the sixth century'. – Peculiar is the way in which Sophocles (*Ajax*, 712) speaks of Ajax as offering the customary sacrifices εὐνομίᾳ σέβων μέγιστα. Still, we are reminded of that moral attitude which we found in Solon's εὐνομία.

The anti-tyrannical *isonomia* of the nobility, carried further by a development which had been prepared by conceptions such as Solon's *isomoiria*, became a new political reality in Cleisthenes' work. As the catchword of democracy it implied an equal share in the Nomos and thus for every citizen 'equality before the law'. That was why *isonomia* was to Herodotus 'the fairest of all names' (3, 80). Eunomia, on the other hand, the ideal of the past and even of Solon, who is sometimes called the father of Athenian democracy, now meant the best constitution, based on inequality. It was now the ideal of oligarchy. The thought of Eunomia, Dike and Eirene as sisters ceased to have any real meaning. It was only consistent with this that an oligarchic party-man, to whom democracy was the contradiction of his ideal of *eunomia*, gave it the name of *kakonomia* (Ps.-Xen., 1, 8). I am also inclined to believe that the common worship of Eucleia and Eunomia (see above p. 73f.) was created by oligarchs of the second half of the fifth century. Pausanias (I, 14, 5) tells us that the temple of Eucleia was built 'for the victory over the Persians, who had landed at Marathon'; probably he misread an inscription, just as he did not realize that the temple was dedicated to Eunomia as well as to Eucleia. Soon after 490 no worship of Eunomia could possibly originate in democratic Athens. Later in the century, however, the oligarchs were accustomed to take the fighters of Marathon as examples and ideals, as is well known from Aristophanes (*Ach.* 181; *Nub.* 986). I assume that they dedicated the temple to their memory, that is to say to their glory (Eucleia) and their state of good laws (Eunomia). That reflects exactly what anti-democrats of the end of the fifth century would feel.[1] No state, however, was more representative of the principle of good order and the overwhelming power both of tradition and law than Sparta, which therefore found the adequate expression of its very nature in *eunomia*.

Thus the Greek dualism between Sparta and Athens, noticeable in the early fifth century in its first and slight beginnings, found its first expression in the new contrast of *eunomia* and *isonomia*. Both conceptions, however, the Euno-

---

[1] As a parallel it may be mentioned that the oligarchs of 411 aimed at restoring the πάτριοι νόμοι οὒς Κλεισθένης ἔθηκεν (Aristotle, *Ath. pol.* 29, 3). I see that A. Andrewes, *l.c.*, p. 102 (Postscript) also assumes that the cult of Eunomia and Eucleia 'goes back to c. 400 B.C.'. But he accepts Pausanias' statement as true. It seems unlikely, though perhaps not impossible, that Eunomia was added to an existing cult of Eucleia.

mia of Sparta and the Isonomia of Athens, rested on the same foundations. With all their contrasting qualities and their contradictory nature they implied one and the same fact, the rule of law. The Greeks never used the word *nomokratia*. But Nomos became the fundamental idea on which the Polis rested, whether it was constitutionally an oligarchy or a democracy. Compared with the absolute character of Nomos, the conceptions of Eunomia and Isonomia were qualified and relative. For that reason they disappeared during the fifth century from the front line of actual politics.[1]

The political philosophers, on the other hand — first the Anonymus Iamblichi (Diels II, 332, 22, 26) and later Plato and Aristotle — again speak of *eunomia*. To them it is an ideal of a public life directed by good laws, but not necessarily tied to an oligarchic constitution. Thus Eunomia was almost identical with Nomos itself.[2] At the same time, the moral implication remained valid, that even the best laws have no meaning and power unless the citizens obey them (cf. Diog. Laert. 3, 103). During the Hellenistic Age the whole idea underwent a sort of revival. For then the expressions used in practical politics — at least as far as those of the Greek city-States were concerned — were strongly influenced by theory, particularly by the doctrine of the 'mixed constitution'. Frequently now, *eunomia* was again coupled with *eirene* and became almost a synonym of another catchword of that age, *homonoia* or 'internal peace'. This shows that in spite of all changes the early meaning of *eunomia* was never lost, and also that it served political theory as an expression of that order which failed to realize the new political forms and possibilities displayed in the Hellenistic monarchies and the Roman Empire.

---

[1] It was different with *autonomia*, which did not imply any special kind of Nomos, but expressed merely the fact that a Polis had its own and independent Nomos. Autonomy, as is well known, became one of the most important political catchwords, used during the Peloponnesian War by Sparta as a weapon against Athens. Later, especially after the Peace of Antalcidas, it was the essence of Persian political propaganda amongst the Greeks.

[2] For evidence of the fourth century and the Hellenistic Age, cf. Keil, 39ff. A late example, not mentioned by Keil, shows that εὐνομία even invaded the field of pure public law; in a Cretan inscription of the first cent. B.C. (from Latmos: *G.D.I.* 5075, 35) we find magistrates who are called 'the elders ἐπὶ τῆς εὐνομίας'. Cf. S. A. Xanthoudides, *Rev. ét. gr.* XXV (1912), 42ff.

VII

A TOTALITARIAN STATE[1]

TOTALITARIAN and authoritarian are comparatively new expressions in the political vocabulary. But the idea is old, almost as old as human history. It is essentially one and the same form of political community which is described by either of the two words. To define it briefly, an authoritarian State is a State based upon obedience, a totalitarian State is one in which this obedience covers every aspect of a citizen's life — in fact his 'total' life. There are authoritarian elements in every form of political community, and in one way or another every State has to be totalitarian. Otherwise there would be anarchy. But it makes all the difference how deeply the duty of obedience invades public and private life, and what share other principles are allowed to have in the structure of State and society — above all, whether the governing men and institutions are under some public control. Much also depends on the answer to the question what the ultimate authority is to which a dictator or a ruling group of men refer as the true basis of their position and power. It may be the will of God or the will of the people or neither of these. Obviously there are certain threads connecting even the authoritarian forms and that form in which the will of the people and its control of the government are the decisive factors. There seems to be something in common even between totalitarianism and democracy.

But this conclusion, although justifiable to some extent, does not agree with the essential facts. The popular verdict, as so often, is right. There were and there are States in which the principles of unlimited obedience and total surrender of the individual to the State have reached such an extreme of consistency and perfection that no comparison with any form of constitutional government seems possible. The State of the Pharaohs with its bureaucracy and masses of slave fellahs was something of the kind. In a sense, the monarchy of the Ancient East as a whole was essentially authoritarian. The State was

---

[1] A broadcast talk in German, delivered in Prague in 1934. Unpublished. The paragraph on the statuette of Heracles is a later addition.

based upon the belief that the king ruled by the special grace of the gods as a being far above human standards. It is different when the theocratic element, which was alive in all the Eastern States, led to the highest god himself being considered the true king. The covenant between God and the people of Israel rendered all human monarchy a sort of substitute, and obedience to God and his laws was inseparable from the idea of a people's unity and community. No authoritarian principle within the human group could possibly grow from such a soil.

But it was not in the East that the first truly political structure of communal life was created, even though the technique of administration and jurisdiction had there reached a very advanced stage. The true creators and exponents of all possible forms of political order were the Greeks, the first 'political' people in history. It was in their numerous States, all of them limited to a narrow space, that for the first time political will and political ideas, both in the community and the individual, came into their own. Here for the first time the problems of a variety of possible constitutions were experienced as well as those of the relations between State and society, between leadership and general will, between community and individual; and here the first attempts were made to solve them. In Greece therefore we also find the State in which the conception of authority was consciously and exclusively accepted as the guiding principle in the purely political field as well as in the education of the citizens.

This State was Sparta. There has been an unending discussion since ancient times as to what name should be given to its political form, its constitution. Ranke, in his *Political Conversation*, says: 'Imagine aristocracy with all its typical qualities, and yet you will not have an idea what Sparta was.' But if Sparta was no aristocracy, was then the enemy of democratic Athens a democracy? Or was the State of the ephors, whose office meant opposition to the kings, a monarchy? Or was it, as Aristotle believed, a mixture of all the three elements, monarchic, aristocratic and democratic? I do not think that there is a definite answer to these questions, and if we are not too legally-minded we shall not worry. Whatever we decide to call Sparta's constitutional form with its peculiar and contradictory features, its true foundation was the unique form of life that it developed. This is what really matters. And it was shaped throughout by the totalitarian principle, and the complete submersion of society and individual in the State. It is for this reason that modern totalitarians have claimed Sparta as the model or ideal of their own endeavours. Whether this is justified or not, whether Sparta was a good or a bad example, whether later totalitarianism was and is her true successor or bad imitator — these are questions which will necessarily arise but cannot yet be answered.

The State of which I am going to speak was called 'the Lacedaemonians'. Lacedaemon or Laconia was the name of the region; its central settlement alone was Sparta. But the Spartiates, the citizens of Sparta, were the only full citizens of the State and ruled it, a minority within the whole population. The original inhabitants of the central areas, the plains of Laconia and Messenia, were subjugated and suppressed; as Helots they were serfs without any rights, the victims of every kind of injustice, even of organized and unpunished murder. The people living in the villages and towns of the surrounding districts, on the other hand, the so-called Perioeci, though free as individuals and, in fact, Lacedaemonians, had no political rights; they served the State as soldiers but not as citizens. The rule of a minority, the oligarchy of the Spartiates, was the expression of the strong political energy, the elemental egotism, and the general psychology of a small group which claimed for every one of its members the right of demanding unrestricted obedience and even servitude from the rest of the population, although these were Greeks like themselves. The authoritarian principle was employed by a group of men who felt themselves a unity, who were, in fact, unique and separated from others by their very nature and their way of life.

The Spartiates were not, as is usual in aristocracies, a noble upper class of the people. They were themselves the people. Descendants of the early Dorian conquerors, they were and remained warlike conquerors, masters and oppressors. They alone were the citizens of the State, a few thousand men only and yet representing the whole. Thus, without being an aristocracy, they formed an aristocracy. And they alone were those Spartans whose way of life has become famous throughout the ages. Within their own community they followed to the utmost the same authoritarian principle by means of which they ruled over Helots and Perioeci. As a matter of fact, the chronological order was actually the other way round. While developing earlier features of communal life, the Spartiates consciously and consistently created a totalitarian State.

The Spartiates called themselves *homoioi*, peers or equals. There were no different social strata within their community; they were the people and nothing but the people. Since this people of equals ruled the State it is even possible to speak of Sparta as a democracy. The equality of all Spartiates in rights and duties, originally also in property, was their *Magna Charta* as it resulted from their history. The fact that the kings, the council of the elders, and the assembly of the people, were all elements of government, can be traced back to the social structure of the early tribe when the gathering of the warriors by their own free decision followed the councils of the old men and the commands of the elected war-leader. In historical times the kingdom had become hereditary, and the elders formed the Gerusia as an elected body of fixed number, while the importance of the sovereign embodied in the popular assembly declined. This assembly as we know it in Sparta had no right of discussion, and could only accept or decline any proposals as a whole. When they had to vote or to elect their officials they did so by a very crude form of acclamation without counting the votes. The democratic element was, after all, not very manifest. But it would certainly be mistaken to call Sparta a monarchy because some of her great kings dominated the political stage, or an aristocracy because of her conservative policy. The most significant fact in the constitutional history of Sparta is the creation of the ephorate, the board of the five all-powerful heads of the executive. In them democratic and authoritarian principles were combined in a unique way. It was the people which every year, in a revival of its ancient power, elected the ephors from its own ranks as the highest authority in State and society. Since the office was annual and there was a board of five, no individual leadership was possible. Something of the will of the people was actually embodied in the ephors. And in spite of their almost unlimited power they remained responsible, and had to submit to some possibility of control. Although they remained the most powerful men in the State, their leadership was ultimately based on democratic principles. Sparta never had a dictator.

The political constitution of Sparta became truly important only through the social structure of the Spartiates and their way of life. Out of the fundamental features of tribal and warlike life, which even in peaceful and peacefully creative times never ceased to permeate the social body, the ephors of the sixth century B.C., deliberately and systematically, created that elaborate and rigid structure of people and State which was ascribed to a legendary lawgiver Lycurgus. In this structure, early and primitive forms of communal life were combined with an artificial order that was based on certain biological foundations and imposed with deliberate strictness. Sparta was, in a degree unknown elsewhere even in Greece, a community of *men*. Women, marriage, family life — they all played a secondary part and therefore lost much of their original value and sanctity. Not the number of children counted, but their sex, their health, their physical strength. The cruel methods of Spartan eugenics are well known. When a child was born the State decided whether it was to live. Weak boys and a large proportion of the girls were exposed and died in the wilds of the mountains. Although no particular interest was taken in securing legitimate offspring and morals were rather loose, the community virtually lived on through propagation within a closed and gradually narrowing circle. In order to be a Spartiate it was not necessary to have been born in wedlock, but it was necessary to own an allotment of land and to have gone through the public education, both reserved exclusively for the Spartiates. Very rarely the son of a Spartiate by a Helot woman was admitted, a foreigner hardly ever. Thus Sparta unintentionally preserved a fairly pure 'race' among her citizens. A small people of warriors provided for its biological existence by a sort of artificial eugenics which practically excluded any substantial change. This was perhaps the most decisive reason for Sparta's quick decay.

We must now speak of Spartan education, the so-called *agogê*. From his seventh birthday every boy belonged no longer to his mother but to the State. Divided into small sections and age-groups, the boys lived a strict communal life and had a common education under the official leadership of selected young and older men. The sections were called 'herds', and the youngest leaders 'cattle-drivers', expressions which are typical of a system of education which forbade the slightest appearance of individuality and personality. The boys were trained in the use of weapons, in music and dancing, but above all in self-command and self-denial, obedience and discipline. Homer's poems were known, and the exploits of his heroes were an ever-living example. But very few of the boys could read and write. Blind obedience was the supreme duty, but besides the duty there was *eros* — love. The erotic relations between the boys and their leaders were manifestly and intentionally shaped by educational aims, and in a sense they belonged to the same moral category as the well-known reverence of Spartan youth for old age. The ultimate aims, however, of the whole educational system, the first system of State education that ever existed and largely the model for later attempts, was to create good soldiers who, strong in body and mind, would serve the community with absolute loyalty. Education, therefore, did not end when the boy had grown up. Common life continued, even for some time after marriage. And until death every Spartiate shared his meals with his group which in peace as well as war formed the smallest cell of the community. People and army were one, and this involved at the same time the eternal suppression of the other sections of the population. Civil life was determined by political and military necessities, and the ultimate duty of every citizen was to be prepared to die for Sparta. Shame and punishment awaited those who survived a defeat. The freedom of a personal and heroic decision was merged in the compulsion of common and undiscriminating patriotism. Sparta shaped a unique type of man, a type of undoubted greatness and striking one-sidedness, which lived on in numerous legends and anecdotes. It also found expression in those famous 'laconic' utterances which by their very briefness reflect the soldierly spirit of the Spartiates. The three hundred who fell fighting at Thermopylae, 'obedient to the law', are eternal witnesses of this human type, although we should never forget that their heroism was not based on free decision, but was dictated by obedience, tradition and — fear.

In one of our museums stands a fine little bronze statuette, which was made in Sparta, probably late in the sixth century (Plate I). It shows Heracles, the great mythical hero of the Dorian tribe — but what a Heracles! He wears as usual his lion's skin and carries bow and arrows. There is, however, nothing of the hero about him, nothing of the greatness and the freedom of the demi-god who liberated mankind from all sorts of evils. The hero has become a soldier, wearing over the lion's skin a hoplite's cuirass — which is entirely alien to Heracles — carrying the quiver like a soldier's knapsack, holding his club in the right hand, and marching along in strict military discipline. We know of a few similar statuettes, one almost a twin figure, but they are just Spartan soldiers and not mythical heroes.[1] Even though we may attribute the similar attitude of these statuettes partly to their archaic style and the traditions of a school of sculptors, the predominant impression and the fact that Heracles is represented go beyond an explanation on merely stylistic and aesthetic lines. It is the type of the Spartan soldier which is represented in these figures, also in that of Heracles. Possibly the latter was modelled after a figure in the temple of Heracles in Sparta, of which Pausanias tells us that it was 'a statue armed as a hoplite'. But then this statue too was true to type. Heracles, as we see him here, is, it seems, doing his drill in the barrack-square. No more striking illustration, I believe, can be found of the very spirit of Sparta.

It was possible to educate the Spartiates to become the most consistent type of the political soldier because they were not distracted from this kind of activity by any labour. Men who in peace-time were engaged in no other occupation than athletic exercise and hunting were physically as well as psychologically much better prepared for warfare than the peasants, craftsmen and traders of the other Greek States. The Helots as agricultural serfs and the Perioeci as craftsmen and traders — the latter as far as these professions were needed at all in the primitive economy of Sparta — accomplished all that was necessary in the economic field. The districts of the Perioeci surrounded the land of the citizens, thus separating not only the Helots who tilled it, but also the Spartiates, from the outer world. In a double sense a security ring was drawn round Sparta. The Spartiates were compelled to live in Sparta itself and not allowed to cross the frontier of the State without

[1] Heracles statuette: M. Bieber, *Die antiken Skulpturen des Kgl. Museum Frideri-cianum in Cassel*, p. 51, Taf. 38, fig. 114. (The club has disappeared, and the rod which he is holding now is a modern addition.) In general, cf. A. Furtwängler in W. Roscher, *Lexikon d. griech. u. röm. Mythologie*, I, 2149, and *Olympia*, Tafelland IV, Taf. VII, fig. 42; E. Langlotz, *Frühgriech. Bildhauerschulen*, 88.

special permit. Foreigners who entered the country could be expelled without notice. Economic barriers were added to this. The State alone owned gold and silver, or was at least supposed to do so, while a minimum of domestic trade was upheld through the famous iron money which was without value abroad. Sparta lived in almost complete autarky as a self-contained body, and this economic fact grew into the strongest possible isolation of life and mind.

Education and economy, politics and private life, everything was strictly organized and governed, and together they all formed a unit, separated from outside. When the ephors entered on their annual office they regularly announced that the Spartiates had 'to shave their moustaches and to obey the laws'. This startling combination needs some explanation. During the sixth century the Greeks in general changed their fashion of beards; previously they had a full beard but the upper lip shaved, later they had both beard and moustache. Sparta, in retaining the old fashion, separated herself from the other Greeks; it was a small point but apparently it had become a symbol. We realize at the same time to what extent the State had a hold on everybody and everything.

The second part of the ephors' demand, obedience to the law, was the ultimate basis and background of Spartan life and Spartan character, something impersonal and even metaphysical. The totalitarian principle in Sparta was so far from implying lawlessness that it led to the most rigid rule of law. There were no written laws in Sparta, there was only the *Nomos, the* sacred law, representing order and compulsion by divine will. The authoritarian State found its last justification beyond all human arbitrariness. Neither the kings nor even the ephors were the true exponents of the authoritarian principle, but tradition and discipline as sanctioned by the gods. In later times Sparta alone among all the Greek States had frequent and friendly relations with the State and people of Jerusalem; it may well be that the Spartans, proud of their sacred, artificially preserved *Nomos*, felt that they had found a similar way of life under the equally rigid and sacred law of the Jews.

In Sparta the rule of law implied that the whole existence of every citizen stood, to an extent hardly ever surpassed in history, in the service of the State. No value was relevant outside the State, neither property nor art nor thought. The individual Spartan believed he was free, because he was a member of a community of free citizens and soldiers. But there was no freedom whatever of the individual, and freedom *in* the State left no room for freedom *from* the State. The people as a whole, the *damos*, was the sovereign of the State, to whom later even a statue was erected. But though the commands of the officials, as it were, represented the will of the people, they were none the less commands to which every citizen owed the blind and complete obedience of a soldier.

This was a fertile soil for misuse and corruption. The full and ideal identity between State and people was never achieved, if only because of the narrow and egotistic *Herrenmoral* of the Spartiates in their relations with all other Greeks inside and outside the State. The Spartiates never lost their fear that the enslaved and maltreated Helots might revolt (as they did several times), and rarely was a State more hated by the outer world than Sparta by the other Greeks after she had 'liberated' them from Athenian tyranny. Moreover, when there was no longer any economic equality among the Spartiates, the conflict between those who still maintained the old standards, and those who did not, became so sharp that the unity of the Spartiates themselves had gone. Yet the germs of decay lay still deeper; they grew from the very nature of the State and its identity with society. If it had been possible for the system to be perfect, Sparta might never have experienced the conflict between public will and individual will. This conflict, after some preliminary stages, became real and fatal at the end of the fifth century when Lysander, the conqueror of Athens, led Sparta to the summit of her external power and at the same time to the turning-point of her inner fate. The appearance of great personalities who free themselves from the traditions and standards of the community and find successors among many smaller men is a common and creative element in general history. In Sparta the necessary conflict between State and individual was bound to be completely unproductive, simply because outside the Spartan way of life and outside the law it was impossible for any Spartan to achieve anything of lasting and creative character. The individual became a rebel without knowing for what higher purpose he revolted. Moreover since the State was based on the principles of authority and leadership, an insurmountable barrier arose between political leadership as an institution, and political leadership as an outcome of nature and genius. The negation of all individual freedom led to intellectual barrenness, just as the narrowness and isolation of breeding and education, that is to say of inbreeding both biological and spiritual, led to biological and moral degeneration. The totalitarian State was achieved to an extent which was probably possible only in a community so small in space and numbers. But this totalitarianism was identical with the end of total life. While from the democracy of Athens, even after its decline and breakdown, the greatest minds arose, Sparta after the sixth century brought forth no artist, no poet, no thinker. And many of her generals and kings were bad and corrupt men. The efficiency and bravery of Sparta's soldier-citizens were everywhere respected or feared. But even this could not prevent her political and even military decline and final doom. Eventually Sparta survived merely as the lifeless museum of its own past and of the idealized Lycurgan order.

Sparta had made the great attempt to build up a unique but one-sided example of a social community. In spite of a reality frequently deficient and disappointing, the ideal of Sparta's political structure and the human type of the Spartiate were impressive. The ingenious attempt, half Utopian and half realistic, to turn an ultimately democratic community into a totalitarian State ruled by the despotism of its own laws, became the more striking when Athens, by the destruction of her public spirit through party struggles and the unrestrained freedom of the individual, had met with disaster. It is for this reason that Sparta, although an increasingly idealized Sparta, became the starting-point and centre of political theory. The development, which reached its culmination, though by no means its end, in Plato's imposing and bewildering picture of an ideal State in the *Republic*, led far away from reality. It is significant that, as far as the picture of Sparta had creative effects, they were achieved only through the medium of the Athenian mind and Athenian freedom. Sparta herself remained utterly and completely barren. Thermopylae remained an eternal symbol — but what nation's history does not show similar and even greater examples of heroic sacrifices? The true glory of Sparta was that she created the first and classical form of an extreme type of State and an equally extreme type of man. Greatness cannot be denied to Sparta and the Spartiate. But in this first and greatest of all authoritarian and totalitarian States all the springs of creative life dried up completely. The fate of Sparta confirms our belief that compulsion and obedience, though necessary means in all political life, never suffice as a goal for the endeavours of men to build a real community. Sparta set up, not an example to be imitated, but a danger-signal to be avoided.

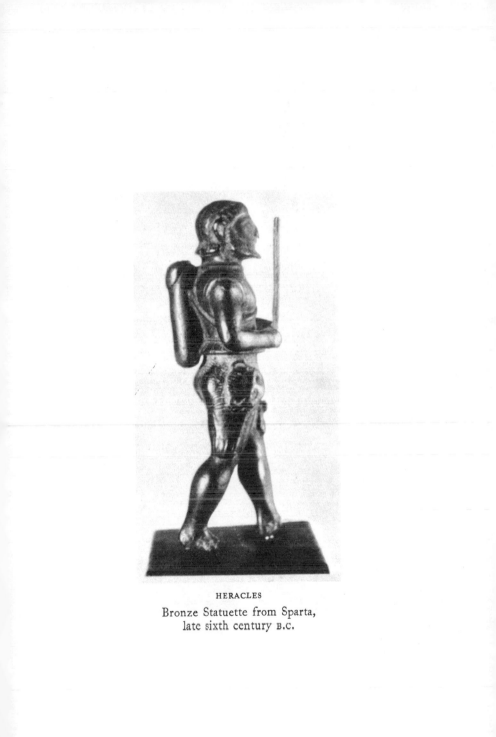

HERACLES

Bronze Statuette from Sparta,
late sixth century B.C.

HERALDIC COINS 594-556(?) B.C. (a-f: GROUP B, g-h: GROUP DⅢ)

PEISISTRATUS 560-527 B.C. (i: GROUP E, j: GROUP G)

k

ALCMAEONIDS
IN EXILE?
514-510 B.C.
(GROUP J)

ISAGORAS 510-507 B.C. (l-n GROUP K)

CLEISTHENES AND AFTER 510-490 B.C. (o: GROUP L, p: GROUP N)

ATHENIAN COINAGE

ATHENIAN COINAGE
Between 594 and 490 B.C.

VIII

ATHENIAN COINAGE

SLOWLY but steadily — sometimes with startling progress — numismatics has become a branch of true scholarship, outgrowing its original character as an esoteric and pedantic hobby. Mommsen was the first who fully realized the importance of coins as a historical source, and since his time there have frequently been published numismatic books — including catalogues like the imposing work on *The Roman Imperial Coinage* by H. Mattingly and E. A. Sydenham, now in progress — which are not merely concerned with such things as weighing and measuring, but are examples of the highest standards of historical scholarship. This kind of work has proved to be of exceptional importance and has yielded a rich harvest, because it was based on material not yet adequately exploited, and because the numismatists had the advantage of being trained in the most accurate of methods. At the same time, as a reaction against inevitable over-concern with detail, they tried to acquire a wide historical outlook. We see this in C. T. Seltman's recently published *Athens, its History and Coinage before the Persian Invasion* (Cambridge, 1924).[1]

The title of the book puts *History* before *Coinage*. That is hardly justified. The book was written by a numismatist and archaeologist, and its most important results are based on the knowledge and the judgment of a specialist. The primary matter of concern is the coinage. But the discussion of the development of early Athenian coinage often involves a new approach to an intricate and obscure subject, and has grown into a real commentary on political and social history, shedding new light on the dark sixth century B.C. Mr. Seltman's book is of the greatest importance for the historian. It will provoke criticism and opposition, but urges us to continue the work on the new foundations which the author has laid. We historians have every reason to be grateful. The following review will, I trust, even in its criticism be taken as a token of grateful appreciation.

[1] The review was published in the *Historische Zeitschrift*, vol. 135 (1926).

Plutarch tells us that Theseus coined money with the sign of an ox, and Mr. Seltman in his first chapter tries to confirm this mythological anachronism by archaeological evidence. It is certain that cattle once were the principal measure of value, and thus fulfilled one important task of money. B. Laum in his valuable though often uncritical book *Heiliges Geld* (1924) has given extensive proof of this. I also agree (and have, in fact, thought for a number of years) that the peculiarly shaped copper ingots, found in various places of Minoan or Mycenaean civilization, must be explained as ox-hides and not as double axes. But there is no real link between these ingots and Attica, and it seems arbitrary to think in this connection of Athens and Theseus. Plutarch's statement can and must be dismissed as erroneous, but can be explained without reference to the evidence of the Mycenaean Age.

The history of early Athenian coinage presents a difficult task. It is true of all early Greek money that the devices on the coins are almost the only evidence from which conclusions can be drawn as to their date and frequently also their place of origin. Here is a wide field for all sorts of arbitrary conjectures. Mr. Seltman, however, has made a very careful examination of the various dies, not only of the more spectacular anvil-dies of the obverse, but also of the punch-dies (*quadratum incusum*) of the reverse, and has arranged the coins in clearly separated groups. He is convinced that by this method an irrefutable chronological order can be established. He probably is too sure of the results of his method, but there is no doubt that he has found the right way of approach. The distinction between the various groups (A — Q) is probably in all essentials justifiable, even though their chronological arrangement is sometimes doubtful.

The real history of Athenian coinage begins with a question, equally important from the economic and the political point of view. Were coins issued in Athens before Solon? Most of the German numismatists who deal with the question deny it. Mr. Seltman tries to show that the well-known coins with an *amphora* (Group A) are Athenian and pre-Solonian; he takes the *amphora* as the symbol of Attic oil-trade. But there is no real proof that the type of *amphora* on these coins is the same as that on another coin which is definitely Athenian, or that it is fundamentally different from a very similar design on coins of the island of Carthaea which is explained as a wine-jar. The question, I believe, is not yet finally answered. In the laws of Draco (621 B.C.) we read of fines of 'twenty oxen'. As Seltman remarks, it is unlikely that Athens had coined money at that early date. Even the classes of assessment in Solon's constitution were still based on an income expressed in bushels of grain. There is, on the other hand, ample evidence for a fairly progressive state of Athenian economy in Solon's time. It is reflected, for instance, in a number of individual laws of Solon and·some passages of his poetry, as well as in certain economic facts such as the assessment based on income and not on property, and the catastrophic bankruptcy of the farmers. During the seventh and sixth centuries, Athens went through a process of transition by which a purely agrarian community was turned into an important centre of trade, and traffic by exchange replaced by traffic in cash. Soon Athens needed coins of her own, though for a short time it may have been possible to use the money of the more advanced Aegina. As far as I can see, pre-Solonian issues in Athens cannot be taken for granted; but they are possible, and any doubts, such as those expressed by Beloch, as to whether Solon himself issued coins, are not justifiable. He actually changed over to a new standard, replacing the Aeginetan or Pheidonian standard by one which is either called Euboeic or, as Seltman prefers, Attic.[1]

With the next group we come to a discovery of fundamental importance. We have a large number of coins which, on account of the varying emblems on the obverse, are known as 'heraldic' coins (*Wappenmünzen*). It has been usual to assign them to various cities, in particular to cities in Euboea. Mr. Seltman has shown that coins with different emblems have the same punch-die on the reverse, and has rightly drawn the conclusion that they come from the same mint. Furthermore, he has compared the emblems on the coins with those on shields of hoplites in contemporary Athenian vase paintings. He can identify a fair number of them and thus prove beyond any reasonable doubt that all these coins were Athenian. He recognizes in the emblems the family arms of the various clans of the Athenian nobility, and although some of the individual

<hr>

[1] Aristotle, *Ath. pol.* 10. Cf. O. Viedebantt, *Forschungen*, 45ff.; *Antike Gewichtsnormen*, 34ff.

attributions remain uncertain, the whole theory is a happy solution of a very intricate question, and one which reveals completely new aspects to our understanding of the archaic period of Athenian history.[1] Mr. Seltman has, for example, definitely proved (p. 20ff.), with the help of a passage in Aristophanes and its scholion (*Lys.* 664ff.), that the *triskeles*, a wheel formed by three human legs, was the coat-of-arms of the Alcmaeonidae. The somewhat later emblem of a real wheel probably belonged to the same clan, although its derivation from the earlier emblem (p. 33f.) is not entirely convincing. The Peisistratidae had perhaps a horse as their arms, the Eteobutadae most certainly a bull's head. The *amphora*, on the other hand, is taken as a symbol of the State, as the 'civic badge', such as later was the head of Athena; Seltman assumes that the *amphora* was the emblem used in Solon's own coinage. As I stressed before, there is, in my belief, not sufficient evidence to make this certain.

Mr. Seltman points out in great detail how the variations of the heraldic symbols can serve as illustrations of the domestic quarrels and changing forces in power. Many of his conclusions are, naturally enough, conjectures rather than statements of fact, and the historian cannot always agree. I for my part, for instance, do not think it is possible to date as early as immediately after Solon's legislation the re-grouping of the population into the partly regional, partly social sections of 'plain' (*pediaci*) and 'shore' (*paralii*). The archonship of 580 must have preceded the break-up of the nobility which is revealed by the new groups with their regional bases. The constitution of 580, when the highest office was temporarily divided among five *eupatridae*, three *agroici*, and two *demiurgi*, is regarded by Seltman (p. 27) as the result of the political success of what he calls the 'agricultural party'. He boldly combines this more than doubtful interpretation with a coin the emblem of which, a cross-bar wheel, is explained as the wheel of an agricultural vehicle. This theory is, to say the least, questionable. But the real difficulty in drawing historical conclusions from the numismatic discoveries is one of chronology. Unfortunately, the views of the numismatists, who naturally must have the first say in the matter, differ widely.

[1] From the standpoint of numismatics a similar verdict has been given by K. Regling, *Philol. Wochenschrift*, 1925, 219f.—Cf. the specimen on Plate II.

Seltman rejects the method and the results of Svoronos, and in most instances he is probably right. A coin of the Eteobutadae, for example, which Svoronos calls pre-Solonian, can safely be attributed to the time of Peisistratus (p. 48). On the whole, however, even Mr. Seltman has not found the key that will unlock all doors.

It is of particular significance that coins with different emblems show identical (not only similar) punch-dies. The conclusion seems appropriate that they not only are contemporary, but — coming from the same mint-master — also prove a political collaboration between the clans concerned. The group D III is important. Coins with the head of Gorgo, a bull's head, or a wheel, all have the same reverse punch. More likely than not they reflect the coalition of Eteobutadae and Alcmaeonidae by which Peisistratus was expelled for the first time. The Gorgoneion, as Mr. Seltman is probably right to assume, was a symbol of the State above the clans and parties, the badge of Athena as opposed to Peisistratus' head of Athena and her owl. It seems likely that another family joined the coalition, as a partner of secondary importance. Its arms were the head of a panther, which appears, curiously enough, in the *quadratum incusum* of some of the coins with Gorgo or wheel. We shall hear more about this family later. Another coin, which seems more or less contemporary, rather surprisingly combines a bull's head and an owl. But this owl looks to the left and is quite different from that of Peisistratus' coins; it is perhaps the arms of a branch of the clan.

The satisfactory explanation of the heraldic coins confirms the important part played by the great families in the politics of the sixth century. Mr. Seltman has well stressed the contrast between these coins and the coinage with the head of Athena and the owl, which was first issued by Peisistratus. But I doubt whether the earliest 'owls' (group C) were a private issue (p. 40). The double emblem of the goddess and her bird was 'the pride of the humblest as of the noblest citizen', and thus a clear answer to the many family emblems of the issues of Peisistratus' opponents. The wavering policies of the various factions among the nobility were to be replaced by a policy which aimed at representing the State as a whole, though, as far as Peisistratus was concerned, a monarchic State. Thus, from a psychological point of view, the owls were not merely a private affair. Nor were they so legally, although the legal position is somewhat obscure. We are used to seeing in the right to coin money an expression of political sovereignty. But the heraldic coins bear no indication whatever as to which State they belong; their symbols refer only to the clans. The question arises whether we have to modify our general views on the connection of coinage and public law. Regling (*l.c.*, 220) points to other Greek coins with varying symbols as an analogy. But they have, besides the varying signs which are understood to be signs of the mint-masters, either a main symbol (as in Abdera, Peparethus, and also Lampsacus and Lesbos) or a secondary one (as in Cyzicus and Phocaea) which clearly represents the State. A third possibility (as in Thebes and Rome) is that the legends show the name of the State or the official characters of the mint-master. Although Seltman does not discuss these difficulties, he obviously hits upon the right solution by explaining the heraldic coins as illustrating a continuously changing policy. If a clan coined its own money, its relations to the State were not characterized by a natural and acknowledged subordination to the State. On the contrary, the noblemen, though less as individuals than as clans, professed a strong degree of independence; they were lacking in 'Polis-consciousness'. Such relations can hardly be expressed in terms of any strict law, but they are nevertheless historical facts. It is true that the nobility of the sixth century was very much more closely bound up with the Polis than, say, the Homeric princes. To realize the immense difference we need only think of Theognis, extreme aristocrat as he was. It is also true that the united society of the nobility in early Athens had broken up into regional groups. Yet, the great clans were still so powerful and independent that their conflicts threatened to disrupt the State both politically and geographically. Thus it could happen that money with different emblems was issued at the same time — that is to say money belonging to the State and yet by its whole appearance advertising the power of the great families.

Political sovereignty and the right to coin were united in the rule of Peisistratus and the issue of his 'owls'. But the chronology of the various groups of these owls is open to certain doubts, although the groups as such seem stabilized by Seltman's method. Two of these groups (E and F) are taken as

the money which the tyrant, during his exile and even afterwards, issued from the mining mint of Mt. Pangaeus. The
attribution remains doubtful despite Seltman's very ingenious
arguments. We must distinguish this case from that which we
have just discussed. Then, in a State in which public law was
still somewhat incomplete and unstable, powerful clans put
their coats-of-arms on the public coins. The case now presented is that of a single man, living in Thrace as a political
exile or simply as a private individual, ambitious to become the
ruler of Athens, who issues coins with the symbol of the State
— although we may admit that this was also the symbol of his
personal rule. In this second case, the issue of coins is so far
separated from legal sovereignty that I cannot accept Mr.
Seltman's theory. I have considerable doubts both about the
private issue mentioned above and about the Pangaean
coinage.[1] Seltman's own list of a hoard found on the Acropolis
contains seventeen and four pieces respectively of the two
Pangaean groups, and only two of the Attic issue (group G 1)
which dates after 546. Mr. Seltman, it is true, maintains that
the two coins belong to the earliest specimens of the group;
but as far as I can see, no certain chronology is possible
within the limits of the group itself which covers the whole
period from 546 to 527. On the whole, Seltman's dating of
the Peisistratus coins raises many doubts, and they are not
dispelled by the fact that he finds himself in complete agreement with Professor Adcock's attempt at dating the periods of
Peisistratus' exiles and tyrannies. It is well known that the
evidence for the chronology of these events in Herodotus and
Aristotle is contradictory. I know of no less than fourteen
different attempts to put the dates in order. Adcock accepts
the two dates 556 and 546 for the beginning and end of the
last exile, as they were set forth by scholars who deny that
there was an earlier exile at all, and he combines these dates
with an earlier exile which, however, in his scheme dwindles
down to a few months in 560. I do not think that this theory
is more convincing than most of the others.

Seltman, moreover, associates (p. 46) a recently discovered
relief of an archaic statute-basis with Herodotus' story of the
flower-girl Phye who, disguised as the goddess Athena, led
Peisistratus to the Acropolis. In this identification Seltman

---

[1] Cf. also Regling, l.c., 222.

follows Svoronos, and it is at first sight a very attractive idea indeed. But it cannot be maintained. The person on the chariot, which a warrior is just mounting, wears, apart from a long floating garment, helmet and shield. That would be nothing unique for the charioteer in a mythological scene such as we should naturally expect here. For the disguised girl Phye, on the other hand, it would have been essential to make it absolutely clear who she was supposed to be, and that means that she would have to wear the *aegis*, the skin with its fringe of snakes and the head of Gorgo which Athena carried over breast and shoulders. The person on the relief certainly does not wear anything of the sort, and Seltman's guess that the shield on her back may have shown the Gorgoneion is pure imagination. I may add that, as far as I know, it would be completely unique at that time to depict in a piece of sculpture an event which was almost contemporary, the date of the relief being about 520 B.C. The general subject, on the other hand, of a chariot and warriors was quite common in a mythological scene.

It is impossible, within the limits of this review, to discuss all the points of numismatic and economic interest in Mr. Seltman's book, such as Hippias' so-called reform of the coinage; the discovery of the fact — or, to be more cautious, of the probability — that there were two Athenian mints, one in Athens, the other in Laurium; or the explanation of the olive leaves which adorn Athena's helmet on the coins in later years as a reminder of the victory at Marathon. Every problem is clearly advanced towards its solution, although sometimes there remain doubts. For instance, the chronological distribution of the dies (usually three each year) is far from certain, and so are the synchronisms between some of the coins and various reliefs and statues.

A unique group of electrum coins (J) deserves special mention. They have various symbols, some the official badge of the owl, others certain coats-of-arms such as a bull's head or the Alcmaeonid wheel. Although almost all of these coins were found in Attica, Seltman sees in them the coinage of the emigrants who during the last years of Hippias' reign lived in Delphi under the leadership of the Alcmaeonid Cleisthenes. While Regling denies the possibility of such an issue by exiles, I agree with Mr. Seltman in regarding it as possible, one reason being the dominant position of some of the leading noble families. Electrum coins in Athens itself would be, to say the least, rather out of place. It is possible that Cleisthenes — who later became the heir of the tyrants by overthrowing them, and then renewed Peisistratus' money, the owls, in the money of the democratic State — issued coins of his own as a weapon in the fight against tyranny. Seltman's explanation, though its argument may not be quite conclusive, is very attractive.

Most interesting and surprising is the reconstruction of the events immediately after the expulsion of Hippias (p. 85ff.). Isagoras, the opponent of Cleisthenes among the emigrants, played a leading part — according to Seltman, for about three years. This assumption is based on a group of coins (K) which always have the Gorgoneion on the obverse, while on the reverse we find the head of a panther or occasionally that of a bull. Gorgo and panther made their reappearance from an earlier group (D III, see above p. 109), which bears witness to the anti-tyrannical coalition of the 'fifties. The bull too appears in both issues, only the wheel of the Alcmaeonidae is now missing. The style of all these coins is close to that of the last issue of Hippias, and Seltman's conclusion that this group represents the coalition of 510 is well-founded. No connection had so far been found between the panther, the most frequent type on these coins, and any outstanding family; it is natural to assume that the panther was the device of Isagoras. Seltman ingeniously confirms this hypothesis by a theory which, though in itself perhaps not entirely convincing, makes good sense in combination with the lesson of the coins. According to Herodotus (V, 66) Isagoras belonged to a family which worshipped the Carian Zeus, and Seltman makes it probable that his sacred animal was a panther or a lion. It seems less likely that, as Seltman asserts, the Eteobutadae changed sides from Cleisthenes to Isagoras. It was Cleisthenes who became separated from the bulk of the nobles, among whom the Eteobutadae were one of the most distinguished families.

With the new insight, which we owe to the coins and their interpretation by Mr. Seltman, into the nature of the revolutionary events of 510 we must, I believe, slightly differ from his views. Modern scholars agree in general that Aristotle must have been mistaken when he called Isagoras 'a friend of the tyrants' (*Ath. pol.* 20, 1). Now we realize that he was, in fact, the head of a coalition of noble families against the tyrant, and that Cleisthenes, that is to say the Alcmaeonidae, probably first belonged to the coalition, but soon found himself in opposition to their ideas; thus Cleisthenes had to give way. The two men were not simply personal foes. Whether the earlier enmity between *paralii* and *diacrii* on the one hand, and the *pediaci* on the other, was an essential factor, is doubtful. Decisive, at any rate, is the fact that the Alcmaeonidae pursued a policy which clearly comprehended the State as a whole, while most of the other nobles still clung to their old clans and factions. It was by an inner necessity that Cleisthenes became the enemy of the nobles and the heir of Peisistratus. He is, it is true, the real father of that Athenian democracy which saw in Peisistratus the hated tyrant. But at the same time he continued the work of Peisistratus, though not, as Seltman thinks (p. 94), because 'the days of the great tyrant were still remembered as days of peace and prosperity'. We must not forget that Cleisthenes' political work had an appearance very different indeed from that of tyranny. While he followed Peisistratus in his hostility to the noble families and his general emphasis on the whole of the State, he clearly separated himself from the tyrant in other respects. Cleisthenes was much more than a mere organizer. He was a great statesman, who relied on a creative combination of traditionalism and revolutionary rationalism. In other words, without uprooting the past he looked forward to the future which, he was sure, would be determined by his own work. This work made it possible for the State of the tyrant to grow into a democracy.

The three last chapters of Mr. Seltman's book are digressions, one on metrological questions which are so specialized, and at the same time so obviously in a state of transition, that they cannot be discussed here. An important detail is the description and convincing explanation of some iron *oboloi* from Sparta, now in the Fitzwilliam Museum in Cambridge. They enable us to refute once and for all the view, almost generally held till recently, that the Spartan iron money consisted of 'sickles', such as are depicted in a number of dedicatory inscriptions. The succeeding chapters deal with 'Mines and Trade', and with Miltiades' realm on the Chersonesus. Several coins with a quadriga or a horseman are attributed to Miltiades, but the attribution does not convince.[1]

The richly illustrated text is followed by a thorough and excellent catalogue of all Athenian coins before the Persian War, the whole covering almost 500 items, by an index and twenty-four beautiful collotype plates. The book, while a pleasure to look at, is an important work of reference, a great help to both numismatists and historians. It represents at the same time a most valuable piece of research, full of new ideas and important results.

---

[1] See this volume, p. 123.

I X

EARLY ATHENIAN COLONIES[1]

ATHENS holds a special position among the Greek cities which founded colonies. She began her colonization much later than the great mother-cities of Ionia and Greece proper. This is partly due to the fact that the Athenians in the eighth and seventh centuries B.C. still found sufficient land in Attica, which after all, though not very fertile, was of considerable size. Besides, the social class which alone was likely to emigrate, the poor peasantry, were under increasing political and economic pressure from a united nobility. The landlords might expel individual small farmers from house and field, but they would not allow the serfs, the so-called *Hectemoroi*, to join together, even if only for the purpose of emigration. Athens, moreover, was by no means the only State which did not found colonies of its own. Others, although they had abundance of population and scarcity of soil, are never mentioned as colonizing States. It can be assumed that frequently people of one State joined individually in the enterprise of another State, and for the Athenians the Ionian city of Chalcis in Euboea, one of the leading colonizing communities, was close enough.

When Athens eventually began such activities herself, the general movement was nearly over. This is one of the reasons why modern scholars often think of Athenian colonization in a different light from the general trend. Moreover, since the middle of the fifth century Athenian colonization, fairly well known through literary and epigraphical evidence, was carried out almost exclusively in the form of cleruchies. Some scholars, probably influenced by the later tendency of the Athenian League or Empire to follow a policy of power and territorial gains, insisted, with varying determination, on regarding the whole process of Athenian colonization, including its earlier stages, as a work of State organization and political purpose. It became quite usual to speak of the foundation of a 'colonial empire' or at least of 'foreign possessions' of Athens.

[1] Published in *Eunomia* I (1939). See note on p. 63. I have added a few notes.

This view led to surprising consequences. In general, the normal form of colony or *apoecy*[1] (ἀποικία) as an independent Polis was clearly distinguished from the *cleruchy* (κληρουχία), a colony of men who remained citizens of the mother-State and were often little more than a mere garrison. But in dealing with Athenian colonization most modern scholars have confused the two forms, even when the official title was mentioned in an inscription. Recently, on the other hand, an attempt has been made strictly to separate the two forms and to maintain that in Athenian colonization the apoecy was the only form used in earlier times, even as late as in the first half of the fifth century.[2] A new investigation of the matter will, it is hoped, clear the way to a new and better understanding.

SIGEUM AND CHERSONESUS

The earliest Athenian colonizing party of which we know was sent at the end of the seventh century to Sigeum in the Troas under the leadership of Phrynon, a winner at Olympia.[3] It seems certain that this story, the historical truth of which has been doubted by some modern scholars, was already known to Herodotus, though he does not say so expressly.[4] The enterprise consisted in the foundation of a real colony, performed in the usual manner. It was a favourite custom to take an Olympic winner as οἰκιστής, or official founder. Such an action can be imagined in pre-Solonian Athens more easily than political expansion and the creation of Athenian possessions on the shores of Asia Minor. The well-known inscription of Phanodicus (*Syll.* 2), with its text in both the Ionic and Attic dialects, fully supports our view. If some of the Sigeans mentioned here were accustomed to speaking Attic, it is clear that the Athenian colonists had become citizens of Sigeum.

The new colony roused the resistance of Mytilene which, as a leading State among the Aeolians, opposed the immigrants and for some time occupied the territory. Whether this

---

[1] I apologize for introducing this ugly word which is needed, if the different forms of colonies are not to remain indistinguishable.

[2] Cf. H. Berve, *Miltiades.* (*Hermes, Einzelschriften*, Heft 2) (1937).

[3] See, e.g., Strab. XIII, 599f. Diog. Laert. I, 74. Cf. J. Toepffer, *Beiträge zur griech. Altertumswissenschaft*, 45ff.

[4] V, 94f. Cf. Berve, 27f.

occupation implied some sort of real possession we do not know. Further fighting followed between Mytilene and Athens which, as the mother-city, had a natural interest in protecting the young State. In one of these battles Alcaeus lost his shield (frg. 49). Eventually a verdict of arbitration by Periander put an end to the war. Peisistratus, so Herodotus tells us, regained Sigeum and ruled it through his son Hegesistratus. Later on Hippias found here a refuge and a new seat of rule.

The question arises whether under the Peisistratidae the relations between Athens and Sigeum were closer than those commonly existing between mother-city and colony. To accept as an alternative only the possibilities of either personal or legal relations is to overlook a third possibility. Just as probably between Sigeum and Mytilene, the relation may have been of a political character and therefore neither personal nor legal. Athens was ruled by a tyrant. But tyranny was not a form of constitution in the definite meaning of the word. It implied rather a position of the ruler outside the constitution. It was, on the other hand, a political fact, and a powerful fact at that. Therefore it has to be understood as an aspect of the State, and not merely as a concern of the individual. It is a mistake to take the State and the tyrant as completely separate factors. Our sources for most of the tyrants are largely hostile, but everything they report shows that, in spite of occasional escapades, tyrant and tyranny, as if compelled by their historical position, form a necessary stage in the development of the Polis. Although some of the tyrants were strong in ambition and will-to-power, they were unable to achieve even their most personal aims in opposition to the Polis — whether they realized this and acted of their own free will, or not. Peisistratus' coinage with the head of Athena,[1] and the fact that it was the tyrant who introduced the festival of the Panathenaea, speak for themselves more clearly indeed than anything that can be deduced — quite apart from the reliability of such deduction — from the words of Herodotus. It is very likely that even under the Peisistratidae the colony at Sigeum was not an extension of Athenian territory. But at least as long as they ruled Athens, their rule over Sigeum had

---

[1] Cf. C. T. Seltman, *Athens, its History and Coinage*, 54ff. See also this volume p. 109ff.

to serve Athenian interests, even though the colonists were no longer Athenian citizens. Most likely, Sigeum kept its former status; it was an apoecy, not a cleruchy. But it was closely connected with Athens, not only by cult and sentiment but also by political ties.

For the first time we realize that it is insufficient simply to distinguish between apoecy and cleruchy. The legal type could be largely modified by political circumstances; and if Sigeum was legally an independent Polis, that is no reason to doubt that Peisistratus' policy, in which it played a part, was consistent and far-seeing. Before investigating further the colonizing activity of the Peisistratidae it seems appropriate to mention a factor which strongly influenced the politics of that age. What exactly was the position of the individuals who as tyrants or noble lords directed Athenian policy? This question has recently been answered in a very definite way.[1] It has been said that the 'great lords' were engaged in a purely family policy the aims of which lay entirely outside the State. And this very policy is supposed to have made possible, and at the same time to have completed, the rise of the Polis. Just like the Peisistratidae in general, according to this view, the Philaidae, the family to which Miltiades belonged, with their occupation of the Chersonesus, merely accomplished a private enterprise which did not imply any extension of Athenian power. In order to prove this, it was first necessary to show that the family of the Philaidae was entirely independent of Peisistratus. Undoubtedly the two families were rivals, but it depended on circumstances whether this fact would exclude collaboration, perhaps even some relation akin to vassalage, or not.[2] Herodotus, in introducing the elder Miltiades, says (VI, 35): 'Peisistratus then was the sole master of Athens, but Miltiades, son of Cypselus, was likewise a great lord' (ἐδυνάστευε). It is equally understandable that Miltiades did not like living under the tyrant, and that Peisistratus gladly seized the first opportunity to remove him from Athens.

---

[1] H. Berve, l.c., and previously in *Die Antike*, XII (1936), 1ff. Cf. my paper in *J.H.S.* LVII (1937), 147ff., and G. Mathieu, *Rev. de phil.* XII (1938), 56ff.

[2] There was no real vassalage either in this case or at any time among the Greeks. The younger Miltiades, however, as ruler of the Chersonesus, became a vassal of the Persian king. This was his legal position; it had nothing to do with his personal feelings. Vassalage could be enforced upon a man against his own wish. I stress this to refute remarks of Ed. Meyer, *Gesch. d. Alt.*, III, 115, and Berve, 46.

But it is a mistake to regard this as the only reason for the expedition to the Chersonesus. Even if we do not think of sea- and trade-policy or of expansive imperialism, it must have been foremost in Peisistratus' mind to avoid having a hostile and powerful rival so close to Sigeum which he had refounded. The tyrant could have banished the Philaidae from Athens just as easily as he expelled the Alcmaeonidae and other families of the nobility. If he acted differently he did so because he did not wish Miltiades to be banished. He allowed Miltiades to take with him whomever he wanted (Herod. 36, 1); this means that Miltiades' expedition was actually sanctioned by Peisistratus as an Athenian enterprise. We hardly need the confirmation in Marcellinus' *vita Thuc.* 7 that Miltiades went out οὐκ ἄνευ γνώμης τοῦ τυράννου; this late tradition may ultimately derive from Herodotus, but the facts remain true in any case. There was probably no legal act, therefore no decree by the people, but the tyrant's sanction had made the campaign a political, and not a private, enterprise. Miltiades had first been invited by a Thracian tribe, the Doloncians, who asked for help against their neighbours. But he performed his work of colonization not only as their elected leader, but also as a true *oecistes*, sent out from, and supported by, Athens. When later the sons of Peisistratus gave the younger Miltiades a trireme so that he might safely succeed to the vacant rulership of the Chersonesus (Herod. 39, 1), this too was not merely the outcome of their wish to remove him as soon as possible from Athens. The gesture — and certainly it was little more than a gesture — was intended to improve the situation on the Chersonesus, the occupation of which was necessary both for Athens and the Peisistratidae. Meanwhile, of course, the importance of the Straits for Athens had considerably in- creased.[1]

It can therefore hardly be denied that it was the very fore- sight and will of Peisistratus, and not an egotistic and private will-to-power on the part of the elder Miltiades, that caused the occupation of the Chersonesus. The Philaidae, too, were Athenians, and the later history of the younger Miltiades — from Lemnos to Marathon — shows that he never lost his essential connection with Athens, even though as the ruler of the Chersonesus, the chieftain of the Doloncians, and the son-

---

[1] Cf. recently A. W. Gomme, *A.J.Ph.*, LXV (1944), 329.

in-law of a Thracian dynast, he outgrew the pattern of an Athenian citizen. The rulers of the Chersonesus, despite all their independence, remained Athenians, and it was from and by Athens that the continuity of their rule was secured.

THE POLITICAL ORGANIZATION OF THE CHERSONESUS

The question remains open whether the Chersonesus was occupied as an apoecy or a cleruchy. As is well known, the younger Miltiades after his return to Athens was accused 'of tyranny on the Chersonesus' (Herod. VI, 104). This, no doubt, does not mean 'tyranny on Athenian soil', but it does mean 'tyranny over Athenian citizens'.[1] The natural conclusion is that there were Athenian citizens on the Chersonesus. But a different opinion has been expressed, based on the assumption that Miltiades' acquittal confirms that he had been a tyrant over Chersonesites, and not over Athenians. Otherwise 'he would have had to be condemned'. But what do we know of the many possibilities of refuting such a charge? As personal enemies accused Miltiades, so he will have had enough personal friends to defend him. Moreover it would have been absurd to make a charge in a case for which an Athenian court had no competence whatsoever. It is, on the other hand, very arbitrary — to say the least — to interpret the words of Herodotus as if the charge was rejected at once and no trial took place.[2] Herodotus employs the usual legal phrases which cannot mean anything but an acquittal.[3] In fact, the story of the trial makes it most likely, if not certain, that there were Athenian citizens on the Chersonesus.

Before going further we had better mention what is known or can be assumed about the political organization of the Chersonesus. Undoubtedly the Athenian colonists were settled in a number of different cities. This remains true even though our evidence, which as a whole probably goes back to Ephorus (frg. 40; Ps.-Scymn. 699ff.), does not make it quite clear which of the cities were founded by Miltiades. The names of these cities do not generally appear before the middle

[1] Cf. Berve, 23, who is right here against U. Kahrstedt, *Nachr. Gött. Ges.* 1931, 161.
[2] This is Berve's strange view, which on p. 24 is taken as possible and on p. 66f. as certain! Cf. also A. v. Blumenthal, *Hermes* 72 (1937), 476f.
[3] ἐδίωξαν τυραννίδος . . . ἀποφυγὼν δὲ . . . Cf. also, e.g., VI, 82, 2.

I

of the fifth century, and certainly not in Herodotus. Instead we hear of Chersonesites or Cherronesites (Χερρονησῖται), and it was an obvious suggestion that this fact signifies a united State. Is this view supported by our evidence?

Herod. IV, 137 calls the younger Miltiades 'strategos and tyrant of the Chersonesites', just as Chersonesites offered sacrifices and celebrated competitions in honour of the oecistes Miltiades after his death (Herod. VI, 38). In both cases the whole area is indicated. There is some political meaning particularly in the first passage, but the power which united the Chersonesites under one 'general and ruler' was confined to the person of Miltiades. It may be doubtful, as we saw, even with regard to the ancient Polis of Athens, whether it is an adequate assumption to contrast the tyrant as an independent power with the State itself. But to draw the opposite conclusion with regard to the much less stable conditions on colonial soil is certainly misleading. The attempt to prove from the position of the ruling family that there was a united State is mistaken, the more so since the Philaidae remained Athenian citizens. The name of the Chersonesites is used, naturally enough, to indicate the whole territory and its population for which, in fact, no other name was available.

Herodotus also tells us (VI, 39) that after the arrival of the younger Miltiades 'the leading men among the Chersonesites gathered together from all cities' to condole with him upon the loss of his brother Stesagoras. I cannot understand how this passage could be used to support the view that the Chersonesus was united in one Polis. Herodotus' words prove, if anything, that there were independent cities, and that again it was only the position of the ruling family which was conducive to unity.

Another example is Herod. IX, 114ff. He describes the Athenian attack on Sestos in 478 B.C., and several times (118, 120) he calls the defenders of the place Chersonesites. But he had stated before (115) that many people from the neighbouring cities (ἐκ τῶν ἄλλων τῶν περιοικίδων) had flocked to Sestos. Thus the Chersonesites whom he mentions were not only the Sestians, but also people from the whole district. Moreover, in the succeeding chapters at least two of the Chersonesian towns, Elaeus and Madytus, are mentioned in a way which seems clearly to indicate that they were independent cities. And when as defenders of Sestos, apart from Persian and allied soldiers, 'the native Aeolians' are mentioned (115), this indicates the origin of the men, not the political community of the Sestians. None of all these passages is evidence of a political unity in the Chersonesus.

Hardly more is proved by the one extant coin with the legend XEP,[1] showing on the obverse the Milesian lion which was also the arms of Cardia in the Chersonesus, a Milesian colony,[2] on the reverse the head of Athena. There are extant a few similar coins, but without the inscription.[3] The coin proves that there was a State οἱ Χερσονησῖται, but it does not prove that this State represented the whole united peninsula. It could just as well be a federation, a κοινόν,[4] or one of the cities in the area. And the latter seems to be certain according to a fragment of Hecataeus (F.Gr.H., 1, F 163, from Stephanus Byzantius) in which the Cherronesioi (Hecataeus' form, contrasted with Herodotus' Chersonesitai) are mentioned as living south of the Apsinthians. The latter were the enemies of the Doloncians, and Miltiades had built against them the big wall across the Isthmus in the North-East of the peninsula. On each end of this wall was a city — Cardia in the North and Pactye in the South. Hecataeus speaks of a πόλις Χερρόνησος ἐν τῷ ἰσθμῷ, and Berve, taking it as one of Miltiades' foundations, traces the same city in a scholion to Aristophanes (equ. 262): Χερσόνησος τῆς Θράκης χωρίον καὶ πόλις, ὑποτελὴς τῶν Ἀθηναίων, εὔφορος εἰς γεωργίαν, ὅθεν καὶ ἐσιταγώγουν οἱ Ἀθηναῖοι. The combination of χωρίον and πόλις is peculiar; but whatever this means, the whole passage with its description 'fertile in agriculture, whence the Athenians also used to bring corn', seems clearly to refer to the whole peninsula which contained a Polis of the same name, and not to the one town which did not even lie on the shore. Thus the Chersonesus of the scholion is identical with the Χερρονησῖται who in the Athenian tribute lists appear down to 448-7 with the considerable sum of eighteen talents, and not with the Χερρονησῖται ἀπ' Ἀγορᾶς of later lists who paid only one talent. Whence the scholiast derived his knowledge I do not know; it was, at any rate, no longer true when the

[1] C. T. Seltman, Athens, pl. XXIV, A 331, P 417. This is the only coin which can with certainty be attributed to the rule of the Philaidae.
[2] Cf. S. Casson, Macedonia, Thracia, and Illyria, 223ff.
[3] Seltman, A 332, P 418-9, η, θ, ι.
[4] Cf., e.g., the Arcadians and their coins; Head, H.N.², 448; Busolt-Swoboda, Griech. Staatskunde, 1396ff.

Knights was performed.[1] The men ἀπ' 'Αγορᾶς were probably the citizens of a small 'market-town' on the wall south-east of Cardia, and it is possible that this was on the site of an earlier Polis called Chersonesus which had been destroyed by the Persians; but Herodotus (VII, 58, 2), when speaking of Xerxes' campaign, already knows the Polis Agora.[2] It has been assumed that the expression Χερρονησῖται ἀπ' 'Αγορᾶς covered a Polis which included Cardia and Pactye, since Cardia does not appear in the tribute lists, and the case of Pactye is at least uncertain;[3] but this remains doubtful. Of the Polis Chersonesus we have no evidence apart from the Hecataeus fragment, although the coin I mentioned makes it likely that the place had Milesian as well as Athenian settlers. Nothing, however, shows that this Polis had any political importance or that it was the residence of the Philaidae. The city was founded to safeguard the wall, and thus, flanked by Cardia and Pactye, to protect the Chersonesus. That is all that we can assume; everything else is mere conjecture. The most unlikely conjecture, not supported by any of the arguments mentioned, would be to take the Polis Chersonesus as the leading Polis of a united State which covered the whole peninsula.

Perhaps even the XEP-coin gives evidence rather against than for a political unity. For one can hardly imagine a reason for all the towns in the Chersonesus using as a symbol of common coinage the Milesian lion. These towns were either founded by Miltiades or they were earlier Aeolian colonies. Cardia, the only Milesian colony, may have had close relations with the small nearby town of Chersonesus. It is, at any rate, remarkable that even later Cardian coins have the Milesian lion.[4] The head of Athena, on the other hand, not only proves that Athenian colonists had settled here. It is also obvious that Miltiades the founder took over the emblem which Peisistratus had made characteristic of his coinage and the very symbol of the State. Thus Miltiades' policy, much in the same sense as

---

[1] Aristophanes apparently mentioned the Chersonesians only as a specimen of the allies who were exploited by Athens. That he should be referring to the small Polis is even less possible than in the case of the scholiast.

[2] In spite of Herodotus' evidence, and without giving any reason, Berve (17) denies that a Polis can be called Agora!

[3] Cf. H. Nesselhauf, *Untersuchungen zur Geschichte der delisch-attischen Symmachie*, 126.

[4] Cf. Head, *H.N.²*, 259.

that of the tyrant at home, was an Athenian, and not a private, policy. The head on the coin of Chersonesus is similar to the type used by Cleisthenes; it definitely shows that the rule of the Philaidae was characterized by its bonds with Athens, and indeed with the Athens of Peisistratus and his successors.

This conclusion remains valid for any answer to the question who the Chersonesites actually were. It is worth while to look more closely into Hecataeus' words. It has long been seen that the original order of the words was destroyed by Stephanus Byzantius who pressed the quotation into his scheme of (1) name of Polis, (2) name of citizens, and compared the latter with the form used by Herodotus. The phrase was originally: Ἀψινθίοισι πρὸς μεσημβρίαν ὁμουρέουσι Χερρονήσιοι· ἐν δ᾽ αὐτοῖοι πόλις Χερρόνησος ἐν τῷ ἰσθμῷ τῆς Χερρονήσου. Hecataeus distinguishes the peninsula and the Polis of the same name, and equally the inhabitants of the peninsula and the citizens of the Polis. The latter are at the same time part of the former; for it is expressly stated that the Polis was situated in the territory of the Chersonesians (ἐν αὐτοῖοι). This combination cannot be understood unless 'Chersonesians' was the name of actual citizens on the one hand, and an unpolitical name of merely regional and ethnical significance on the other; it is the same use of the word that we have in Herodotus and probably also in the scholion to Aristophanes.

This use, once again, makes it almost certain that there was no common and united State. The last and perhaps strongest support of the opposite view, which remains to be dealt with, is the fact that in the tribute lists down to 448-7 Chersonesites are mentioned who paid a tribute of eighteen talents. This, at first sight, seems a clear indication that there was a political organization of the whole Chersonesus, but it has been usually and satisfactorily explained by some sort of federation, perhaps only for the purpose of paying taxes and tribute, a συντέλεια.[1]

[1] Cf. Nesselhauf, 36, 1. 126ff. Casson, 223. H. Kolbe, *Deutsche Literatur-Zeitung*, 1938, 966., I am very glad to find my results in general in conformity with the magnificent work done by the editors of the *Athenian Tribute Lists*, I (*A.T.L.*), which was published shortly after my paper came out. But I see a difficulty in their treatment of the Χερρονησῖται of the earlier period who paid eighteen talents. On p. 449 these are classified as a syntely which included several towns, among them the Χερρονησῖται ἀπ᾽ Ἀγορᾶς; on p. 564, on the other hand, all Χερρονησῖται are supposed to be the people of Agora only, whether they paid one or eighteen talents. The 'huge reduction' in 447-6 is explained merely by a reorganization following the arrival of Athenian settlers. It is true that in the lists from 447-6 to 442-1 the tributaries, although clearly identical

To assume a *dioecism* for 447 which would have followed an earlier *synoecism* is simply a vicious circle; for, since our literary sources (Plut. *Per.* 11, 5. 19, 1. Diod. XI, 15, 1. 88, 3) show nothing of such a dioecism, it is only a guess from the tribute lists, that is to say it is based on the hypothesis of a synoecism. The individual cities of the Chersonesus appear in the tribute lists after 447,[1] indeed with small contributions; this can be, and has been, explained by Pericles' new colonies of Athenian cleruchs. It does not prove anything for the earlier status.

It will be useful to investigate more closely the general picture of the settlement on the Chersonesus.[2] Miltiades founded or reinforced the following places: Cardia and Pactye in the East near the wall; to them Chersonesus = Agora is to be added; Elaeus and Crithote, the 'oil city' and the 'barley city', in the South-West near the entrance to the Hellespont. In between, on the shores of the Hellespont, were the Aeolian city of Sestos, which was probably not under Miltiades' rule, and Madytus. Other places, for instance Νεάπολις ἀπ' 'Αθηνῶν, which is mentioned in the tribute lists, cannot be identified with any certainty. But even from these few places the double aim of the settlements is manifest: protection against the hostile tribes in the North-East, and acquisition of an area from which oil and grain could be exported. An additional aim was, of course, to get new land for Athenian citizens. But on this side of the wall lived also the Doloncians and many non-Attic Greeks (cf. Plut. *Per.* 19). While Sigeum was a purely agrarian colony, this is not true to quite the same extent of the Chersonesus. And the Doloncians inhabited the very territory in which, especially at the two ends, the Greek cities were situated. It would not have been possible to distinguish be-

with the people of Agora, are called Χερρονῃσῖται only, and it is argued that 'it is most improbable that the name should change its meaning'. But there were always two meanings side by side, and I believe that the syntely was called by the ethnicon which I traced in other sources. This is the way the name is used, e.g., in the Carian syntely of Χερρονήσιοι; another parallel is the appearance of the Λήμνιοι in 452-1, while since 447-6 they are separated into 'Ηφαιστιῆς and Μυρινᾶοι. We naturally ask why the expression Χερρονησῖται ἀπ' 'Αγορᾶς was introduced at all, and the only answer I can think of is that it became desirable, in order to avoid confusion, to distinguish between the inhabitants of the peninsula who had previously formed a syntely, and the citizens of the Polis Chersonesus = Agora.

[1] Only Alopeconnesus appears before this date, according to the *A.T.L.* in 452-1 and 450-49. But at least the earlier year is uncertain; only]εσιοι is preserved. In 450-49 Αλοπε[is read. For 451-0 cf. Meritt, *Anat. Studies to Buckler* (1939), 187.

[2] Cf. the map in Casson, *l.c.*, 211, and in general the Gazetteer in the *A.T.L.*

tween the territory of the cities and the land of the Doloncians, if the cities had really formed one united State.

The colonization of the Chersonesus can hardly be understood, unless it is seen — as was usual among earlier scholars — as part of the general policy of expansion during the reigns of Peisistratus and his sons. This policy so clearly tended towards the Northern shores of the Aegean Sea and the Hellespont (Rhaecelus, Pangaeum, Chersonesus, Sigeum; slightly later, Lemnos and Imbros), that it must be understood as governed by the intention to create a coherent sphere of power. This power rested both on the men who found here home and food, and on the gains which Athens received in products from the mines and the soil. There can be no doubt that Athens had to import corn even at that early date. It is a mistake, as Professor Hasebroek has shown, to speak of a 'policy of trade'. But though we agree that the foreign policy of Athens at that time was not guided by motives of commerce, it surely rested on certain economic possibilities and necessities. It follows that, once again, we have to recognize in the political factor the force which moved as well as shaped the actions.

From all the foregoing it seems evident that the unity of the Chersonesus, as far as it was political, was entirely based on the position of the Philaidae. And this position is well characterized by the later charge of tyranny against Miltiades. In his position, State policy and family policy were inseparably combined. Miltiades, as I put it previously,[1] 'as a princely dynast exercised the rule of Athens over the Chersonesus'. We shall later ask ourselves[2] whether the word 'rule' with its general implications of public law is quite appropriate; but the facts of actual power are, I believe, rightly expressed by those words.

There remains, however, the question how it happened that the unity of a tyrant's rule changed into the unity of an organization which served at least for the payment of the tribute. It would be easiest to explain the later form if there had been a united State from the beginning. But none of the arguments in favour of this assumption has proved valid; some of them indeed almost contradicted it. It must be admitted that there is no definite proof for any other form of organization. But since we were forced to deny that in earlier times the town of

[1] Cf. my *Ost und West*, 117.   [2] See page 136.

Chersonesus was ever the political centre of the peninsula, it is impossible that after 490 the small town of Agora had such a position. And, without this, the conclusion drawn from the tribute lists has no foundation whatever. Possibly there were no Athenian colonists at all in the Chersonesus between 493 and 479. But its political importance, made clear by previous experience, must have incited the Athenians when Themistocles and, above all, Cimon were their leaders, to continue or renew their hold on the Chersonesus. The fact that this statement is based on an *argumentum ex silentio* does not contradict it; and when the Delian League was organized, the unity of the Chersonesus as a sphere of Athenian power and influence had to be restored, now probably in the shape of an alliance.

APOECY AND CLERUCHY

Legally, the Athenian allies were autonomous. This is a cogent reason for assuming that the Chersonesites, whatever their political organization, were no cleruchs; their cities must have been real ἀποικίαι. But, as I mentioned earlier, the usual distinction between apoecy and cleruchy, though testified by Athenian official language (IG.I², 140, 9), does not suffice to cover every instance. We have to retain the distinction as it stands in certain cases; for it is entirely valid from the purely legal point of view, when it is asked whether a colonist was a citizen of Athens or of a different Polis. But if the truly political factors are taken into account, and the fact that there was more than one type of cleruchy and apoecy, then we arrive at quite different conclusions.

Before we go deeper into this matter, it will be better first to discuss another early Athenian colony, that on Lemnos (and Imbros). We make this seeming digression for the following reason. In 447 the tribute of the whole Chersonesus was lowered and collected from the individual cities, probably without a renewed assessment for the Hellespontian district.[1] The last tribute of Lemnos (nine talents) of which we know belongs to 452-1. After 447 the island appears in the lists divided into two cities, Hephaestia and Myrina,[2] and at the

---

[1] Cf. Nesselhauf, 116, 128.
[2] The reading in 453-2 (V, 17): hεφαισσ]τιες seems, to say the least, uncertain.

same time the tribute was lowered to $4\frac{1}{2}$ talents. It is just possible that this happened as early as 450 when the tribute generally was reduced; but if we consider the division into single cities both in Lemnos and the Chersonesus it is much more likely that the procedure followed parallel lines in both places. It is only natural that the geographical coherence of the line Lemnos-Imbros-Chersonesus was reflected in a coherent policy. Pericles in 447 sent cleruchs probably to both ends of that line; in this way the changes are most easily explained. In the same way the earlier situation on the Chersonesus, difficult as it is to explain, will be more easily understood in connection with that of Lemnos.

Lemnos — and Imbros too, though it is not mentioned by Herodotus — was conquered by the younger Miltiades probably between 510 and 505.[1] He sailed from Elaeus (Herod. VI, 140), expelled the 'Pelasgian' inhabitants and gave the island to Athenian colonists (Herod. 136); but he did not act as an oecist. This settlement, too, has been considered an apoecy, not a cleruchy.[2] To prove this, the strongest counter-argument must be refuted, a Lemnian inscription of the early fifth century,[3] containing a list of names, apparently of men killed in battle, arranged according to the phylae of Cleisthenian Athens. Previous commentators assumed that these men were Athenian citizens. Now it is maintained that the Cleisthenian phylae, like all phylae, are tribal or belonging to a clan (*gentilizisch*), or, as in this case, 'quasi-tribal' — at any rate, independent of citizenship. I cannot imagine a more manifest misrepresentation of the Cleisthenian order, in which not only citizenship in general, but even the membership of a phyle was exclusively fixed by the fact of the deme in which a man was registered. I am convinced that it is wrong to say that the Cleisthenian phyle was 'in its idea a kinship group'. The phyletae worshipped the hero given to them as divine representative of the phyle by Delphi, but they never saw in him a common ancestor. The very meaning of Cleisthenes' reforms is destroyed unless we maintain the view that in practice as

[1] Cf. E. Obst, *Pauly-Wissowa*, XV, 1686. Berve, 49f. Gomme, *Hist. Comm. on Thuc.*, I, 375, 1, regards only 510 and 495 as certain limits.

[2] By Berve, who categorically denies any cleruchy for early times, and that despite Salamis (cf. Busolt-Swoboda, 871, 2. W. Schwahn, *A.J.Ph.*, LIV, 1933, 39ff.) and Chalcis (Herod. V, 77, VI, 100; Aelian. *v.h.* VI, 1).

[3] Cf. Picard and Reinach, *Bull. corr. hell*, XXXVI (1912), 330ff.

well as in principle the *ius sanguinis* was replaced by the *ius soli*.[1] Communal life was now centred in the local village or borough, the deme, and it is from and through this community that Cleisthenes' work got its driving force and the chance of lasting success. There should be no doubt that those Lemnians were Athenian citizens.

Several passages, however, in fifth century sources cannot be understood unless Lemnos and Imbros were in a high degree independent. They are frequently mentioned as allies of, and thus clearly distinguished from, the Athenians.[2] To overcome this obstacle, we must learn more of the nature and the variety of possible forms of cleruchies — which frequently have not been fully recognized. A number of excellent articles has been written on the subject of the cleruchies.[3] But since our evidence is fairly ample for a later period only, scholars, naturally enough, in trying to explain the whole phenomenon, chiefly used these later sources and did not sufficiently take into account any changes which might have happened in the course of time. It is true that 'a history of the Athenian cleruchies cannot be written'.[4] But it seems worth while to elaborate certain types and tendencies, which have been partly noticed before, but have not been put into historical order. Some scholars realized that cleruchies were not always of the same kind, and distinguished at least two forms; but no generally convincing criterion was found for this distinction. Whether the military character of the cleruchies, or their importance for social policy, was more stressed — no clear principle was followed, largely because the apoecies were included. This is true, for example, of the theory of Eduard Meyer, who distinguished between a cleruchy with military contingents of its own and one which remained inside the armed forces of Athens, and identified the former type with

---

[1] It is true that the principle of residence in the deme was confined to Cleisthenes' generation; all the descendants belonged to the same original deme wherever they lived. This fact would mitigate the strictness of the local principle, but it certainly did not refute it. Mr. Gomme, in his very friendly review of this paper (*J.H.S.* LIX, 1939, 295), objects to my protest against the view that Cleisthenes' phylae were kinship groups; but he is nevertheless convinced that the Lemnians were Athenian citizens.

[2] Berve, 52f., has collected the evidence.

[3] Most important: A. Boeckh, *Staatshaushaltung d. Athener*[3], I, 499ff., II, 100ff. A. Kirchhoff, *Abh. Preuss. Akad.*, 1873, 1ff. P. Foucart, *Mém. acad. inscr.* Sér. I. vol. IX (1878). E. Schulthess, *Pauly-Wissowa*, XI, 814ff. Busolt-Swoboda, 1271ff.

[4] Schulthess, 821.

the apoecy.[1] It must be admitted that in literature, even in
Thucydides, the expressions for the colonists themselves
(ἄποικοι, ἔποικοι, κληροῦχοι) are sometimes confused, although
their original meanings were evident. But, since in official
language both forms could be clearly distinguished (IG. I², 140,
8f.), we have to accept them as separate forms, or else show
that other forms were covered by each of them.

The decree on Brea (Tod, no. 44), at any rate, was concerned with an apoecy, and not a cleruchy. That is expressly
stated in the inscription. It is also essential to notice that the
oecist had full freedom in organizing the colony; only the
composition of the colonists was, in an amendment, confined
for social reasons to the two lower classes, the Zeugitae and
Thetes. Certain regulations and fixtures of a religious character had also to be given. In addition, Athens took care that
the cities ἐπὶ Θράκης gave each other mutual military support.
This regulation shows that the colony was to be part of the
empire, and the fact that the Thracian district is called by its
official name, confirms that Brea became one of the allies. In
the tribute lists, however, it does not appear; it probably had
the same privileged position as, for instance, Amphipolis.[2]
There are other characteristic features. The Athenian State
financed the whole expedition; the γεωνόμοι, who had to dis-
tribute the land of the colony, were installed beforehand, as a
purely Athenian board, 'one from each phyle'; Athenian
citizens who were on active service were given a chance to
join later; in the safety regulations (13ff.), and apparently also
in the lost beginning of the decree, it was made clear that Brea
depended on Athens even outside the religious sphere; finally
it seems that an existing settlement was occupied, and the
previous inhabitants were probably expelled. In all these
features this apoecy appears rather akin to the type of cleruchy.
We must conclude, at least for the middle of the fifth century,
that is to say for the Athenian Empire as shaped by Pericles,
that it would be just as mistaken to identify the apoecy with
any form of cleruchy as to assume that the distinction between

[1] E. Meyer, Forschungen zur alten Geschichte, II, 182f. Gesch. d. Alt. IV, 19f.
Neither is a clear distinction made in two dissertations which are frequently quoted:
R. Dahms, De Atheniensium sociorum tributo (Berlin, 1904), and M. Wagner, Zur
Geschichte der attischen Kleruchien (Tübingen, 1914).

[2] This explanation is given by Gomme, l.c., who is probably right in objecting to
the view which I had expressed that Brea was too small and too poor to pay tribute.

apoecy and cleruchy was quite clear-cut and excluded transitional forms.

The apoecy of Brea is distinguished from the average colony of other States (and times) by the fact that it was to a large extent politically dependent on the mother-city; its autonomy was restricted. A similar position, only the other way round, could arise for a cleruchy. In principle, every cleruchy, being a colony of Athenian citizens, was nothing but a part of the Athenian State. The extreme case of this is when the cleruchs merely formed a garrison, and the land distributed to them might be even farmed out. This is what happened in Salamis, Chalcis, Lesbos. Frequently, however, the cleruchy was, in a high though varying degree, independent and autonomous. The later records from the fourth century onwards give us some opportunity of seeing features deriving from the conditions of the fifth century, such as municipal government and an army, evidently also taxes of their own (cf. Ps.-Aristotle, *oecon.* II, 1347a, 18ff.). In those late sources the — Athenian — demos of a cleruchy is frequently mentioned.[1] In earlier times this formula was probably not used so consistently or with the same fixed legal meaning. But in another way the independence of the cleruchy may have been even more definite in the fifth century. Thucydides, at any rate, mentions the Lemnians and Imbrians by name, like any other autonomous Polis, as the closest allies of Athens. And in Athenian inscriptions the names of those killed in war could be registered, arranged by the Attic phylae, but nevertheless with the heading 'Lemnians from Myrina' (IG.I², 947). They are called Lemnians, not because they were Lemnian citizens, but because they belonged to a contingent of Lemnian soldiers. The arrangement of a second inscription (IG. 948) shows that it would be a mistake to think the Athenian phylae had been transferred to an autonomous Polis Lemnos. It is only under the name of the phyle that, as a subdivision, the word Λήμνιοι appears. These men were Athenian citizens. The evidence from the fifth century is too scanty to enable us to decide whether as in later times almost the whole apparatus of government as used in Athens was repeated in each cleruchy. But the details are of minor importance; the type of cleruchy is obvious.

It then became an easy matter to call this sort of cleruchy a

---

[1] e.g., ὁ δῆμος ἐν Ἴμβρωι. with or without Ἀθηναίων. Cf. IG.II², 1224ff., 3203ff,

Polis. Legal thinking, especially in public law, was frequently not very clear and definite. We sometimes find a cleruchy described as a Polis, though naturally only when there was at the same place no community of local citizens besides the cleruchy. As we saw before, a few passages in Herodotus cannot be understood unless we assume that what he calls a Polis was a cleruchy. The same is true of the passage from Ps.-Aristotle's *Oeconomica*. Moreover, in the honorary decree for Comeas (IG.II², 672, 8, 44) the two cleruchies at Lemnos, Hephaestia and Myrina, are expressly called πόλεις. In this record of about 280 B.C., there is some confusion even in official language. There is no longer a strict distinction between the two types, and support is given to our view that by then 'apoecy' and 'cleruchy' had come nearer in meaning to one another.

To distinguish the type of an independent cleruchy from that of a military one, we define it as a community of its own, or, as we may perhaps say, a 'municipal cleruchy' (*Gemeindekleruchie*). The cleruchs in such a community were bound to Athens since they remained Athenian citizens. But in practice they could never exercise their political rights. Moreover, they were peasants bound to the soil,[1] and frequently supervised by Athenian officials. Thus they stood outside the freedom of an Athenian citizen, even outside any true citizenship. It is the personal position which distinguished these colonists both from the military cleruchs and from the citizens of an apoecy. Their independence remained most precarious, and it would be, of course, mistaken, to regard their community as a State on its own. It is a type which does not fit into the normal scheme, according to which a community either was, or was not, an autonomous Polis. But the type can be found, and we must understand it by political rather than legal standards.

We realize that 'the middle position between autonomous communities and members of the Athenian State' (E. Meyer), which is typical of some cleruchies, brings them nearer to the type of the apoecy. Or to put it in a more general way, there were several intermediary forms between the pure cleruchy and the pure apoecy.[2] This may explain the differences be-

---

[1] Cf. IG.II², 30b, 4.7.

[2] This view comes close to that of Schulthess (828) who rightly denies that there ever was a general statute on cleruchies, and believes in an individual arrangement for each case. Schulthess's theory, however, does not show the historical basis of the facts.

tween various theories intended to distinguish between the types of colonies. In using the same terms, scholars are often speaking of different things, and therefore overlook the variety of facts and misunderstand their respective statements.

To simplify matters and to point to the essential results of our discussion, it seems desirable to distinguish four types: the cleruchy as a garrison, and as a municipal community, the apoecy as a dependent colony within the empire, and as a normal colony. If we look at these types from a historical, and not a systematic, point of view, it is evident that a garrison originally could occur only in the immediate neighbourhood of Athens (Salamis, Euboea). At a greater distance a garrison was possible only when set within the framework of the empire, and this is equally true of the dependent apoecy. During the early period of Athenian colonization, that is to say before 478, no form of colony could possibly come into existence other than either the municipal cleruchy or the pure apoecy.[1]

The arguments *pro* and *con* which we have discussed so far, as to which of the two types prevailed in early colonization, have not proved really cogent, although some of them very clearly pointed to the early existence of cleruchies. To decide the question we have to deal with two more points. The first is the interpretation of Thuc. VII, 57, 2, where a survey is given, somewhat strange in its wording, of the States which fought against Syracuse: 'The Athenians themselves, being Ionians, readily went out against the Dorians of Syracuse; and the Lemnians, Imbrians, and Aeginetans who then lived in Aegina, and also the Hestiaeans from Euboea who were colonists (ἄποικοι), took the field with them as peoples still speaking the same language and using the same customs. Of the rest some joined in as subjects, others as autonomous allies, and some also as mercenaries.'

The group to which special attention is called are Athenian colonists. The inhabitants of Hestiaea are particularly mentioned as ἄποικοι; here the earlier inhabitants had been expelled (Thuc. I, 114, 3). This is supposed to have been also the case in Aegina, though Thucydides calls the colonists there

---

[1] Sigeum was an early apoecy, with its usual features, but to some extent lacking in full political independence because of the family rule of the Peisistratidae. Cf. above, p. 118f.

ἔποικοι or οἰκήτορες (II, 27; VIII, 69, 3). Apart from these two the Lemnians and Imbrians are mentioned. They all have something in common, but this is not their political form, which cannot have been that of an apoecy because this expression is applied with some emphasis to the Hestiaeans only.[1] In fact, Thucydides tells us plainly enough what they had in common; it was their language, the Attic dialect, and their 'customs' (νόμιμα). I do not think this characterization would be meaningless if they were Athenian citizens. Thucydides intends to give the reasons why these cities — whatever their legal position, with which he is not concerned — were put into one category, clearly to be distinguished from allies and subjects. If Lemnos and Imbros were municipal cleruchies Thucydides' phrase is adequate; but the circumstantial expression shows at the same time that the official nomenclature was vague and, in fact, inadequate. The very general term 'customs' probably indicates the constitutional forms and habits. A number of cleruchic decrees, though of a later date,[2] show that the form of the prescript of Athenian decrees was taken over, and this implies important political institutions. In the fourth century when Lemnos, Imbros and Scyros had again lost their short-lived autonomy (Xen. hell. IV, 8, 15; V, 1, 31), there were cleruchs in Lemnos who had kept their Attic *demoticon*; we know of them through inscriptions.[3] And the Cleisthenian phyle gave the name to the prytanies which functioned in turn. All this is exactly as in Athens itself. The cleruchy in Lemnos was composed of Athenian citizens and governed by Athenian institutions. There is no reason whatsoever why the position should have been different about 500 B.C.

The second point still to be discussed is that of the tribute, a question much disputed till recent times.[4] If a strict legal distinction is made between cleruchy and apoecy, then there can be no tribute from the cleruchies; for the φόρος is a burden on the allies, and not on Athenian citizens. It seems, however, not impossible that a community which had troops

---

[1] Mr. Gomme reminds us that the difference in the status of these colonies is also stressed by the fact that Lemnos and Imbros paid tribute, and Aegina and Hestiaea did not. See next page.

[2] Cf. H. Swoboda, *Griech. Volksbeschlüsse*, 40. Busolt-Swoboda, 1277f.

[3] Busolt-Swoboda, 1273, 1.

[4] We can expect a full discussion in the second volume of the *A.T.L.*

of its own might also find itself in the position of an ally and be compelled to pay tribute. The apoecy of Brea, on the other hand, was not completely autonomous and did not pay tribute. I do not venture to decide the question whether there were not, after all, non-Attic natives in Lemnos and Imbros who paid tribute; but I consider it unlikely. I think it is quite understandable that, when the Delian League was founded, existing municipal cleruchies had to join the ranks of the tribute-payers, simply because they had replaced important States which otherwise would have been liable to contribute ships or to pay tribute. The possibility cannot be excluded that these quasi-independent cleruchies, some of which might even have lost their original character and become independent Poleis, were treated in the same way as the autonomous allied States. Later cleruchies, beginning with those of Pericles, all of which were founded chiefly for the political and military security of the empire, naturally did not come in for the payment of tribute. They sometimes actually caused the tribute to be reduced, because the original population had to surrender part of their land.

I regard it as certain and easily intelligible that Lemnos, after Miltiades had conquered it, became a municipal cleruchy. It is less certain whether the Chersonesus was in the same position. But if we consider that in the sixth century an apoecy could by no means be governed in the same way as it was in the Athenian Empire, and if we realize, on the other hand, in what position of political dependency the Chersonesus was kept, then it seems natural to assume that here, too, were cleruchies. Perhaps it is better not to speak of Athenian rule or Athenian possessions. There was probably a certain difference between the status of Lemnos and that of the Chersonesus, rooted largely in the circumstances of the time when these colonies were founded. The Chersonesus was an offspring of tyranny, Lemnos of the free Polis. Miltiades on the Chersonesus was the lordly dynast, similar to the tyrant in Athens and at the same time his counterpart: in Lemnos, though he acted independently and spontaneously, he was a general who afterwards surrendered the island to his native Polis. It is absurd to take this as 'a wooing of Athens' or — years before the outbreak of the Ionian revolt — as a preparation for his return. It reflected, in fact, his personal and political position, exactly as his different behaviour in the Chersonesus reflected his position then and there. In both cases Miltiades' attitude, as at each period it resulted from his feelings as well as from political considerations, was essentially determined by his connection with Athens. We learn something about this connection through a well-known red-figured plate, probably belonging to the twenties of the sixth century. Here a horseman is depicted in Thracian costume, and the usual love-inscription runs: ΜΙΛΤΙΑΔΗΣ ΚΑΛΟΣ.[1] It is not the political forms that have changed between the two dates, but the position and attitude of Miltiades. I am inclined to think that the form of colonization was very much the same in both cases.

It is, however, unlikely that both forms were simply identical. For one factor was different, and this largely determined the nature of the settlement. In Lemnos the pre-Athenian population, on the whole, had to leave the island, while in the Chersonesus not only was nobody expelled, but the elder Miltiades was even called in to save the inhabitants from external enemies. Both Greeks and Thracians lived together under the Philaidae, and of course later also. Thus it is likely that the ethnical composition of the various Chersonesian cities was by no means everywhere the same. Consequently the political form, too, may have varied. The coin from the city of Chersonesus can hardly be explained unless citizens of Milesian and Athenian origin lived here together, and both must have been citizens of the new Polis. The new foundations, on the other hand, like Elaeus, Crithote, Madytus and Neapolis, will have been cleruchies of the independent type, the kind we have to assume on the Chersonesus, according to our previous investigations.

THE PARIAN EXPEDITION

The nature of Athenian colonization, and the part played in it by some great individuals, have been discussed, as far as our sources make it possible. Before trying to sum up, we ought to consider one more event, the expedition to Paros in 489 B.C. This strange enterprise of the victor of Marathon probably belongs to our subject, but its meaning and relevance are especially difficult to understand. Later sources explain it in a

---

[1] 'Miltiades is beautiful.' Illustration, e.g., in Seltman, *l.c.*, 142.

rational, but obviously misleading way. As it is emphasized by several scholars (How and Wells, Berve and others), this must be said of the story which Ephorus tells us (*F.Gr.H.*70, F 63). Before Themistocles created the fleet, the Athenians could hardly think of occupying the Cyclades, even though the State sometimes, with private support, provided for a fairly large fleet. For the historian of the fourth century, however, this was a natural thing to imagine, and he would also think that the failure of the expedition was due to treason on the part of the leader. The trial in particular which immediately followed the campaign must have led later generations to regard Miltiades as a man similar in character and destiny to Themistocles and Pausanias. Herodotus' report is free from such an unhistoric adaptation to later standards; it is, in fact, the *lectio difficilior*.[1] There is no doubt that his story is to be preferred.

But he, too, already knew different stories. He tells us (VI, 134, 1), though this is at variance with his own succeeding narrative, that there was a uniform story 'by all the Greeks' about the origin and the beginnings of the enterprise; but as to the course of the fighting and Miltiades' final failure he gives only one version, that of the Parians who produced religious reasons. We do not know why he did not mention the Athenian version, or any other if there was one, nor do we know what these versions were like. The facts mentioned should, however, induce us to be very careful in trying to find the historical relevance of Herodotus' text.[2]

'Miltiades told the Athenians he wanted seventy ships, an armed force, and money, without informing them what country he was going to attack. He only promised to enrich them if they would follow him. For he would lead them against a land whence they might easily carry off ample gold. With these words he asked for the ships, and the Athenians were induced to grant [everything he wanted]. Miltiades, having got the armament, sailed against Paros' (VI, 132).

It cannot be doubted that the original initiative to embark on the expedition came from Miltiades. But when he later recounted, as the motive for the war, the story that the Parians had accompanied the Persians to Marathon with one trireme

[1] This is well remarked by Berve, 97.
[2] Cf. R. W. Macan, *Herodotus IV-VI*, vol. II, 251f.

of their own, he turned the whole enterprise into an act of vengeance on the part of Athens. Herodotus, on the other hand, regards this as a mere pretext, and maintains as the true cause that Miltiades personally had been wronged by an individual Parian. This, of course, is irrelevant gossip. Herodotus clearly had the wish to incriminate Miltiades, which provides one more reason for being critical of everything he tells us, or seems to tell us, about the personal character of the whole expedition.

The Athenian assembly conceded to the victor of Marathon the right to lead a campaign against a country not known to the people. If this story is true,[1] it was certainly an unusual procedure; but it can be explained by the 'miracle' of Marathon. The people had unlimited confidence in Miltiades, who perhaps gave tactical reasons for keeping the goal of the expedition secret.[2] But since the people granted ships, money and an army, we must ask whether in these circumstances the enterprise was still what has been called a personal affair of Miltiades. The troops can only have been citizens, not mercenaries who might have been 'granted' like ships or money. But citizens, and they even in considerable numbers, could hardly have joined as soldiers and sailors, unless the people had decided officially upon a campaign, even though against an unknown enemy.

Thus the whole enterprise, and in particular the part played by Miltiades, appears in a different light from what Herodotus suggests, or what those suggest who go still farther than Herodotus. Miltiades was the military leader; he had given the people certain promises and had won them over to his plans. The situation is very much the same, all differences being admitted, as that of Alcibiades when he persuaded the Athenians to go to Sicily. But it was the people that decided on the final decree, and the official motivation of the war, as later given by Miltiades, was in accordance with this fact. It was the same people that for this very reason put Miltiades to trial in their own court, a trial which Miltiades in no way tried to evade. We do not know whether Miltiades' original aims were chiefly personal, and whether he used the public weal largely as a

[1] It is doubted, e.g., by Gomme.
[2] Cf. Macan, 254. Much later something similar occurred in Sparta, although the situation was different (Thuc. V, 54, 1).

pretext to foster his own power. But even if this was so, and Herodotus' allusions were, in a way, to the point, we shall find that events were stronger than men, and that the State forced upon the individual the obligations towards the community.

The charge of 'deception of the people' (ἀπάτη τοῦ δήμου), with the prospect of the death penalty, was not concerned only with the waste of public money, but meant deceitful injury to the community itself. The death of many citizens during the campaign would incriminate Miltiades more deeply than the loss of the promised gold. The essential point, at any rate, is that he was charged with ἀπάτη and barely escaped death, the penalty of fifty talents being the very high fine which was to take the place of execution.[1] In the ancient law, mentioned by Demosthenes (XX, 100, 135: νόμος ἀρχαῖος) — whether previously existing or introduced only to meet Miltiades' case — the death penalty was prescribed for the mere breach of a promise given to the people. Rightly understood, this law shows with what an almost brutal firmness the Polis forced the individual to complete responsibility and unrestricted submission. The trial by the assembly of the great victorious general, just like Cleisthenes' introduction of ostracism, is an expression of the strong will of the Polis to suppress the *hybris*, and the egotistic will to power, of the great dynasts.[2]

The Parian expedition, like the earlier colonizing enterprises, cannot be separated from the general trend of politics. But it has not yet been shown that this event had anything at all to do with colonization, whether apoecy or cleruchy. Some historians think that Miltiades wanted to create in Paros a sort

[1] Fifty talents is a large sum. But the explanation given in the text seems quite adequate. If the same amount was sometimes used as a penalty or as a bribe, it is generally mentioned as the highest possible amount (e.g., Herod. V, 51, 2. Plut. *Per.* 35, 4). Moreover, the gradual devaluation must be taken into account. It alone explains the almost proverbial use in Aristophanes (*Vesp.* 669. *Thesm.* 811). The Philaidae were a very rich family, and we need not doubt that Cimon could pay the heavy fine, and nevertheless remain a rich man. No further explanation is actually needed, and the attempts to find one are rather pathetic and even comic, whether made by Cornelius Nepos (7, 6) who thought the fifty talents was the compensation for the expenses of the expedition, or by Berve (101) who calls them 'the minimum gain of the expedition which was to be divided between Miltiades and the people'!

[2] Ostracism was not put into use for twenty years. This is a proof of the strength of the Polis, not of its weakness. It would have been the latter only if there had been domestic strife on a large scale between 507 and 490. But the contrary is true (cf. *Ost und West*, 107ff.).

of family stronghold, such as the Peisistratidae had done in Sigeum, or he himself in the Chersonesus. But the island of Paros was barren, and a settlement of citizens almost impossible. Our sources do not give the slightest indication of anything of the sort. But Miltiades' aims are expressly stated; he promised the Athenians gold. What he afterwards demanded from the Parians, was silver — a hundred talents. This payment was hardly the wealth the Athenians had hoped for and had been led to expect. The sum as a whole, though a heavy fine, is too small for this, and besides, it was not gold. Paros had no gold. This is a geological fact, not 'a subjective assumption' as we have been told. In Herodotus' time Paros paid an annual tribute of sixteen, later even of twenty-five talents, a very large sum indeed. But this does not prove anything about Miltiades' time. For meanwhile Parian marble had become a most valuable article of export, which it certainly was not in about 490. At that time Paros was an island of only modest wealth. There was gold on the Thracian shore and at Thasos, a district well known to Miltiades. Paros was the mother-city of Thasos, but it is most unlikely that for this reason Paros had a large treasury of gold; for Thasos did not, of course, pay any tribute to Paros, and in general Greek States of that period did not usually collect public treasures. Neither is anything known of Paros as an important centre of commerce at that time.[1]

But to conquer Paros might have been of strategical and political importance, at least for a man whose real aims included Thasos. That is why I had assumed[2] that Miltiades — for reasons not known to us, but perhaps indicated in what I have just mentioned — considered Paros a necessary stage on his way to the further and more ambitious aim of winning the Pangaean and Thracian mines.[3] Herodotus (VII, 112) tells us that in 480 these mines were in the hands of Thracian tribes.

[1] Nepos in his very poor biography of Miltiades (7, 2) calls Paros *insula opibus elata*. But this, even if it were true, does not say that it was an important trade centre (against Beloch, II, 1, 83). It is probably nothing but a conclusion from the very story of Miltiades' expedition.

[2] *Ost und West*, 123.

[3] Cf. on them Casson, *l.c.*, 59ff. – It may be worth while noticing that eighty years later, in 411, Paros and Thasos were connected by a *sympoliteia*, which is mentioned again in a source of 339 B.C.; cf. O. Rubensohn, *Athen. Mitt.* XXVII (1902), 198, 273ff., 285f.; H. O. Raue, *Untersuchungen z. Geschichte d. korinthischen Bundes*. Diss. Marburg, 1937, 58, note 82.

Athens had lost them when the Peisistratides were expelled. The idea may easily have suggested itself to Miltiades, who had various and close connections with Thrace, that he might try to recover these possessions. Personal interest, once again, was closely bound together with the interest of the State. The Parian expedition can be taken as part of the history of Athenian colonization, if we accept what has been said about the intentions behind it. They clearly continue the expansive policy of the Peisistratean age.

CONCLUSION

To sum up the results of our discussion of the nature and history of early Athenian colonization, there is, above all, the fact that through all changes and differences a policy was maintained which was dictated by a conscious political will. As a whole, this is indeed the view generally held by scholars of one or two generations ago, although in details some of their views must be revised. The opinion expressed more recently that there were fundamental and incompatible differences between 'archaic' and Periclean policy is, to say the least, much exaggerated. This view misunderstands the constant and characteristic nature of Athenian colonization, as it was first seen when Solon induced the people to occupy Salamis. It was continued in the family policy of Peisistratus, and the ambitions of the Philaidae served the same purpose. By this colonization, new soil for Athenian citizens was provided, Athens procured rich supplies of corn and metals, and gained new spheres of political influence. The usual form of colonization, the apoecy, was accepted, but underwent a political development. At the same time the new form, the cleruchy, was created to meet the needs of the State as well as of its leading men. In Sigeum the political bond was secured by the 'branch' of the ruling family. In the Chersonesus the situation was somewhat different, since here a rival family was concerned. Peisistratus probably saw in the fact that the majority of the emigrant settlers remained Athenian citizens, a safeguard against the growing independence of the Philaidae. The social and economic aims of the colony were achieved just as well as in an apoecy, but the new community was at the same time included in the political scheme of Peisistratus' able and intelligent statesmanship. Possibly he was the inventor of the cleruchy type of colonization, and Miltiades merely knew how to unite under his own rule the various settlements which need not have been of identical type, just as he united Greeks and Doloncians. Finally, in Lemnos, when the 'Pelasgian' inhabitants had been expelled, independent cleruchical towns were created. It is likely that the type of the 'municipal cleruchy' developed only gradually and participated in the development of Athens from tyranny to a free community of citizens. There is therefore nothing anachronistic about it all. Colonization by cleruchies was an early attempt of the Polis to grow beyond its natural boundaries. It also disclosed a tendency, typical of the tyrants, to replace the mere splitting-off of the citizen population through the foundation of new colonies by a political bond between mother-city and colony. Athens in the sixth century, from Peisistratus to Cleisthenes, had reached a political maturity which can be equally discerned in other connections. It is the result of a real inner tradition, bearing witness to the unique greatness of the Polis of Athens, and not only an assumption by modern scholars, that the features of fifth-century policy had their true origin in the policy of sixth-century Athens.

X

TRAGIC HERACLES[1]

HERACLES AND TRAGEDY

HERACLES, the hero who fought with his hands or with such primitive weapons as club and bow, who accomplished the 'twelve labours', who delivered Prometheus from the eagle, who finally after a life of toil gained immortality and married Hebe or Eternal Youth — this son of Zeus and demi-god, compelled by Hera's jealousy and hatred to serve a weak and evil man, yet always emerging triumphant, this is the Heracles of most of the old myths and of most of his cults. Immensely strong and a great fighter, he was the ideal of an age and a civilization for which bodily strength and untiring courage were essential features of a true man. Naturally enough he became in later times the protector of young men in the gymnasium and the palaestra.

Mythology for the Greeks was, to a large extent, their early history; it was in fact the history of a people whose characteristic way of thought was unhistorical. This explains why for them mythology was never at an end. It remained the ever-growing and ever-changing domain of poets and thinkers, as much in later times when the stories about gods and heroes had ceased to be the subject of simple and naïve belief, as in the happy age of Homer and the Homerids. The tale of Heracles, like other mythological stories, was extended and enriched. One poet gave him miraculous strength while still a babe in the cradle, and made him strangle the serpents sent by Hera. The catalogue of his labours grew, new countries and new deeds were added, and Heracles' exploits finally covered more or less the whole of the known world. He purged land and sea of monsters and evils, a real benefactor of mankind. But was the cause of all this hard toil and fighting nothing but the hatred of a goddess who after all acquiesced in the vast offspring of her husband's amorous adventures? Some poets found this an

[1] Reprinted from *Durham University Journal*, XXXV (1943).

insufficient cause for such great ordeals, and invented stories of Heracles' own misdeeds, such as the murder of Iphitus. The most notable of these stories was that which described how the young hero, married to the daughter of the king of Thebes, in a sudden fit of frenzy killed his own children. Another poet wished to represent the mighty man as the servant not merely of a smaller man, but actually of a woman, and thus wrote the story of Omphale. On the other hand, Heracles remained the great representative of noble and courageous youth, and it was entirely in the line of previous developments of the legend that the sophist Prodicus invented the moralistic story of Heracles at the cross-road.

Whatever happened to Heracles, he always in the end ascended to Olympus, redeemed from his hard life upon earth. He was a great hero indeed, yet his was no tragic fate, for there was the 'happy end' to all his toil and struggle. This end was described in slightly different ways, but it seems clear that the last of his labours would inevitably lead him along the path to eternal life. Either he slew the dragon and won immortality by carrying off the apples of the Hesperides; or he descended into Hades, in order to bring up to earth the terrible watchdog of the nether world, and overcame death by returning from that country from which no mortal man had ever returned. After fulfilling his last labour he sacrificed himself in the flames of a pyre on the summit of Mount Oeta, thus rising to the gods.

Only when this sublime story was combined with the intrigue of the Centaur Nessus, and Heracles became the victim of his innocent wife Deianeira, did the myth come really close to tragedy. Here then was not only toil and labour, but also suffering. Heracles suffered in body and soul. The godlike hero was a human being, and his fate seemed that of mortal man. Originally, however, the story of Nessus and Deianeira belonged to Aetolia, and had nothing to do with the Thessalian legend of Heracles' end on Mount Oeta. In that Aetolian story Heracles won Deianeira and slew Nessus, but we do not know what followed, if indeed anything followed at all. Was the tale of the poisoned garment an original feature which only later was combined with the Oeta story? We cannot say, but we may assume that mere suicide was never the end of the godlike hero.

In dealing with the story and figure of Heracles as they were revealed in early epic and lyric poetry we have to realize how restricted and fragmentary is our knowledge. Most of our sources belong to later times when the myth had, or at any rate might have, undergone new changes. In maintaining that the Heracles of the earlier stages down to the fifth century B.C. was a great hero, but no tragic figure, we are supported by the fact that 'tragedy was somewhat shy of Heracles' (Jebb). It seems certain that in none of the many tragedies which are lost to us was the legend of Heracles made the very basis and content of the play. There were no Greek tragedies on the subject of Heracles except Sophocles' *Trachiniae* and Euripides' *Heracles*. We shall appreciate the reason for this, when we understand by what means and for what purpose the two tragedians finally made Heracles a tragic figure.

To answer these questions is the object of this paper, though it cannot do more than outline the essential facts. Before we proceed, however, let us look for a moment at the problem from a different point of view. The 'strong man' did not excel in heroic deeds only. There is a stock type of strong man or giant in the fairy-tales of most peoples, and the strength of his arms is matched by his prowess in eating and drinking, and for that matter he is also a great lover. The glutton Heracles, favourite type of comedy and satyr-drama, derives from the same great figure as the redeemed benefactor of mankind. It was usual with the Greeks to make fun of their gods, and Hermes the thief, the sensual and intoxicating Aphrodite, or the voluptuary Dionysos were as old and as real as their severe and sublime counterparts. But no god, however much he might suffer, was ever tragic. The Heracles of comedy is confirmation of the fact that the hero's fate was not tragic, unless it became involved in human frailties and human crimes. Heracles, whether hero or glutton, was always superhuman and therefore essentially untragic.

The attentive student of Greek Tragedy at the present time cannot but be aware of the open conflict between two schools of thought and criticism, the 'historical' and the 'literary'.[1] Now,

---

[1] This essay is especially indebted to the following books, different as they are in outlook and results: H. D. F. Kitto, *Greek Tragedy* (1939); K. Reinhardt, *Sophokles* (1933); H. Weinstock, *Sophokles* (1931); G. M. A. Grube, *The Drama of Euripides* (1941). I am all the more anxious to emphasize this indebtedness, because I often differ widely from these writers in important, even fundamental, matters.

there should be no doubt that any real attempt at understanding a work of literary art must be literary, in the sense of having to treat its subject as a work of art. To this extent the 'literary' outlook is undoubtedly right, especially if we bear in mind that historical interpretation has frequently failed to realize the marked divergence between the realities of life and of the stage. Even in Athens drama was not politics. On the other hand, to understand a poem involves understanding the poet's mind, and it is hard to believe that there was ever a poet, at all events a Greek poet, who consciously acted as a 'pure artist', as a servant of *l'art pour l'art*. It is even more difficult to imagine a poet, however great a genius, whose mind was entirely out of touch with the ideas and problems of his contemporaries. Man is both creative and a creature, an independent individual and a product of the forces of nature and history. Any poet's mind must, at least unconsciously, reflect some of the essential features of the time and place in which he lives. The real problem therefore cannot be stated (as Kitto, for example, maintains) in terms of the exclusive contrast between historical scholarship and literary criticism; it demands for its solution that we show by every means available why the poet has written what he has written.

We do not know when the *Trachiniae* was performed, and we can only conclude from a few hints that the date of Euripides' *Heracles* is probably about 420 B.C. But this lack of chronology ought not to trouble us. I do not myself believe in the results, contradictory as they are, of 'literary' research into the question of chronology, and I propose to neglect this question altogether. I have no doubt that one of the two plays about Heracles was written with some reference to the other, but which of them was the earlier, which the later, remains an open question. I have of course, as others have, a view of my own on the relative chronology of the two tragedies, but I cannot prove it. For the same reason I shall also omit the question of the relative chronology of the *Trachiniae* within Sophocles' work. I believe that the material which would enable us to trace the development of the poet's mind and art is far too slight for this purpose, even if the seven and a half out of about one hundred and twenty plays may be considered as in a sense representative. Nobody could give a coherent picture of Shakespeare's artistic development, if he knew no other of the thirty-seven plays but, let us say, *Richard II, Troilus and Cressida, Hamlet,* and *Twelfth Night* — all masterpieces, and the proportion to the total even more favourable than in the case of Sophocles. But quite apart from our fragmentary knowledge of the poet's work, the question in itself is much more complex than is usually realized. General conditions and the individual qualities of the poet are intermingled in every conceivable way, and it is impossible to isolate questions of technique, style, characters, or ideas, and find a single or even a predominant line of development. To draw characters, to indicate dramatic action, to outline human problems, and so on, were all parts of the same process of poetical creation. When modern research revealed the poet's intentions now in this and now in that direction, it was natural to overstress the specific points. But after all there was one creative mind at work — a fact which is recognized by the Greek word for a poet as one who 'makes' or creates.

SOPHOCLES' 'TRACHINIAE'

The *Trachiniae* is a play about two persons, Heracles and Deianeira. This is a simple and obvious fact, and any explanation which evades it is wrong from the start. Sophocles did not write a drama with the intention of misleading his audience, and that would be the case if either Heracles or Deianeira were of subordinate importance only. Similarly the *Antigone* is a play about two persons, while the *Ajax,* on the other hand, is a tragedy of a single individual, in spite of the fact that Ajax dies in the middle of the play. But whereas the double fate in the *Antigone* is, in fact, one fate of two persons, interconnected throughout the play in what is a real struggle between two beings, two souls and two wills, the double fate in the *Trachiniae* implies two fates. Not only is Deianeira dead when Heracles first enters the stage; though perhaps this is not so important as would appear, because in the large first part (Deianeira's part, which is about three-quarters of the play) the absent Heracles is always present in the mind of every single person on the stage. But Deianeira is never once in Heracles' mind, neither before nor after the disaster, except for the short moment when he wants to punish her. The tragedy of Heracles is that of his own nature and his own actions; its very core is his greatness which makes him believe that he is entirely independent, a law unto himself. The tragedy of Deianeira is that of Heracles' wife, and though her character and her actions determine the outcome, she is essentially dependent on Heracles, a married woman whose whole life is shaped by this fact, and by this fact alone. Heracles' self-centred mind on the one hand, Deianeira's loving dependency on the other, exclude any common fate as well as any real struggle between them. I doubt even whether it is justifiable to take them as representatives of their sexes. Although, no doubt, Heracles is exceedingly masculine and Deianeira not only very feminine, but, as we saw, suffering because of her marriage, generalization leads nowhere, especially since the alleged two principles of manhood and womanhood never come into conflict with each other. No, there are two human beings, connected by the tie of marriage, but without real common existence, and destined to perish just because of these facts. Although I believe that the great figures of Sophocles' tragedies are more than mere 'characters', and that the *Trachiniae* is not only an expression of Sophocles' 'interest in the situation created by so unusual a character as Heracles' (Kitto), we must try not to apply ideas and standards which are alien to his men and women. They cannot be understood by psychology only, for Sophocles is not interested in psychology for its own sake. Heracles and Deianeira suffer, because they are what they are. But why and when and how these human beings are both characters and creatures, fashioned by the poet's genius from the facts of eternal nature as well as of the contemporary background — that is what we have to show.

Deianeira's tragedy seems at once simple and beautiful. Her marriage to Heracles had been deliverance from fear and terror rather than fulfilment of happiness, and her married life had been sorrow and anxiety. She loved Heracles, and when he was away on his labours (and he was away most of the time), she had longed and grieved for him. But she never realized what it meant to be married to 'the famous son of Zeus' (19, 566, etc.), to a man who was not simply 'the best man of all' as she calls him (177), to a man who was undoubtedly great, strange as the form may be which that greatness took. If she for her part was nothing but the loving wife, it is this very quality which gives her her unique charm and makes it so easy for us to forget that her tragic mistake contains an element of sheer foolishness. We can understand the jealousy of a middle-aged woman towards her youthful rival, even if we believe that up till then Deianeira has always regarded her husband's numerous love affairs as natural and inoffensive. Indeed the very mention of them discloses a petty and bourgeois mind, which is in fact opposed to the average attitude of both mythical and historical Greece. When Deianeira applies the love-charm given her by the dying Nessus, she does not fully believe in its helpfulness and is somewhat afraid of it. The poet makes this quite clear (582): 'May I never know nor understand wicked daring, for I hate women who dare. But if by using love-spell and charm on Heracles I may prevail against this girl, well, everything is ready — unless indeed I seem to be acting foolishly; if so, I cannot have finished with it too soon.' She wants to be confirmed in her half-belief by the chorus, and she is easily confirmed, or rather before any further doubts may be discussed, Heracles' messenger Lichas re-enters and Deianeira is compelled to proceed with her plan, to lie and to conceal, and to rely on the silence of the chorus. 'For if you do something secretly, even if it be shameful, you will never be brought to shame.' (596). With this rather repulsive piece of conventional morality Deianeira definitely reveals more of her character than is usually admitted.

But what is done cannot be undone, and things take their inevitably disastrous turn. Deianeira had used a flock of wool to anoint Heracles' robe with the fatal poison, and when she sees the wool crumbling away in the blaze of the sun, she at once realizes that she has done a frightful deed (706), as in fact she had half-consciously feared before. It will be evident by now that her tragedy is not quite so simple and so beautiful as is frequently believed. The tragedy of the loving wife who destroys her beloved and herself is touching and moving, but there is sufficient indication of wrong-doing, or perhaps rather of human imperfection and weakness, apart from mere error. Is there nothing wrong in foolish action which may even be considered as an immodest encroachment upon the realm of daemonic powers? Is there nothing wrong in a narrowness of mind which finally declares that it is unbearable to live with an evil reputation, if one is actually not evil (721)? There is something very conventional about Deianeira, and it is obvious

that this contrasts very sharply indeed with the nature of
Heracles. To Deianeira love is all in all, and this gives her
greatness; she has the kindest of hearts, as her first meeting
with Iole proves; but she shrinks from responsibilities, and is
incapable of understanding anything above the average level
of human, we may even say of bourgeois, life. She could have
been greater only at the cost of being less human and, I dare
say, less lovable; this cost the poet did not choose to pay.

Sophocles has twice contrasted a pair of sisters, one of
whom is strong and active, the other weak and passive. His
interest and sympathy are, of course, with Antigone and
Electra rather than with Ismene and Chrysothemis. The
former pair are heroines of strong will-power and equally
strong belief in a right which is more than their personal right.
Only in fighting for the unwritten laws of a sacred world
order do they win the right and the duty of action, even to the
last terrible consequence of murder. The others, however, are
true to their sex; tender and weak in body and spirit, they have
neither the power nor the right to act heroically. Here, we
feel, lies the true reason for Deianeira's deficiency. She acted,
but not in the defence of sacred and eternal laws (for instance,
the sanctity of marriage), but for her own private happiness,
for her undisturbed position as Heracles' wife. This may be
natural, but in the end it is selfish, and it shows, once again,
that Heracles' wife never knew what sort of man Heracles
actually was, and that his fate was determined by the gods and
was not to be altered by magical tricks. For her ignorance she
pays dearly, and not only with her death; the weak woman
gains the strength to kill herself and to die where her life
had centred, on her marriage-bed. What is more cruel and
even more sad is that she has no place in the thought of the
dying Heracles. Her silent departure from the stage, when she
goes out to die, seems to repeat itself, when she is forgotten as
soon as Heracles learns that she did not want to kill him.
Nothing could be more tragic than this last touch which
reveals the utter futility of everything Deianeira had thought
and felt and done. Her endeavours not only were futile, they
could not be anything but futile. The question whether she is
guilty or not, is not to the point, and the chorus's common-
sense statement (727) that those who erred unintentionally
should be judged more leniently, is at once rejected by

Deianeira herself. Her tragedy is a love tragedy, but not in the Euripidean (and modern) sense. It is not love that destroys Deianeira; she is no Phaedra, no Medea. It is her tragic fate to be married to a man whose nature she does not understand, and to be involved in daemonic events which she does not understand either. This explains also what we called her foolishness in regard to Nessus' advice. It accounts, on the other hand, for her irresponsible yielding to private feelings, justified as they may be; she overestimates the importance of personal thoughts and rights, and all this leads to disaster. Deianeira in all her loveliness and tenderness is neither *the* woman nor *the* married wife, nor again is she just the mythical person who happens to bring disaster upon Heracles. She is a creature of Sophocles' own times, the product of a society which still believed in gods and oracles, but had lost, chiefly by indolence and weakness of mind, its real contacts with the great divine forces which rule the world.

Sophocles, in creating the human beings of his plays, did not wish like Euripides to discuss the problems of the day, nor in fact to discuss problems at all. He wanted to show the eternal position of man as it was revealed in countless individual lives and destinies. He moulded his characters and contrived their situations according to his knowledge of human nature, but in doing so, like the great and serene poet that he was, he trans-ferred into witnesses of eternal truth the human beings of his own environment. Deianeira, like any other of his great creations, is alive and eternal because she embodies eternal life in contemporary shaping.

Deianeira's fate is at the same time indissolubly connected with, and in clear contrast to, that of Heracles. All that we have said about her will be elucidated and confirmed by the story of Heracles. We have seen that originally his fate was untragic, and it cannot be supposed that he became tragic merely by the jealousy of his wife. In order to take hold of the poet's intentions and ideas, it is usually helpful to show whether (and if so, how) he changed the traditional legend in essential features. The first instance of the kind which we can point to in this place is the fact that Sophocles puts between the death of Nessus and the use of the poisoned garment the whole married life of Heracles and Deianeira. This fact is just as important for Heracles as for Deianeira, though in a

different way. Only thus could his true nature be revealed by a
life-long experience. This at once leads us to the second
important change in the myth, the change in Heracles'
character. Sophocles' play is based on belief in the myth, in all its
features, even its most archaic and grotesque. But the hero who
has passed through all his labours and who, except on the last
occasion, has always gone forth as if to conquer, not to die
(160), does not appear as the great saviour and liberator of
mankind, apart from his own rather boastful self-praise near
the end of the play (1058ff.). Throughout the time before he
enters the stage we are hearing about him, but all that we hear
is about his strength, about some of his deeds which are in fact
ruthless misdeeds, and about the harshness and savagery of his
nature.

The third important alteration of the traditional legend,
perhaps the most important, though they are all closely
related, is concerned with Heracles' death. I shall come to this
later.

Heracles had once saved Deianeira from her terrifying
suitor, the river god. But he has not made her happy. Not
only do they now live in exile on account of his murder of
Iphitus. But their life together was constantly interrupted by
his going away. He was, of course, compelled to leave her by
the tasks the gods imposed upon him, but we soon realize that
many of his adventures were caused entirely by his own character. All the messenger-speeches in the play — whether
truthful or not, they are completely unbiased — agree in
describing Heracles as a fiendish or, to say the least, a most
unpleasant person. His murder of Iphitus was a vile and
treacherous act of vengeance (270). When Eurytus refused to
give him his daughter Iole as a mistress, Heracles found a
petty pretext for waging war against Eurytus, destroying town
and people, raping Iole and sending her to his own house. He
was honest enough (479) not to deny his love for Iole; he had
nothing to do with Lichas' attempt to conceal the bitter truth
from Deianeira; not even for a moment did he think of his
wife's feelings. All this is quite different from mere rudeness or
carelessness, and can hardly be explained in terms of the
'natural man', the 'bad husband', or the like. Most of the
commentators remain at this level when they try to outline
Heracles' character. Nevertheless, Heracles is not a philander-

L

ing brute, even though Deianeira sees him somewhat in this light. Bitterly, in spite of her usual restraint, she complains of that Heracles who 'is called' good and true (541). But the essential quality of which we get a glimpse is his complete lack of sympathy with, or interest in, other human beings, his extreme self-centredness and egotism. Is this just human selfishness, or is it something more?

Heracles is afflicted with intolerable sufferings. The natural reaction of the audience should be pity, pity even to such an extent that it might have been thought necessary to counteract it by making Heracles' character as little lovable as possible. This argument is sometimes used, but it involves a serious criticism of the poet as a poet. True, we do not feel pity, rather awe and perhaps even a certain amount of impatience. But this does not follow from the unpleasant character of the hero, but from the fact that we see fate working, and feel that there is a tragic and bewildering dissonance between the man and his fate. On the other hand, whatever character Heracles may have was certainly not introduced for a subordinate purpose only, like that of giving the audience not too severe a shock. Heracles is what he is, because this is an essential part of the idea of the play.

So when Heracles kills the innocent Lichas, when he boasts of being the saviour of Hellas, when he is burning to take vengeance on Deianeira and distorts the meaning of his labours to such a degree that he sees Deianeira as one of the monsters he slew (1110f.), we are not really moved. It is all so far beyond normal human standards that only by realizing this can we find a way to real understanding. Heracles, who in the usual legend did miraculous deeds and so became the bene-factor of mankind, is here turned almost into the opposite, into a man who follows his own nature and desires without restraint, commits outrageous misdeeds, and thus becomes a danger and a menace to other people. Deianeira dies, Lichas is destroyed, Hyllus and Iole are made unhappy, others perish, and all because of Heracles. The tales about the monsters he slew are almost forgotten, and his strength, his terrifying greatness have turned against his fellow-beings. He is entirely amoral, daemonic, a superman, not in the sense of a genius, but as a being outside the rules and laws of human society, relying upon laws of his own making.

This picture of Heracles culminates in the last dialogue with his son. Here the overwhelming force of the dying hero becomes more manifest than ever. Entirely self-centred and therefore unable 'to give himself' to someone else (1117), entirely lacking in self-knowledge and therefore unable to realize that he has brought misery upon himself, he gives his last orders as a powerful *pater familias* who, without the slightest sign of paternal love, imposes upon Hyllus duties intolerably harsh.

Deianeira is forgotten at the very moment that Heracles learns she was innocent of murdering him, and that he himself according to the oracles is doomed. He now faces his fate and ceases to struggle against it, because he recognizes the power of the gods and the truth of their oracles. But again it is only Heracles who is in Heracles' mind. He orders Hyllus first to bring him to Mount Oeta to burn him there. When Hyllus shrinks back, Heracles agrees that his son shall merely make the arrangements, without himself being compelled to kindle the flames. Then he orders him to marry Iole. Again Hyllus refuses, not as we might well think, because he considers it immoral and incestuous to marry his father's last paramour, but because she was unconsciously guilty of the death of both his parents. In dealing with his father's request Hyllus is thinking and acting along the lines of conventional Greek religion, and is therefore afraid of pollution as caused by the murder of his father or marriage with a polluted person. This is the impiety (*dyssebeia*) which he fears, and only Heracles' repeated command of which the gods are taken as witnesses removes the obstacle.

But why does Heracles give these orders? To take the second one first, it is a fact that the legend knew of Hyllus and Iole as the parents of the famous Heraclids. But nobody would have thought of this, if Iole had not been further mentioned. When Sophocles took this mythical fact into account, he did so for a special purpose. The poet once more wished to impress on the audience the nature of the hero, to show him in his boundless and unscrupulous self-centredness. Nobody should possess the woman who had been Heracles' last love, nobody but Heracles who lived on in his son. Ajax, before his end, thinks of his little son, the only heir to his greatness. The same desire for survival appears here, but is turned into an outrageous demand. Heracles does not care for Hyllus nor any longer for Iole; he does not object to the allegation that she is 'among his worst enemies' (1237). He is only concerned with himself, and with securing a worthy, in fact the only possible, continuation of his race which would enable him, as it were, to live on in both persons, son and mistress.

The other request to put him on a pyre on Mount Oeta follows the traditional legend, and at the same time makes it possible to remove the dying man from the stage. This, however, is not the only significance of the demand. In the legend Heracles did not die, but was borne from the flames to the gods, a god himself. This legend was well known (and is, of course, essential in Sophocles' *Philoctetes*), but is it possible to assume that without the slightest hint given by the poet every spectator would supply the story? It surely is not, and Sophocles makes it quite clear that he did not think of this form of the legend. The oracles had foretold Heracles' death, and 'nothing else was meant but that I should die' (1172). When he is being carried off, he repeats (1256): 'This is the end, the very last end of Heracles.' If there is any meaning in these words (and I am sure there is a good deal), they can only mean that there will be no redemption. Heracles, the son of Zeus, is going to die, a mortal man, a doomed man.

This is the third important change in the myth which I mentioned earlier. It was necessary, and it proves finally that Heracles' character is more than an essay in psychology. Life ends with death, and death brings peace and deliverance from pain. The oracles are fulfilled, though differently from what Heracles had expected. He now faces death with the hope of being strong enough to suffer without showing that he suffers, asking his 'stubborn soul' to be joyful, because the end is near. Death is the end, and not a new beginning. There is no redemption, no transfiguration. There can be none, because to the last Heracles does not rise above his own nature. There are no gods waiting for the hero, willing to receive him as one of their own. Death is for Heracles neither purification nor punishment; it is the end of his life and his sufferings, and nothing more. Sophocles has turned Heracles' character almost into the opposite of what it originally was, and he does the same with his death. It is all entirely logical and consistent. The superman, who has lived his life in the vain attempt to follow only his own desires and his own laws, is in the end not superhuman, is a man who has to acknowledge that the gods always had his fate in their hands. Heracles realizes this, but he does not change his mind. He does not surrender, he does not recognize any other limit to his greatness than death. He dies as he has lived, as superman, but the pitiless form of this end is a clear sign of the poet's own last verdict. There is no hope and no truth in man's own self-centred greatness.

The death and tragedy of Heracles are the work of the gods. With a full and sounding accord, at the same time refuting an incidental bitter criticism of the gods by Hyllus, the last words of the chorus bring the play to an end: 'there is nothing that happened that is not Zeus.' The fate to which Zeus gives his name is more than blind destiny. It is a task which the gods impose upon men, and it is Heracles' personal tragedy that he who had fulfilled so many tasks with the strength of his arms, did not fulfil the task set to his soul. The man who takes himself as the only centre of his thoughts and deeds, the man who cannot give himself to others, whose strength and courage destroy as much as they save — this man is doomed to perish. I cannot believe that all this is expressed solely for the sake of the story and the plot. This Heracles, in spite of his strange mythical features, is alive with the spirit of the great individualistic movement of the fifth century. What we recognized in the case of Deianeira becomes much more evident and full of deeper meaning in that of Heracles. There is a lesson to be learnt. Selfishness, or rather concentration on one's own person, in a word individualism, is not the right path for human beings to follow. There is no excuse, neither in conventional mediocrity, nor in the belief in the right of the superman, the great individual, to dictate his own will to the world. Man perishes, if he relies only on himself. No daemonic nature, no human greatness frees man from the eternal obligation to be part of a world 'which is Zeus'. Man is not the measure of all things.

EURIPIDES' 'HERACLES'

In passing from the *Trachiniae* to Euripides' *Heracles* we pass from a tragedy of character and fate to melodramatic theatre. The tyrant Lycus, blacker than black, the noble and courageous Megara, Amphitryon the venerable old man, Iris the hateful servant and imitator of her mistress Hera, or again scenes like the entirely unexpected appearance of the daemon of madness — these and other features all betray intentional simplification and a genius for theatrical effectiveness. Even Heracles himself, after the beautiful scene of his return, when he first learns about the danger of his family during his absence and then utters boastful threats, seems the hero of an adventure-story rather than the great figure of Greek myth.

All this may be important for understanding the nature of Euripides' art. But it does not go to the core, and it does not reveal the poet's true intentions and deeper meanings. Once again, the approach must be made by stating what essential features of the traditional legend have been altered by the poet. In the first place, Heracles' madness and crime are not a prelude to, and the cause of, his labours, which in fact represent a not very satisfactory punishment for a most terrible deed. To make his madness truly tragic, it had to be inflicted upon the great victorious hero who had just fulfilled the last of his ordeals and might hope for a future life of peace and happiness. A second feature is Lycus, a figure invented by Euripides, and necessary for the plot as the persecutor of Heracles' family. We shall see whether he is of still further importance. The third feature — the introduction of Theseus — is of a different order. He brings the solution of a tragedy which otherwise would have ended with the hero's suicide. In persuading Heracles to live on, Theseus reveals what in Euripides' opinion should be the true attitude of a great man in disaster. We realize that this is at the bottom of the chief innovations in the legend — the reaction of Heracles as he is overwhelmed at the very summit of his career by a tragic and disastrous fate.

In the first part of the play Heracles is absent, and it is indeed this absence which is responsible for the terrible danger threatening his family. It also forms the background to various scenes which are conspicuous for their rather stale and boring rhetoric. Apart from the growing certainty among all

the persons on the stage that Heracles is dead (a belief necessary for his return to make its full effect), there is one predominant impression which we derive from this part of the
play and which is decisive for our judgment of the whole, the
impression of the greatness of Heracles. He is great in every
way, a hero of outstanding achievements, the benefactor of
mankind, the pride of his aged father, the centre and standard
of life for his wife, a good son and husband, and, above all, a
loving and beloved father for whom his children are longing
unceasingly. The outrageous abuse of him by Lycus serves
to enable Amphitryon, Megara, and the chorus to bestow upon
him all the praise which culminates in the beautiful First
Stasimon, the song of his labours. This Heracles is the very
pattern of human greatness and kindness, and thus, in spite
of the poet's art, is in a way melodramatic. No event will prove
his greatness more decisively than his return from his last
labour, from Hades. This, both in the context of the play and
in its deeper meaning, is the victory over death.

However, the man who while absent was unable to protect
his own family is brought to realize that he has no faithful
friends (558), and he even doubts the value of all he has done
before (575). These are the first signs that greatness is
nothing absolute, that it depends on circumstances and has a
measure of uncertainty which may prove to be dangerous.

There is no other preparation for what is going to follow.
All attempts to show Heracles as having lived throughout
between genius and madness, or as a man with an easily disturbed mind, have failed. Madness comes upon him from
without, and not as a necessary psychological development.
The chorus had just rejoiced in the 'change from evils' (735)
which had brought back Heracles, the legal king, and had
restored belief in the justice of the gods (814). Nobody in the
audience will have been mistaken about the tragic irony of this
song, though nobody knew what was going to happen. The
sudden appearance of Iris and Lyssa, as real as any of the
numerous 'appearances' in Euripides' plays, is a complete
surprise which had to be introduced by a sort of second
prologue. The only link which connects it with the earlier
part of the play is the fate of Heracles, as expressed in the
incomprehensible paradox that the saviour has become the
destroyer.

The report of Heracles' madness and his murder of wife and
children, and the scene in which he awakes to realize what he
has done, are masterpieces of dramatic art and psychological
insight. The hero's madness is in fact the very centre of the
play. But impressive as it is, it is by no means made clear
why it had to happen. Iris, Hera's mouthpiece, explains the
situation in her own way. First Heracles had to fulfil his
labours, then he was free to endure new suffering (827ff.),
and suffer he must, for 'the gods will be as naught, and mortal
men great, if he does not pay the penalty'. Penalty for what?
The labours were finished, and they were themselves a penalty.
Heracles has not committed any crime, he has shown no
hybris. Lyssa herself describes him as a benefactor of mankind
and even as a pious restorer of the worship of the gods (851ff.).
And we remember that he himself, with his children clinging
to him, had found in his love for them the thing which makes
all men equal (633). Heracles was very far from being overbearing or self-centred. No fault, no crime, his greatness alone
is the reason for Hera's envy and hatred.

There may be one objection to this argument. Heracles,
as Iris says, must pay the penalty. The same expression occurs
more than once in the play, but always with regard to Lycus
(169, 734, 740, 756). Lycus' case, of course, is clear. He is
punished for his crimes, and rightly so. It can perhaps be
understood why Iris applies the same expression to Heracles,
for it involves a certain claim on her part to exercise justice,
even without the slightest hint at what the crimes of Heracles
have been. The idea that Heracles suffers in order to pay the
penalty does not occur again, and we could leave the matter at
that, as a point of minor relevance, if it were not for one very
strange fact. When Heracles kills his children, he believes
them to be the sons of Eurystheus. But though his madness
accounts for the error, it does not equally account for his
impulse to kill the children of his enemy. Several commentators have seen this and concluded that he acted on the
same lines as Lycus had done, in truth with even less excuse,
for he had no need to fear Eurystheus' sons as Lycus had feared
those of Heracles.

This explanation, which puts Heracles in a parallel position
to Lycus', leaves us at a loss. It is incompatible with the whole
play, and in fact cannot be sustained. Heracles' madness

begins when he interrupts his sacrifice with the words (936):
'Why do I offer this fire of purification before having killed
Eurystheus?' The desire to kill the man who by the will of the
gods had been his master — and an unpleasant and outrageous
master he certainly was — did not enter Heracles' mind as long
as he was sane. His slaying of Eurystheus' children is even
more a consequence of his madness. It might have been in the
general spirit of Greek mythology to kill one's enemies and
their offspring, but it is certainly not so in Euripides' play
with its standard of rational morality. Assuredly, Heracles is
not put on the same level as the wicked Lycus, whose deeds
derive from cold-blooded cruelty and calculating fear. If we
talk of 'excuse', it is entirely on behalf of Heracles who has no
good reason to fear Eurystheus' sons, but whose mind is
deranged. What is proved in fact is that even the great soul of
Heracles can be turned to amoral cruelty and madness by the
dark forces of fate.

Again therefore, and this time with truly fatal consequences,
the uncertainty of human greatness is revealed. It is due to
the inscrutable actions of fate, of the gods. Who are these
gods? Who is this jealous and cruel Hera who caused Heracles
all this evil and will 'dance for joy' like a country girl (1303)?
'Who could pray to such a goddess?' This is the decisive
question for the understanding of Heracles' tragic fate, but
the answer is not simple.

The third and last part of the play, the Theseus scene, is
from the artistic point of view a weak and flat anti-climax.
But for the meaning of the play as a whole it provides all the
clues. The elaborate discussion between Heracles and
Theseus, the purpose of which is to lead Heracles back to life,
aims at solving the two essential problems which are set by
Heracles' fate. The first problem is that of the nature of the
gods, and the second, which is, so to speak, the practical
counterpart of the first, is how far man may find it possible to
live without the gods.

As against Theseus' genuine but conventional belief in
the truth of the poets' tales about the gods (1315), Heracles
suddenly discovers that they are untrue. 'The god, if indeed
there is a god, has no needs' (1345). Euripides is not just an
atheist. He accepts the existence of gods, though with doubts,
but he denies the truth of their characters as revealed by the

myths. This means that the gods have nothing to do with the cruel fate which Heracles has to suffer.

Here we may shortly deal with a special question which has unduly disturbed some of the commentators on this play. I mean the problem of Heracles' two fathers. There is no intention of ridiculing Amphitryon. The idea that Zeus has made him a funny sort of cuckold is entirely alien to Greek thought. But there is no attempt either to conciliate the two claims of fatherhood. Amphitryon boasts of Zeus' partnership, but again and again shows love for Heracles as his true son. To the chorus Heracles' greatness is proof that he is Zeus' son, but they address him almost in the same breath in both relationships (1071, 1086). Heracles loves Amphitryon as his father, but in his distress he at the same time reproaches Zeus for having begotten him as Hera's foe, and declares that he prefers Amphitryon (1263ff.). We see then that the impossible fact of the double fatherhood is not only mentioned, but emphasized throughout the play, though it is of no importance whatever for its inner problems. Obviously the motif was used with no other intention than to rub in the impossibility of the legend as one of the many untrue stories about the gods.

This whole trend of thought was, of course, nothing new in the Greek mind. As early as in the sixth century Xenophanes had attacked the anthropomorphism of the conventional religion, and Euripides' contemporary, the great sophist Protagoras, had professed to know nothing about the gods, 'neither that they exist nor that they do not exist nor what their nature is'. Euripides thinks more or less along these lines of scepticism and moralism, but his manner of attack is slightly different. He is deeply concerned with the fact of the senseless and unjust fate of mankind. Those entirely amoral deities who are believed to be responsible for this fate cannot be true and real gods. Since however the most terrible fate, indifferent to any human greatness and goodness, remains a fact, the gods, being beyond human passions and deficiencies, have nothing to do with fate. We may think that the undisturbed gods of Epicurus are here foreshadowed.

Man however has to struggle against fate. Amphitryon has given the watchword (105): 'He is the best man who trusts in hope; to see no way out is a bad man's part.' This saying becomes decisively true, when Heracles, the murderer of those dearest to him, is determined to commit suicide. In fact, there seems to be no other way out. Then Theseus steps in, and the second theme of the last scene becomes predominant. Theseus brings the most generous offer of help, being neither afraid of Heracles' misery and crime nor of pollution. He believes that the gods rule in spite of their sins and faults (1316ff.), and if they wish they can be our best helpers (1338). But if they do not, then man is in need of man, of friendship. 'Put your hand upon my shoulder, I will be your guide' (1402). Friendship between man and man, service of one human being to another, this is the true help in misery and despair. Not in Theseus', but in the poet's, mind this is the inference to be drawn: man can rely only on man. We must learn that we are men, that even the greatest of us is helpless against fate, and helpless if alone. In a world of injustice, misery and uncertainty the only certain and true thing is friendship. Friendship enables Heracles to recover his greatness of soul. Instead of despairing he overcomes his tragic fate, determined to live on. Although his future life will be without heroic deeds, even without any real content, it will be life nevertheless.

There is a deep meaning in the way in which friendship resolves the whole tragedy. Yet even the most wonderful friend cannot undo the terrible deed which Heracles has done. And if the solution falls somewhat short and does not seem to be on the same level as the awful greatness of Heracles' fate, this may perhaps prove that Euripides' art in this last part of the play is not adequate to his intentions. On the other hand, it may equally well show that we for our part do not yet fully understand the poet's mind.

Theseus promises Heracles that he will be worshipped throughout Attica. But the hero of the play is not a god or a demi-god. He is a man, a great man, and what matters is that there is one way of life only, one based entirely and exclusively on human nature. The disharmony of a world in which a blind fate destroys good and great men must be resolved into the harmony of human greatness and unselfish love between human beings. Euripides denies the right of mere individualism, but he equally denies superhuman guidance and ordering. The gods as they appear in his plays are real, not as gods, but as personifications of the great forces which rule the world, blind, amoral forces which may bring good or evil. Man must rely on himself and his fellow-men to build his world, proudly and courageously defying the blows of fate. In a new sense, Protagoras' sentence becomes true: Man is the measure of all things.

CONCLUSION

If our interpretation of the two plays is essentially right, we can combine the meaning of both tragedies by saying that the tragedy of Heracles is the tragedy of human strength and greatness, and its eternal struggle against a stronger and greater fate. There are two possible 'solutions'. Either man recognizes the divine order of the world and believes in its meaning behind and beyond all senseless fate; or he decides that there is no such order and that he has to face fate without any other help than that of his own spirit and the support of his fellow-beings. Beyond the mythical as well as the historical features of the two poets' conceptions, by which the untragic hero Heracles became the bearer of tragedy, we discover eternal ways of human thought and life. We may call them Theism and Deism on the one hand (there is no difference between them which holds good for Greek belief), and Humanism on the other. We realize that Sophocles was pessimistic, Euripides optimistic, though the former saw the world as an organic and harmonic order, the latter as a discordant and senseless chaos. The Sophoclean superman perishes, while the greatness of the Euripidean man finally triumphs over the fiercest onslaught of fate.

It is perhaps significant that Sophocles' hero had no choice. He must bow to his fate and die, and his suicide is only a shortening of his last sufferings. The Heracles of Euripides has freedom of choice, and he learns how to overcome his fate and to start a new life. Fatalism and freedom of will are the watchwords for the two attitudes of mind, but they do not really cover the deeper insight of the two poets. For both attitudes include, as it were, their opposites. In the *Trachiniae* Heracles' character is a decisive factor in bringing about his doom, while the fate of Euripides' Heracles comes entirely from without as a disaster which neither was provoked nor could be influenced by human beings. The fate in Sophoclean fatalism is not blind, but part of a world divinely ordered and with ultimate meaning, while Euripides' belief in the freedom of the human will does not connote the freedom to alter the ways of a senseless and godless world.

Once again, we look at the tragic figure of Heracles in its double aspect, as it stands out against the background of the two poets' philosophies of life. Perhaps I may be allowed to re-state the decisive difference with the help of a somewhat minor factor in each play. The plot of the *Trachiniae* is, so to speak, knotted around the series of divine oracles the truth of which becomes manifest. Not only the fate of Heracles, but also the way in which he faces it, depends on his belief in the oracles. His last orders express the clear decision to acknowledge the true meaning of the oracles and to go forth to his death. In Euripides' play a theme which accompanies the story (though it is less important than the oracles are for Sophocles) is the fight against ignorance (*amathia*). Lycus has to be taught (172, 189), Zeus in withholding his help is accused of ignorance (347), and finally Heracles is told that Hellas would not endure, if he died through ignorance (1254). It is this final ignorance which matters, the ignorance of the last things, of the meaning of the world and the gods and human life. Heracles, in rebutting this reproach, discovers truth and gains his last victory, the decision to live. Faith in oracles on the one hand, and belief in reason and knowledge on the other, lead the hero to his final destiny.

The double example, I believe, makes it obvious that it is not the 'dramatic bias' (Kitto) that decides the difference in the outcome, but the poet's mind and the ideas he wants to embody in the fate of his hero. It is not merely the case of another poet and another dramatic plot, though they play their part in determining the difference of outlook; it is a new generation and a new epoch in the history of the human mind, an epoch in which human reason outgrows and overcomes, for a time at least, the faith in superhuman forces and in the dark secrets of death and after-death. When Heracles rejects suicide, he acts as a true creation of Euripides and of the age of enlightenment.

Heracles has become tragic. The great man meets disaster. Euripides, however, turns death and tragedy finally into life. The great man who at the same time was a family man and a good friend is on account of his own nature not only less heroic, but less tragic. No fate was more undeserved and more cruel than his, and therefore it is horrible — melodramatic rather than tragic. True and complete tragedy is revealed only when disaster and character meet, and loneliness is its true signature. In Euripides' play Heracles goes through terrible moments, in that of Sophocles through a whole life, of isolation and loneliness.

X I

ALEXANDER THE GREAT [1]

ABOUT a generation ago, a well-known German scholar wrote a Greek history from a collectivist point of view. He denied the historical importance of great individuals, and Alexander in his description became something like a half-drunk blockhead who owed his victories partly to his good luck, and partly to his father's generals. His empire, which did not survive him, was a mere accident, and the great change represented by the transition from Greek to Hellenistic history was due to the general tendencies of the time rather than to Alexander and his deeds. These radical ideas were almost unanimously rejected, but to-day it seems worth while to reconsider the question once again. For by now the German love for hero-worship has led to an incredible degradation of intellectual and moral standards and to a disastrous lack of critical judgment. The successes of the man against whom we are fighting have a certain similarity to those of Alexander, and we may ask ourselves whether possibly our traditional and perhaps somewhat conventional view of Alexander was mistaken, and whether he too was merely a conqueror and oppressor of countries and peoples, a savage barbarian who brought defeat and misery to a large part of the world. In a wider sense the question of the part played in history by individuals is at stake, but I am not going to deal with the general problem. In finding out what Alexander did and was, we shall also find an answer which may eliminate some possible doubts on that general question.

Alexander, the son of Philip, king of the Macedonians, was the first Western man of world eminence. The Greeks considered the Macedonians to be barbarians, although in fact they came from the same stock. Barbarians, in Greek opinion,

[1] Address given at a meeting of the Northumberland and Durham Branch of the Classical Association, May 1941. (Unpublished.) This essay repeats certain ideas which I have expressed before, particularly in a chapter of *Ost und West* (1935) and in *Alexander and the Greeks* (1938). But the present paper was written after experiencing the events of 1940 and 1941, and this fact, I hope, will justify its publication.

were all non-Greek peoples, but during the fourth century the outlook changed, and participating in Greek education rather than being of Greek origin came to be the test of whether a man was to be called a Greek or a barbarian. The Macedonian kings had for some time past tried to introduce Greek culture in their country and especially among the ruling aristocracy, but they succeeded only in part. The free peasants and shepherds of Macedon, as well as the independent nobles, were never truly captured by the rational and artistic civilization of Greek town-life, and we may take it as symbolic that the most rational of the Attic tragedians wrote his most irrational and most savage tragedy, the *Bacchae*, when he lived at the Macedonian court. Philip II, following and even exceeding the policy of his predecessors, made use of Greek achievements, particularly in the military and administrative spheres — that is to say in a policy of nationalism and power. He met half-way certain Greek ideas of national unity or Panhellenism and even monarchy — ideas arising from the dissolution and decline brought about by the policy of the Greek city-States, by Spartan militarism, by Athenian democracy, and by the eternal wars between so many of the Poleis. Philip imposed upon the Greeks his political leadership and proclaimed, without finding response, a common war against Persia. Demosthenes, the great defender of Athenian freedom and particularism, died later than Alexander, but his policy had been dead since Philip defeated the Greeks at Chaeronea in 338 B.C.

Two years later, Philip was murdered, and Alexander succeeded him at the age of twenty. He relied on the power which his father had created, and he knew how to consolidate it; but the flight of his thoughts and ideas went much farther than anything Philip had planned. When Alexander actually waged war against the Persian Empire, he felt himself a true Panhellenic leader, going first to liberate the Greek cities in Asia Minor and thus to achieve what Athens had failed to do. Alexander was Greek by education, Aristotle having been his tutor for a couple of years. Not much love, however, had been lost between teacher and pupil, and no real understanding secured. All the young man's enthusiasm for Greek poetry and art did not make a Greek of him. He remained a Macedonian, even in a sense a barbarian, and signs of almost primitive savagery which appeared sometimes explain to some extent, but do not justify, such verdicts as that mentioned at the beginning of this paper. But Alexander was always more than merely a Macedonian, and he was not only a lover of Greek art and literature; he was, almost unwittingly, a true Aristotelian in his untiring search for new facts. This equally led him towards protecting and fostering science and scholarship whenever he could, and was at the root of his attempt to become the master of the earth to its very ends.

Panhellenism was the political idea that ruled the first stage of his campaign. He claimed as his ancestors Heracles and Achilles, and deliberately and consciously followed both of them: the son of Zeus in his untiring labour and bravery, fighting brutal violence all over the world, Achilles as the passionate and heroic protagonist of the Greeks against Asia. Alexander began his Panhellenic campaign against the Asiatic Empire with a visit to Troy, sacrificing to the local gods and crowning with wreaths the tomb of Achilles. His own task was to him a repetition of the Trojan War, and this was not just a romantic and theatrical demonstration, but expressed genuine feeling and his attitude towards reality.

The whole campaign against Persia was decided by three pitched battles, but there were heavy obstacles and delays in between and afterwards, such as the eight months' siege of Tyre or the years spent in conquering the many strongholds in Eastern Iran. Alexander was always in the hottest part of the battle, usually at the head of his cavalry. But he had prepared the scheme of the fighting with the utmost care beforehand. He used, of course, the experience of his older officers, but in an ever-growing degree his military genius emancipated itself from their advice. He was sometimes overdaring and suffered unnecessary losses, but he never made, as far as we can judge, any decisive strategical or tactical blunder.

The Panhellenic idea had its propaganda value. It was also intended to counter the attempts of some of the Greek States to join the Persians against Macedonian supremacy. Greek contingents in Alexander's army were anything but numerous, and from the military point of view the campaign was almost purely Macedonian. Greek mercenaries were even among the enemy's best troops. Those of them who were taken prisoner after the battle at the Granicus were either killed or sent to

M

penal labour as traitors. Thus Alexander also used Panhellenism to denounce his Greek enemies as 'Fifth Columnists', and
to deter other Greeks from serving in the Persian army. It
was a strange and almost unreal feature of this campaign that
the Macedonians were fighting for the Panhellenic ideal which
meant nothing to them, while, on the other hand, the Greeks
took little part in its defence. There was an abyss between
ideology and reality, and then as always the only uniting link
was Alexander himself.

Once master of Asia Minor, Alexander immediately began
to build up the administration of the conquered countries,
combining the Persian provincial organization with the freedom of the Greek cities and with concessions for the largely
Hellenized peoples. The second battle, that of Issus, opened
the door to the East. Darius tried to negotiate and made the
generous offer of the Euphrates as the future frontier. Alexander refused, and his proud letter, preserved in Arrian's
description of the campaign, gives the reason. It is an amazing
document. Alexander was not yet master of the Eastern
Mediterranean, but he claimed to be 'King of Asia', a term
which involved his supremacy over the Persian king who at
that time still held three-quarters or more of his empire.
Alexander no longer felt himself only as the Macedonian king
and leader of the Greeks. His aims reached far into the East,
although he was sufficiently cautious and thorough first to
subdue Phoenicia and Egypt, thus creating a First Empire
encircling the shores of the Eastern Mediterranean as a basis
for further conquests.

It is in the narrative of the years 333 and 332 that for the
first time in our sources an expression appears which was to
be used time and again to introduce new actions of Alexander.
'Longing took possession of him' to do this or that, to found
Alexandria or to make the difficult and to all appearance aim-
less journey to the oasis of Siwa. The word *pothos* (longing),
very likely going back to Alexander himself, indicated his
irrational will, which he probably often had to set against the
opinion of his advisers. It is a very human and rather a youthful word. Caesar believed in his fate, Napoleon in his star,
but Alexander did not act as a tool of a higher power. He felt
his destiny in his own heart, and his personal emotions and
desires, passionate and determined as they were, were his

guide. If ever an individual being, and not collective forces, decided the course of history, it was then. Driven by his own genius, he broke the bounds of Greek *sophrosyne*, or sound moderation, and escaped from the narrow nationalism of the Macedonians, aiming at goals far from the beaten track, but keeping in unwavering consistency to his own way, which led from success to success. The King of Asia knew what he wanted in the end, but he had yet to learn how to achieve his aims. It was the visit to Egypt that showed him the road leading to the greater empire.

Egypt was the first of Alexander's conquests that had an old civilization of its own, and at the same time a population which, though it welcomed Alexander not as a foe but as liberator, was strange and alien. Impressed by the temples and pyramids as well as by the amazing fertility of the country, Alexander realized for the first time outside the Greek world, that it might be better to win over a people than to subdue it. He made sacrifices to Egyptian gods and combined them in one festival with Greek displays and competitions. This was the first, still clumsy and imperfect, expression of the idea that was to govern him later in the building-up of his empire, the idea of blending and uniting Greek and Oriental civilizations. Alexander went out not to destroy but to create.

His longing was to bridge the deep gulf between West and East. Zeus-Ammon, the god of the oasis Siwa, was both Greek and Libyo-Egyptian. His oracle was famous among the Greeks, but the god, who as Zeus had ram-horns, was worshipped by the natives as a real ram. Alexander, who had become the legitimate Pharaoh and therefore the son of Amon-Re, the highest Egyptian god, was addressed at Siwa as the son of Zeus-Ammon. This moment was the reward for the hardships and the loss of valuable time which he had suffered by his march to the oasis. The Greek world received, partly with respect and partly with scepticism, the news that Alexander had been recognized as Zeus' son. And the growing empire was taken under the protecting wing of a god who personified the unity of East and West. Irrational forces which remain difficult to explain created an atmosphere in which Alexander could be at the same time the son of Philip and the son of Zeus, man and *heros*, a people's king and the deified Pharaoh. Alexander went East, both in fact and in mind. At the end of the road the king was to become the ruler of the world and the son of Zeus a god himself.

At Arbela (331) the Persian king finally lost his kingdom, and Alexander entered the great capitals of the East: Babylon, where he worshipped Marduk as the true successor to the old Babylonian kings; Susa, the seat of the Persian government; Persepolis, where he sat on the throne of Xerxes and burnt his palace as vengeance for the burnt Greek temples of 480; and Ecbatana, the Median capital. Now the Macedonian king was truly the King of Kings. He dismissed the Greek troops; the fiction of a Panhellenic campaign was openly renounced. Moreover, even the most extravagant aims of Macedonian policy had been fulfilled. Alexander, when he decided to go farther East, left behind him his old general Parmenio, the exponent of the Macedonian tradition. When Darius was murdered by a rebellious satrap, Alexander as his legal successor punished the murderer according to Persian law. He now set out to become master of the whole realm. He introduced Persian court-etiquette, created Persian regiments and the like. The Macedonians grumbled at these measures, but nevertheless the common soldiers loved their king who even in Persian glamour shared hardship and danger with them. He was generous and he knew how to inspire them, often with a few words only, just as we know that Caesar and Napoleon did. The nobles, however, opposed Alexander's policy as it was expressed by the appearance of king and court. To them the clemency towards the Persians, and even preference for some of them, were real insults. They no longer understood the king who had entered upon a task greater than any possible scheme of Greeks or Macedonians. He had outgrown their nationalism. Revolts and conspiracies followed and Alexander suppressed them with the harshness and arbitrariness of an Asiatic despot. But even in his passion, extreme both in anger and sorrow, he remained noble, he remained human.

During the following years (329-327) Alexander conquered Eastern Iran and Turkestan, an immense territory, partly inhabited by some of the bravest and most warlike tribes whom he considered best fit to share the position of the Macedonians in the army, and among whom he also found his queen, Roxane.

The world from the Adriatic to the mountains of Hindukush was under Alexander's sway. But more than ever was he filled with what we may call a hunger for space. Like every great conqueror, the more he had, the more he wanted. He longed to reach the ends of the earth, and wished to see the miraculous country of India. The world-conqueror once more met with a new world, hostile to him in action and spirit. The pupil of Aristotle, who was accompanied by Greek scientists, learned many new facts of zoology, botany, anthropology, and, above all, geography. He learned that there was no Eastern Ocean, forming the boundary of the earth, but a new continent, and that the rivers of the Punjab flowed southwards towards an unknown sea which separated India from Egypt. Alexander began to build a fleet in order to reach the Southern Sea, but at the same time he still wanted to proceed farther to the East. It was then that for the first time the Macedonian soldiers refused to obey. Although then only a minority in Alexander's vast army, they remained the decisive element. Their physical and moral powers were exhausted, and Alexander, who never was defeated by an enemy, had to give way to his own men. He was, after all, not to reach the Eastern boundaries of the earth.

The Indian campaign culminated in an amazing drive down the Indus with fleet and army through the wonders of the tropical scene — but also fighting hostile peoples and religious resistance which was stirred up by the Brahmans. At last Alexander reached the ocean. With a few ships he sailed out, and with solemn sacrifices celebrated the moment when land was no longer before him. But as always in a new situation he combined personal mysticism with the quick adoption of new and necessary measures. He ordered the fleet under Nearchus to explore the sea-route back to the Persian Gulf, which was to become the future road connecting India with the West. He himself with a large part of the army returned by land, but in the deserts of Baluchistan he met with almost complete disaster through thirst, hunger and exhaustion. There was no practicable land-route to India from the West, and even by sea, though Nearchus found his way, the communication was never very easy or regular. India remained remote, though strongly influenced by Greek civilization during the following centuries, partly owing to the link formed by the Greek colonists in the new towns which Alexander had founded in Eastern Iran.

Their importance is stressed by the fact that down to our own time some of them, such as Herat, Kandahar and Kabul, have been political and cultural centres.

Five years after he had left the heart of his empire Alexander returned. The empire was larger than any before, but the task of building it was far from being completed, and might never be completed at all. There was a dangerous discrepancy between, on the one hand, the immensity of the Eastern countries and the large number of peoples, and on the other, the small body of ruling Macedonians, represented by the king, the officials, and the army, even if they, according to Alexander's wishes, were to be supplemented by Persians and Iranians. Another reason for disharmony was the part to be played by Greek civilization. It was, as the following centuries proved, the only possible common basis on which a universal empire could be built. But Alexander was not aware, as he hardly could be, of the fact that Greek civilization was prepared to follow in the steps of his conquests and to abandon the narrow boundaries of city-State and city-life, that it would be capable of adapting itself to world-wide conditions and of becoming a truly universal civilization.

Alexander had only two more years to live. They were packed with work and plans to consolidate and to extend the empire. In a huge festival Alexander gave away thousands of Asiatic women to Macedonian officers and soldiers; he himself married one of Darius' daughters besides Roxane. The general marriage festival was to be a symbol of, and a lasting security for, the unity of the empire. While the army and even the king's bodyguard were filled with Persians, the Macedonian veterans were bought off with large gifts and sent home. In that situation they regarded as betrayal what otherwise would have been a natural and well-deserved solution. There was open mutiny, and Alexander, full of wrath, threatened to sever himself completely from the Macedonians. In the end, the deep-rooted attachment of the soldiers to the king's person led to a compromise. But Alexander, in his desire to consolidate the empire, had destroyed the instrument of his victories. Macedonians and Greeks alike were now mere tools in the service of the universal empire, which, with all the details of its organization, was built around one centre only, the king. He was not so much the embodiment of monarchy as the one great man who, besides being an Asiatic king, was also the heir of Greek education and Greek individualism. To the peoples of the East he was the legal king, and as such either a god or at least a ruler by the grace of the gods, the link between man and god. To the Greeks he had to be more than the Macedonian king and the ruler of the East, more even than the son of Zeus-Ammon. There was one way open, and, considering the character of Greek religion, it was the natural way to take. Alexander demanded to be worshipped as a god. He thus became the first of many deified kings and emperors in the West. Some of the enlightened Greeks of the time ridiculed his wish. But to the Greeks in general the borderline between great men and gods had never been very strict, either in myth or in recent history. Alexander the god was a product less of Eastern than of Greek religious traditions.

Alexander undoubtedly was an Oriental sultan. He was also a wild conqueror who never found a limit to the extension of his realm. But he was at the same time more than this. In aiming at world-domination he did not merely serve his own ambitions. He always served a larger idea, that of an empire which was to unite the peoples of the earth without forcing any one of them into slavery. It may be doubted whether Alexander believed in the unity of mankind, an idea so important in the philosophy of the following centuries. His was not a philosophical but a political mind, and it seems reasonable to assume that his chief aim was the unity of the territory of the known world, the *oecumene*, rather than that of all mankind. He furthered the unity of a new political organism when he founded new cities, improved traffic and trade, converted the immense treasures of the Persian kings into coins, even when he organized scientific exploration by land and sea. This political organism was *his* empire. The consequence, however, was that under his personal rule the differences between men of different nationalities began to diminish. They were all subjects and no longer free as Greeks and Macedonians understood freedom. Even the ruling peoples, Macedonians and Persians, never became citizens of the empire. Alexander went so far as to plan a mutual transference of European and Asiatic populations, a truly gigantic and despotic idea. But no country or people was ever exploited for the benefit of a ruling nation or of the king himself.

His last plans, if our evidence is correct, were concerned with the future conquest of the Western Mediterranean. A powerful fleet in the harbours of Egypt and Phoenicia, a road along the whole shore of North Africa (the road now partly built by Mussolini and used in the African war), were to be built in preparation for a war to be waged against Carthage and the peoples of the West. They as well as Greeks, Libyans, Ethiopians, and others, sent their envoys to Babylon to pay homage to the great king. Alexander was at the summit of his power. Shortly afterwards he suddenly fell ill and died, at an age at which all the other great conquerors and dictators of history had hardly begun their careers. Before he died his Macedonians passed his bed, man by man, in tears, while he was no longer capable of speaking. Love and loyalty greeted the dying ruler of the world.

When he died the empire was not complete, either in its expansion or its internal structure. The task would probably have been too immense even for him, and even supposing that he had lived for another ten years. The effects, however, of his great creation did not perish as it disintegrated. Unity could not be maintained, and for two generations the Mediterranean world was torn to pieces by the everlasting struggles of his generals and their sons, who became rulers and kings in a new order belonging to a new historical period. But the form and organization of the new territorial monarchies were inherited from Alexander's empire, even in their differences. He had created more than a transitory realm. It was due to him that for many centuries the bond between East and West became firm and indestructible. Old and out-of-date forms of politics and life disappeared, and the world embarked on a new historical epoch, in which were laid the foundations for Roman and mediaeval times. The unity of East and West could never be realized in one man's lifetime, even if he was a genius, but, Utopian as his aims were, they remained a challenge for many centuries to come. Rome, although the heir of Greek culture, divided the world into a Latin half and a Greek half. But behind the division was unity, and both the Roman Empire and Christianity were based on the Hellenistic unity of universal civilization which resulted from Alexander's empire.

Alexander died at the age of thirty-three. His youthfulness even magnified his stature and achievements, stupendous as they were. For more than a thousand years, throughout almost the whole of the mediaeval world, he was a figure in legend and fairytale. He died young, and that proves, as the Greeks used to say, that the gods loved him. Men also loved him, admired and feared him, and even his enemies found little to blame him for. His hunger for conquests, although their scale was terrifying, was nothing by which men of his time or the succeeding centuries would be shocked. His outbursts of recklessness could be extreme, but no-one should be surprised at finding that a volcano has its eruptions. Even in his worst moments Alexander was warm-hearted, greater than other men also in feeling and passion, never cruel, and generous towards even his bitterest foes.

The new historical period which he brought about was not due to any revolutionary scheme or spirit of his, nor did it correspond to his conscious and intentional aims. Alexander, unlike Caesar and Napoleon, was not the child of a revolutionary age. But it was indeed revolutionary that a Macedonian king ruled over the peoples of Asia. It was even more revolutionary that a conqueror who had had a Greek education threw overboard the Greek pride in being the race destined by nature to rule, the *Herrenvolk*, and proclaimed the equality and the rights, if not of all mankind, of the leading nations in West and East. Alexander prepared the soil for the demand that all human beings should have the same share in freedom and welfare. The equality of the many implied the rule of the one man. Yet, although there was not, and could not be, political freedom, there was complete tolerance towards every kind of civilization and religion.

The gigantic effects of Alexander's empire and, even more, of its demolition, were ultimately due to his unique personality and its historical position. He was one of those who embody the leading forces of their times, past and future. He was the heir of the past as the beloved king of the Macedonian people, as an enthusiastic disciple of Greek culture, as the legitimate successor of Egyptian and Asiatic kings. He was, at the same time, the protagonist of the future as the founder of the first territorial and absolute monarchy which grew from the soil of the Western world. He also led Greek individualism to its culmination, overthrowing the pride and prejudice of the Greek city-State as it was still preached by his teacher

Aristotle. He proclaimed the unity of the *oecumene*, and was therefore the first great universalist, the first in a sense whom we may call cosmopolitan. In his person and life as well as in his empire he united East and West, thus consciously fulfilling a task of the greatest historical importance. He was as great as his work. This knowledge will help us to apply the right standards, when we look at other men and other ages.

POSTSCRIPT 1944. G. B. Shaw in his latest book (*Everybody's Political What's What*) has a chapter on *The Military Man* in which he denounces, on more or less equal terms, Alexander and Caesar, Napoleon and Hitler. As to the two latter, Mr. Churchill has rightly protested against the widespread habit of comparing them. But to rank Hitler among the great military men is absurd, and there is no justification for comparing the great Alexander with the would-be great *Führer*. Since I wrote the paper on Alexander, events have proved, not only, as I tried to show, that the two men are of completely different character and calibre, but also that the new conqueror gambled away all his successes. Alexander's empire did not survive him, but a new order arose which determined the course of history. Hitler's new order was dead before his own death. Whatever the future of Europe, it will not be built on the ruins left by a criminal and amateurish megalomaniac. Her fate does not depend on the 'Nordics'; it does depend, like that of the Mediterranean world after Alexander, on the concord between East and West.

XII

ATHENIAN HYMN TO DEMETRIUS POLIORCETES[1]

'
. . . . .

The greatest and the dearest of the gods are present in our city. The same lucky moment has brought them here, Demeter and Demetrius.
5 She has come to celebrate the holy mysteries of Kore; he is present, joyous as befits the god, beautiful and with laughter. An august picture is revealed — his friends all around him,
10 he himself in the middle: they like the stars, but like the sun he.
Hail to thee, O son of the mighty god Poseidon and of Aphrodite!
15 Other gods are either far away, or lend no ear, or do not exist, or care nothing about us. But thee, we see here present, not in wood or stone, but real.
20 To thee therefore we pray. First of all, O beloved, give peace. For thou hast the power. Punish the Sphinx that rules, not only over Thebes but over all Greece —
25 the Aetolian, who sits on the rock, just as the old Sphinx did, and robs and snatches away all our people. I do not know how to fight him. The Aetolians always plundered
30 their neighbours, but now they do the same even to those who live far away. The best would be that thou thyself shouldst punish him. If that cannot be, find an Oedipus, who will either overthrow that Sphinx or turn her into stone.
. . . . . '[2]

---

[1] Published in *Die Antike*, VII (1931). I have added a few notes.
[2] The text was last printed by F. Jacoby, *F.Gr.II*. 76, F 13. In l. 31 the MSS. have σχόλασον, and Kaibel and Jacoby keep it. But can it really mean (the only possible meaning here) 'spare time' in the sense of 'devote thyself to this task'? The word, in particular when used absolutely as it is here, suggests leisure rather than activity. With Diehl and others I accept Toup's correction κόλασον.—In l. 34 the text is corrupt (σπεινον). No emendation is quite satisfactory, and Jacoby therefore puts none in his text. I accept, although with some misgivings, Meinecke's σπίλον (rock, cliff). Wilamowitz reads σποδόν (dust), Mr. Edmonds σπίνον ('a tiny tit'). If σπίλον were right, it would be a certain support for the disputed text in Soph. *Tr.* 678: κατ' ἄκρας σπιλάδος.

This hymn is preserved in Athenaeus' *Deipnosophistae*, the well-known compilation of the third century A.D., and is ascribed to an unknown poet, called Hermocles or Hermippus. The historian Duris, writing in the Hellenistic Age, inserted it in his work to illustrate the decline of the civic virtues of the Athenians. We meet essentially the same judgment in George Grote's *History of Greece*.[1] Convinced Liberal as he was, he regarded the glorification of Athenian democracy as the true meaning of his work. He took our hymn as a confirmation of his view that 'the history of the Greeks as a separate nation or race is reaching its close'. If I venture to deal once more with the hymn I do so because, as Grote says, it is 'curious'. It does not interest us because of any artistic value; most certainly it is not a specimen of high poetry. But with all its shortcomings it is a historical document of particular import-ance, and I shall try to show that it can tell us much more than merely the fact that Athens had lost her military strength and her spirit of political independence.

The extant text is incomplete. An exhortation to the singers to begin their song, and probably, as we shall see, more than that, must have preceded the first lines. A concluding part will have followed in the end, in which the prayer, which in the first place (l.21) asked for peace, was probably carried further by entreating the god to secure freedom and order.

The hymn, translated here in prose,[2] was originally written in a peculiar metre which appears as early as in Anacreon's poems, though in our song it is treated with a certain licence. It consists of a normal iambic trimeter, the verse of tragic dialogue, alternating with a short trochaic line, the *Ithyphallicus*. This line is decisive for the rhythm and the whole character of the song, and accordingly was called after the name of the whole poem, which is an *Ithyphallus*. This name is due to the fact that metre and rhythm were first used in the popular songs of the Phallus-bearers, the men who in Dionysiac processions carried the symbol of the generative power and fertility of man. The Phallus was the most common and most significant symbol

---

[1] Vol. 10, p. 320f., a remarkable passage, even though Grote saw only one aspect of the song.

[2] The numbers on the margin refer to the original lines of the poem. A poetical version by J. A. Symonds is repeated by K. Scott (see next note), p. 229; another one was kindly written for me by Mr. J. M. Edmonds. But I felt that neither was literal enough to bring out all the points with which I am going to deal.

of the deep unity which to the Greek mind existed between religion and natural life. It was a popular symbol with its implications both of sanctity and obscenity. And the hymns which the Greeks sang in its honour were equally popular. This is true of our hymn too, although it was not dedicated to Phallus. Duris tells us that the Athenians used to sing it at home as well as in public. In the translation, though I had to abandon the attempt to repeat the original metre, I tried to copy as faithfully as possible the general style of the Greek text, particularly its simplicity and humdrum triviality. Duris' evidence shows that the song, although a hymn of worship and even a prayer, was also a popular song, frequently sung on occasions other than religious processions. It therefore lost much of its original character as a religious hymn, and it will be more to the point to speak of it as a song than a hymn. It has a very obvious political meaning, as is the case with many popular songs in both ancient and modern times. But the whole spirit which is expressed in its apparently trivial words is a very particular one, and it will be worth while to discuss the song in full detail.[1]

The general situation is clearly indicated in the third part of the song. Alexander's empire had been turned into a system of territorial monarchies. This was done in the long and savage struggle between 'fighting giants', to use Jacob Burckhardt's expression for those early Hellenistic kings. Part of the struggle was the fight for the dynastic heritage of Alexander, the throne of Macedon. Cassander, the fierce son of the old viceroy Antipater, had killed the last members of the royal house, women and children. A few years after 300 B.C. he died, and his death opened the way for the restless energies of Demetrius, who, for his innovations and successes in siege technique, received the surname of Poliorcetes or Conqueror of Cities. He had been without power ever since his father Antigonus lost his life and throne in the disaster of Ipsus (301 B.C.). With varying success Demetrius gradually built up a new basis of power in Greece, where once before he had found followers, particularly in Athens. Now, however, he had to overcome strong resistance

---

[1] This paper was all but finished when I read the two important articles by O. Weinreich, *Antikes Gottmenschentum* (*Neue Jahrbücher*, 1926) and K. Scott, *The Deification of Demetrius Poliorcetes* (*Am. Journ. of Philol.*, 1928). Their points of view are different from mine, but I was glad to find in both papers strong support for my own ideas. A review of my paper by P. Treves appeared in the *Riv. di filologia*, IX (1932), 279f. (cf. also *ibid.*, 194ff., 257).

by many of the citizens before he could occupy the city. He succeeded in becoming king of Macedon, but even then remained the adventurer of his earlier years.[1] For more than six years he was king, although hard-pressed by both domestic and foreign foes. Among the latter was Pyrrhus, king of Epirus, Demetrius' equal in fervid energy and adventurous spirit, but surpassing him in military leadership and resolute statesmanship. Pyrrhus had first married a daughter of Ptolemy Soter, king of Egypt, and later a daughter of Agathocles, the tyrant of Syracuse. He had gained a position and an influence among the new class of kings such as Demetrius never achieved. Despite all the glamour of his personality, and although he had married Phila, the daughter of Antipater, he remained isolated. The relations between these great rulers were essential in shaping the framework in which the small Greek States had to live and act. The Aetolians and Boeotians were Pyrrhus' allies and Demetrius' enemies. Aetolian soldiers held the rock of Delphi as well as the citadel of Thebes (l. 23-26). They were a dangerous menace to the surrounding peoples which depended on Demetrius — in particular to Athens, the neighbour of Boeotia. Athens also suffered badly from the plundering raids of the Aetolian pirates, who extended their activities farther and farther (l. 29-30).[2]

Demetrius' life was filled with love affairs no less than with deeds of war, for both served him in his adventurous policy. When he arrived in Athens — the occasion of our song — he came from Corcyra where he had gone by invitation of Lanassa, the daughter of Agathocles and second wife of Pyrrhus, who found herself neglected by her husband. Demetrius married her. It.was his fourth 'legal' marriage. He then went to Athens where he arrived probably in the summer of 291 B.C., at a moment when the Athenians were about to celebrate the Eleusinian Mysteries. This is the reason why Demetrius is mentioned in our song together with Demeter, the similarity

[1] Treves, l.c., objects to my characterization of Demetrius because he was *sovrano e politico* and aimed at an *Impero assoluto e teocratico*. I do not think that the one view contradicts the other. No doubt, Demetrius had great ideas about his position, and Treves has done well in stressing the evidence for them. But was he for that reason less of an adventurer? My discussion of the song, at any rate, is quite consistent with Treves' opinion.

[2] For the general political situation cf. R. Flacelière, *Les Aetoliens à Delphes* (1937), 65f., 73ff.

of the names giving the combination a kind of playful justification. The people turned to Demetrius because he had the
power (l. 22). Their own weakness found striking expression
in the helpless words: 'I do not know how to fight him' (l.28),
and in a pleasant mythological simile the song puts before
Demetrius the particular political desires of Athens. It would
have been senseless to express the hope that the Sphinx might
throw herself from the rock as the one in the old story had
done. The Athenians prayed to Demetrius that he himself, or
somebody else by his order, might overthrow her or turn her
into stone. The latter version (if the text is correctly restored)
is derived from the view, illustrated by vase paintings, that
Oedipus' Sphinx was visualized as one of the stone figures
which crowned a column, such as were known from graves and
votive monuments (see Plate III). Thebes fell after a long
siege; thus the prayer of the Athenians was partially granted.
But Demetrius was unable to restore peace. At that time the
other rulers were already forming a new coalition against him.
The next year, the Aetolians were still in possession of Delphi,
and Demetrius ordered the Pythian Games to be held in
Athens. A few more years of violent strife followed, and then
the adventurous and glamorous life of Demetrius ended. He
died a prisoner who had lost his throne, and yet his sons and
grandsons were to become kings of Macedon.

The first words of the song praise 'the greatest and dearest
of the gods', who afterwards are addressed as Demeter and
Demetrius. The main theme of the whole song is mentioned
for the first time, that of the god Demetrius. In 307 B.C. he
had driven from Athens the peripatetic philosopher Demetrius
of Phaleron, who then governed Athens in the name of Cassander, and had restored democracy. The Athenians then
greeted their new master together with his father Antigonus
as Saviour and Benefactor (*Soter* and *Euergetes*), and heaped
upon them all kinds of honours, such as are due to gods and
heroes. The two kings became the eponyms of two new tribes,
and thus stood side by side with old Attic heroes. Their golden
statues were set up close to the group of the tyrannicides. A
month of the Attic calendar was called Demetrion, and the
portraits of the kings were woven into the holy robe of Pallas
Athena. Priests and altars, sacrifices and games, processions
and even sacred ambassadors (*theoroi*), such as were sent to

Delphi, were introduced for the worship of the new gods. The gratitude of Athens was expressed in terms of such extravagant flattery that it caused quite a sensation among the Greeks; but although at first people found the Athenian behaviour disgraceful, they soon at various places began to imitate it. This, however, suggests that the forms of worship used by the Athenians were not merely due to the incidental exaggeration and servility of a degenerate community; they were at the same time the expression of new and creative forces which were just emerging into the open.

Our translation speaks of the 'lucky moment' which brought Demetrius to Athens together with Demeter (l. 4). This lucky moment is not Tyche, fate and destiny, but Kairos, the single point in the course of time which one has to seize, the favourable moment which, according to Pindar (*P.* 4, 286) 'in the hands of men . . . hath but a brief limit of time'. It is significant that the event of Demetrius' arrival is thought of as being caused by the *kairos*, a conception in which the fact of the one single moment is combined with the ideas of luck, favour, and grace. The view has been expressed that at that time the conception of *kairos* always involved the urge to use the favourable moment to the utmost of one's power, in other words that human will prevailed over mere fatalism. This view is hardly confirmed by our passage. It is true, there is nothing of that severe fatalism which sees destiny working in even the shortest period of time, but neither is there freedom of will. *Kairos* here is little more than the playful chance of an incidental moment. We must therefore not think of the god Kairos who at that time, as a companion of Tyche, was beginning to be worshipped. A later epigram tells us that Menander, who died in the very year in which our song was written, was the first in literature to speak of his cult. It was about the same time that Lysippus made a famous statue of the god Kairos. Although we must be careful not to assume an influence which cannot be traced in the song, it is good to remember that the Greeks usually regarded as a deity what to us is an abstraction. The *kairos* of our song is the happy coincidence of the Eleusinian festival with Demetrius' arrival, but even this was not a mere chance. Some divine power had its share in it, though the joint appearance of Demeter and Demetrius remains without further significance. Demetrius had actually become an initiate of the

OEDIPUS AND THE SPHINX
ATTIC VASE PAINTING

COINS OF DEMETRIUS POLIORCETES

OEDIPUS AND THE SPHINX
Attic Red-figured Vase Painting, early fifth century B.C.
COINS OF DEMETRIUS POLIORCETES

NEFRETETE

IKHNATON WITH HIS FAMILY
Both works from Tell-el-Amarna,
fourteenth century B.C.

Mysteries as early as 302, and that in a hurried manner which was at variance with all the holy traditions. Moreover, in a fragment of a contemporary comedy Demeter and Demetrius seem to be united in a libation in which a double measure of wine is offered to the 'holy goddess' and the 'sweetest king'. The latter is not addressed as a god in the few extant words, but his divinity is obviously implied. Yet, we must not go beyond that. It was a mistake to assume that in our song Demeter, who comes to celebrate her mysteries, was actually Lanassa. She probably did not even accompany Demetrius to Athens, but stayed behind at Corcyra with some of his troops. The 'happy coincidence' did really refer to Demeter, but the happy moment in particular was that of the arrival of Demetrius, who might help Athens in her plight. The poet does not speak of the god Kairos, and that is the more understandable as afterwards the living god is invoked, the god who is present and truly perceptible with eyes and ears. Still, it is equally typical of the religious mood of that age that the song alludes, though very slightly, to the belief in Chance and Fortune, and very strongly professes the belief in the god Demetrius.

He is called son of Poseidon and Aphrodite (l. 13), but not on account of some freshly invented myth nor because the two deities were sometimes united in myth or worship. The reasons for their parentship are Demetrius' character and position. Everyone knew of Demetrius as the master of the seas as well as the frequent conqueror on the battlefield of love; only now he had arrived in command of a fleet from his latest marriage. Poseidon, on the whole, was a kind of guardian god to Demetrius. That is made particularly clear by the testimony of Demetrius' coins,[1] on which Poseidon is frequently represented at first as the fighting god to whom Demetrius owed his naval victory near Salamis, on Cyprus (306 B.C.), announced to the world by a triumphant winged Nike standing on the prow of a ship.[2] Later Poseidon appears as the ruler of sea and land,

[1] Cf. E. T. Newell, *The Coinages of Demetrius Poliorcetes* (1927). See Plate III, a-c.
[2] This does not mean, as Treves asserts, that I date the Nike of Samothrace as early as that. Archaeologists now agree that the famous statue in Paris is a work of Rhodian origin of about 250 B.C.; it was therefore set up for a later naval victory than that of 306, probably that of Cos, in which Antigonus Gonatas and the Rhodians defeated the Egyptian fleet. Dr. W. W. Tarn dates this battle at 258 B.C. (*C.A.H.*, VII, 713, 862), and proposes a completely satisfactory solution of the whole question: Antigonus imitated his father Demetrius, 'who after Salamis had set up a statue of Victory standing

N

setting his foot on the land, or as the king on the throne, always reflecting Demetrius' own position, whether actually held or only aimed at. But there is no indication that he is Demetrius' father, and it is equally significant that Aphrodite, alleged to be his mother, never appears on the coins. No one was in any doubt that Demetrius was the son of Antigonus. Yet the position is to some extent similar to that of Alexander, son of Zeus-Ammon, who later gave orders that he should be worshipped as a god. The Greeks, thinking as they did in terms of genealogy, were always able to assume divine ancestors for certain contemporaries, because to them myth never lost the character of being present and actual. And these ancestors were needed to give the appropriate background to the divinity of great living persons.

The relationship between Demetrius and the two gods Poseidon and Aphrodite was little more than a kind of playful invention, and not primarily an expression of religion. It was not the same with Alexander to whom the parentage of Ammon was a deep-rooted personal claim. But in neither case did the deification itself remain merely accidental or unique. The well-known phenomenon of the ruler-cult was very typical of the Hellenistic Age. Taken as a fact of general history, it cannot be fully understood unless we take into account the importance of Eastern monarchy for Alexander as well as for the Seleucids and Ptolemies. The kings of the East lived and ruled either under the particular grace of the gods, or as gods themselves. The worship of the ruler, on the other hand, when it was created as here by the Polis, must be understood as a natural, even necessary, stage of Greek religion. One foundation on which this kind of cult was based is the fact that to the Greeks the unity, or rather the identity, of the political and the religious community was a matter of course. In the territorial monarchy, which now was the new and predominant form of State, that unity or identity could not be expressed in any other way than by the worship of the monarch and the dynasty. Even the Antigonids who as the rulers of Macedon for a long time preserved the character of a people's

on a ship, by setting up ... the winged Victory of Samothrace'. There are, in fact, differences between the coin-dies and the statue which make it likely that the former have not been copied from the latter (cf. Newell, 35ff., B. Ashmole, *C.A.H.*, VIII, 675f.).

kingdom, were worshipped as gods by some of the Greeks. A second foundation, again not a product of the great contemporary changes but an expression of the traditional ways of Greek thought, was laid by the fact that the Greeks never completely separated men and gods. In the mythological stories the gods thought and acted very much like men, and in myth as well as cult men were supposed to have risen to be gods or heroes. In the mystical teaching of the Orphics or in the verses of Empedocles we learn of the direct and immediate transformation of a man into a god. The religion of the Delphic Apollo, on the other hand, saw in such a spirit, widespread though it was, the sin of human *hybris*. The primary meaning of the inscription on the wall of the temple of Delphi, the commandment 'Know thyself', was: 'Know thyself as the human being thou art, and obey the gods.' At the end of the fifth century Sophocles was made a *heros* after his death; and Lysander, while still alive, received sacrifices, and paeans such as those sung for Apollo were sung in his honour. The religious forces behind such actions and conceptions are strange and alien to us, but they are religious nevertheless. They were bound to express themselves with new vigour when revolutionary events and powerful individuals gave the times a new shape.

Our song makes particularly clear out of what kind of psychological soil the deification of living men grew from its hidden and modest beginnings to overwhelming importance. At an early time, criticism was directed against the human and all-too-human nature of Homer's gods and those of the Polis. In the sixth century it was Xenophanes who made fun of the anthropomorphic gods: 'Now if horses or oxen or lions had hands and power to paint and to make the works of art that men make, then would horses give their gods horse-like forms in painting or sculpture, or oxen ox-like forms, even each after its own kind.'¹ Ethical thought of a more penetrating kind objected to the mythological stories and frequently altered them. Monotheistic ideas gained ground, and the conception of God was spiritualized — a process which culminated in the metaphysical ideas of Plato and Aristotle. Scepticism and negation, on the other hand, ultimately led to complete atheism. The Polis continued the official worship of its gods; some people maintained the pious beliefs of old; later, the syncretism of the

¹ Translation by J. M. Edmonds in *Elegy and Iambus* (*Loeb Library*).

Hellenistic Age breathed new life into deities who still bore the names of the Olympian gods, but had frequently changed their very nature. All these facts, however, do not refute the view that in truth the gods of Homer and Hesiod had abdicated.

Our song, in a sense, confirms this by a few lines (15-17) which, if they are not simply frivolous, give proof of a considerable amount of indifference. They contain, as it were, a survey of all the negative views concerning the gods, without any attempt to show that any one of these views seems either mistaken or preferable to any other. Perhaps the gods are too far away — among distant peoples such as the Ethiopians or Hyperboreans. Perhaps they do not hear when men invoke them. Perhaps they do not care about men at all. Perhaps they do not exist at all — at any rate, they are of no use to men and do not punish the evil-doer. It has been said that the views here expressed are very similar to those held about the gods by the philosophy of Epicurus. Lactantius says of Epicurus' god: 'Deus nihil curat, ideo incorruptus est ac beatus quia semper quietus.' At the time of our song Epicurus had been the head of a philosophical school for about twenty years; from 306 onwards he taught at Athens. It is therefore quite possible that among other views his were also alluded to in our song, though it seems more likely that we have here rather a confirmation that Epicurus' philosophy had much in common with popular ideas. At that time quite frequently we find the view expressed that the gods neither see nor hear, and that they do not take the slightest interest in the affairs of mankind.

But our song speaks of something more than merely the general, completely negative, conviction as expressed in those three lines. It shows that Greek religion was not simply dead. Even in its decline it remained true to its own nature. From the ineffectiveness of the gods the writer of the song does not conclude that they were either superfluous in this world of ours or of an entirely different nature and purely spiritual. He draws the conclusion that the gods of wood or marble ought to be replaced by a 'true' god, a god really alive. Something similar happened in the case of Asclepius. In the same third century in which rational and scientific medicine was making the most striking progress, the faith in the healer-god Asclepius, who made his cure by appearing in human shape in the patient's dreams, reached its peak of popularity and importance. A religion had broken down, but this did not lead either to passionate atheism or to the fanatical belief in a world beyond our world. Scepticism and criticism had not succeeded in overthrowing the popular view of the gods in their traditional human form; the only thing that the people had realized was that the gods were inactive and ineffective. In a very curious way the intentions of the sceptics turned against themselves. Anthropomorphism was even stronger than the anthropomorphic gods, whose statues showed them in human shape but not alive. These gods were not disclaimed because they were supposed to have human senses and human organs of sense, but because, having them, they made no use of them. The crisis of faith led to increased materialization rather than to spiritualization. There was among the majority of the Greeks a strong urge towards new and intense religious beliefs. The citizens, decadent and selfish, troubled by worries and fears, found some satisfaction in absurd superstitions, magic tricks, and mystic miracles. But, hand in hand with all that, arose the faith in the overruling power of those royal men who from Alexander onwards had changed the face of the earth and kept on troubling the world, whose actions continually and decisively intervened in the lives of States as well as of individuals.

This new faith seems to come close to the theory of 'Euhemerism', which at that time became the fashion among educated people. Its main idea was that the old gods had once been great men who were worshipped as gods on account of their power, their exploits and achievements. This doctrine was a product of rationalistic reasoning. Ruler-worship was a different conception — apparently similar, but actually based on an opposite way of thinking. When people deified men who were living and acting among them, they could do so only because they were moved by irrational impulse. It is difficult to imagine that the exaggerated and degraded flatteries which the Athenians showered, not only on Demetrius himself but even on his mistresses, had anything to do with religion. But in so far as this was part of 'ruler-worship', we must be careful not to regard it merely either as megalomania on the part of the rulers or as servile flattery on that of the subjects. There are analogies such as the position of the Pharaohs, or the Greek belief in heroes and demi-gods. They may help us to understand the whole phenomenon, but they cannot provide a full and satisfactory explanation. Ruler-worship spread all through the world and was of the utmost historical importance. Its effects were to extend far into the future to the pagan and Christian masters of the Roman Empire and even to the absolute kings by the Grace of God in recent centuries. The immense historical effects of the ruler-cult makes it an absolute duty not to exclude its only real explanation. It has been rightly called a 'political religion'. But then it was not only politics, but also genuine religion.

The true god Demetrius is a god just because he is bodily present as a human being, 'joyous, beautiful and with laughter' (l. 7). Demetrius, even after he had passed the age of forty, was famous for his shining beauty. 'His features', Plutarch tells us, 'were of astonishing and extraordinary beauty, so that no sculptor or painter ever achieved a real likeness of him.' Yet some of the more realistic portraits on the coins of Demetrius, which can be found among many others of an idealized and stereotyped kind, give us an idea of a unique mixture of youthful sprightliness and royal dignity. Our song, however, points to more than merely the beautiful appearance of the man Demetrius. The parenthesis 'as befits the god' is significant, and we can translate it even more correctly by 'as the god must be'. We need not think of the laughter or smile of the Saviour child in apocalyptic prophecies such as Virgil's Fourth Eclogue. But we must realize that gay laughter is not typical of all gods. There were many gods who were thought of as looking sombre and frightening or at least solemn, and while the son of Aphrodite might be a laughing god, the son of the earth-shaker Poseidon would not be. One would like to think that *the* god, who is described in this passage, is a definite god. If so, he must have been mentioned in the lost beginning of the song. There seems to be only one possible god. An epigram tells us: 'Bromius loves the singers of songs.' Bromius is Dionysus as the god of 'noisy' worship. The *Ithyphallus* is a cult-song for Dionysus, and it may well be that this form of song would be addressed only to a Demetrius who was at least likened to Dionysus, even though at the same time called son of Poseidon and Aphrodite. This view is supported by other evidence.[1] Instead of repeating it I quote in transla-

[1] For a full discussion of it, cf. Scott, *l.c.*, 143, 148ff., 221ff., 227ff.

tion the striking description of Demetrius, taken mainly from
Plutarch, which Jacob Burckhardt gave in one of his public
lectures: 'He was not a giant like his father, but was of more
than medium height, the heroic and splendid figure of a true
king. Sometimes he was terrifying, on other occasions graceful and captivating. People hastened from far off merely to
see him. He could abandon himself to pleasures, and then
again be absorbed in activity, always capable of keeping both
spheres entirely separate. He was the best companion in drink-
ing-bouts, he loved splendour and even effeminate indolence;
but in war he was sober and sensible, active and of immense
energy. His ideal among the gods was Dionysus, who could
be stormy and violent as well as luxurious and soft. He would
have loved to live such a life as Dionysus might have lived on
earth. Demetrius was one of those who, like Alcibiades, were
dangerous because of their gift — often unconsciously displayed — of charming others and enjoying the pleasures of life
even at an age beyond the time of youth.' It was the appearance
as well as the character of Demetrius which caused him to be
compared with Dionysus, and also his own endeavours to
imitate the god. Apart from Heracles, the great benefactor
of mankind, it was in particular Dionysus who, to all the deified
rulers of Macedonian origin from Alexander onwards, was a
sort of model to be followed and a deity akin to themselves,
and therefore perhaps more than a colourless 'ideal'. It was the
same Dionysus who in the centuries to come took an ever-
growing part in the magic world of ruler-worship and belief in
a Saviour god.

We learn that the Demetria, the festivals held in Demetrius'
honour both in Athens and in other cities, were deliberately
modelled on the Athenian festival of Dionysus; that the Dionysiac *technitae*, the professional actors, took an outstanding part
in them; that there were performances of tragedies and comedies.
The similarity of the two festivals was so great that later
writers could think that the Athenians had replaced their
ancient sacred Dionysia by a festival that bore Demetrius'
name; Plutarch reports this, and it is significant, even if it be
untrue. Another item of Plutarch's knowledge seems a fac
actually confirmed by our song: the Athenians resolved officially
to receive Demetrius with the same honours as Demeter and
Dionysus. These two deities enjoyed common worship in

Eleusis, and it is easy to see that the combination of Demeter and Demetrius was based on deeper reasons than the affinity between their names. At the same time, it becomes even more certain that in the lost beginning of the song Demetrius was addressed as Dionysus.

Here indeed is no mere negation, no scepticism or unbelief. The bonds between the new god and certain deities of old reveal that ruler-cult was derived from genuine forces of Greek life and tradition. There was sceptical mockery and selfish fear, but beneath them were ancient religious conceptions which found new forms of realization. The Greeks, unlike other nations, conceived divine power as something that was close to men, and not remote and distant. The very spot on which Demetrius left his carriage when he entered Athens for the first time was consecrated by an altar of the 'descending god', *Kataibates*, a name otherwise used of Zeus who descended in thunder and lightning. The presence or *parousia* — an idea used in our song several times, though only in verbal form (l. 2, 8, 18) — is the manifestation or 'epiphany' of the god. These are conceptions common to most religions, but in general they belong to the world of visionary revelation. Greek gods, as early as Homer, reveal themselves in a very earthly and human shape. Even Greek religion can be understood as a belief in divine revelation. But it is a revelation of such an immediate and complete reality that it was art that became its true mediator; and it is through the works of art that even to-day we can receive its message.

Dionysus does not appear on any of the many coins of Demetrius. This may have been partly caused by the fact that Demetrius' policy, which was reflected in the types of the coins and after 301 was mainly concerned with regaining Macedon and Greece, could not be attached to the myth of Dionysus to the same extent as, for instance, could the conquest of the world by Alexander. A second reason is that the worship of Demetrius as Dionysus was chiefly favoured by the Athenians, and they always maintained their independent coinage; no coins of Demetrius were ever issued from Athens. But of Demetrius' divinity in general, the portraits on his coins give full proof. Just as the divine Alexander is represented as bearing the ram-horn of Ammon, so Demetrius has a bull's horns growing out of the hair above his forehead — a curious sight

(Pl. III, b-c). Some scholars have taken the horns as a proof of Demetrius' connection with Dionysus, others of one with Poseidon; but neither view has a real foundation. The bull was a very general symbol of divine power. It is not possible to attribute the horns to any single god in particular. But the curious headgear is clear evidence for the belief in the super-human and divine nature of Demetrius. It confirms the fact, expressed in so many words by our song, that, whether as a claim on Demetrius' part or as popular belief, there was a physical unity between the man and the god.

It was a terrible age, those years just before and after 300. War never ceased for Athens, after Demetrius had 'liberated' the city from the peaceful and sensible rule of his philosophical namesake. Naturally the Athenians prayed, above all, for peace. The longing of men for peace, as so often in history, found its expression in a prayer to the 'rescuing god', the Saviour or *Soter*. We think of the *Pax Augusta*, of the Messianic hopes laid down in the mystical books of Hellenistic Jews, of the 'Peace on Earth' of Christianity. Nothing of all this is contained in the prayer of the Athenians; they do not think of a world peace, they are only longing for the moment when peace will return to their own country. And yet, even this prayer sees the god as the bringer of peace, the same god who was worshipped as Preserver and Saviour. A figure is taking shape which was to gain an ever growing importance in the political and the religious world.

But the god who was to bring peace must have the power to enforce it. This is expressed by a line (22) which is ambiguous — probably intentionally so. The words used are not those in my translation 'thou hast the power', but 'thou art the lord'. This means, first of all, that in the view of the Athenians Demetrius was *kyrios*, or lord, over war and peace; he was the powerful ruler whose decision would meet with no resistance. The conception of a lord or master over war and peace was quite common and did not necessarily have any particular or deeper meaning. Xenophon, for example, tells us that Lysander gave this 'title' to the ambassadors whom Athens after her defeat had to ask for the conditions of peace. It was because I wished to avoid any undue emphasis on that line that I did not translate it verbally. For to our mind the word *kyrios* fore-shadows the great development which it was to undergo.

Master of the State — that was the title of the people under democracy, and the title of the Hellenistic king. Master of the world — that was to be the title of the Roman Emperor, and the title of Jesus as the divine Lord of Christianity. We must be careful not to read later developments into a document of an earlier age. But we are justified in stating that the word *kyrios* had embarked on its tremendous career and had started to acquire a religious meaning. Here just as in the other passages which are discussed in this essay, it was the position of the deified ruler of the third century b.c. which revealed the decisive change in men's attitude of mind and the beginnings of new and far-reaching developments.

Even in the simile of the sun and the stars, which at first sight may appear rather trivial, we now recognize something more than a hackneyed comparison. 'An august picture is revealed' (l. 9). The word for 'august' (*semnos*), sacred or venerable, is also used with regard to Demeter and her mysteries (l. 5). Again, the god is celebrated as present by his epiphany, his manifestation. During the last quarter of the fourth century the astronomy of the Chaldaeans and their astral religion began to influence Greece. About 280, the Babylonian priest, astrologer and historian Berossus founded a school in Cos. But even Plato in his old age was deeply interested in these matters, and it was only slightly later that philosophy, particularly that taught in the Academy, could regard the stars and the gods as more or less identical. It is another symptom of the time that Aratus' poem on the constellations, which he wrote about 275, soon became very popular. But for the Greeks interest in the stars did not yet mean astrology. The world of the third century was too deeply in love with life to accept the sombre and fatalistic resignation of the astrologers. Moreover, despite all the Eastern influences, the astral beliefs of the Greeks adhered to the traditional forms of Greek thought. At the same period, astronomy as a science attained results of the highest value. Aristarchus of Samos actually discovered the heliocentric system, which by its very nature was opposed to the fundamentally geocentric teaching of astrology. This may have been one of the reasons why Aristarchus' bold theory did not prevail during the following centuries.

The simile of our song does not reflect all of these developments. The poet certainly did not think of the heliocentric system, although he probably regarded the surrounding stars as the planets, and thus actually made the sun — Demetrius — their centre. His conception is hardly based on more than the popular belief in a close connection between the world of the gods and the sidereal bodies. Such beliefs were even stronger than in earlier times when Helios or Apollo drove the chariot of the sun. A few years later the court astronomer of the Ptolemies placed the 'lock of Berenice' among the stars, and Callimachus celebrated the event in a poem. We may regard this as learned playfulness and a courtier's flattery, but we must also realize that it was derived from the beliefs in astral gods. King Helios, standing at the centre of the circle of the star deities and ruling the world, is a conception which under the influence of Chaldaean and Iranian doctrines gained much ground during the Hellenistic centuries. From this conception was eventually derived the victorious and undefeated sun-god, *Sol Invictus*, a figure of great significance in the worship of the Roman emperors and even of the Christian Church.

Again, we recognize the beginnings of far-reaching inter-connections and developments. The god of the beautiful sun of Hellas was, above all, a 'joyous' god. Dionysus, on the other hand, the god of joy and exuberance, who conquered the world in his triumphant campaigns, embodied even more strongly the idea of a world-wide empire — especially after Alexander's conquest of India had become more and more of a legend. The historian Duris, the same to whom we owe the knowledge of our song, tells us — and the story is told in a slightly different form by Plutarch — what fantastic and magnificent robes Demetrius liked to wear, among them a garment adorned with 'the golden stars and the twelve signs of the zodiac' or, as the other version runs, 'the cosmos and the stars of heaven'. This starry robe, with its pictures ultimately referring to the 'wisdom of the Chaldaeans', was not worn by any of the later kings of Macedon. This is easily understood since their rule was not based on any magical or religious idea. Demetrius' robe is the *Weltenmantel*, the cosmic robe, later worn by the mediaeval emperors, with all its astrological implications proclaiming the man who wore it as the ruler of the world. Once this is recognized as typical of Demetrius, it is no matter for surprise to find that at his festival in Athens the divine king was represented on the proscenium of the theatre as 'supported by the *oecumene*', by the whole known world. The simile of the song, although very little more than a simile, yet reflects the fact that, as we know to-day, in Babylon, Egypt and among the Hittites the king was identified with the Sun-god who rules the world. Monarchy from its beginnings was bound up with that magic sphere which we find alive in as late a conception as *le roi-soleil*.

Let us finally look at the song as a whole. In its form and tenor it was 'old-fashioned', derived from traditional forms of worship, and untouched by the cults and hymns of Oriental and Hellenistic gods like Isis, Sarapis, and others. Their hymns were long-winded and stereotyped litanies, praising by enumeration the virtues of the deity concerned. This ithy-phallic paean is purely Greek, a prayer of the Polis, written for a particular Polis at a particular moment, and not part of a liturgy or of any religious service. And yet in almost every word of it we may find the germs of new ideas and general conceptions. Everywhere forces are foreshadowed which were to become typical of the Hellenistic Age. We have shown this to be true of single words and phrases, but it is also true of the whole song. Demetrius is here almost a syncretistic god, at the same time Dionysus and Helios (and a rather un-Greek Helios at that), the son of Poseidon and Aphrodite, and a partner in the worship of Demeter. The close connection be-tween Demetrius and Athena is not mentioned. He had been made her fellow-god, the co-inhabitant of her temple, as early as 304; he called her his elder sister, probably because as Dionysus he was one of Zeus' younger sons. There is a sur-prising likeness between the head of Demetrius on one of his bronze coins and that of Athena on a contemporary gold coin (Pl. III, e-f), and the fighting Athena appears on some coins in an attitude similar to that of Poseidon (Pl. III, a, d, g). It was perhaps on account of the scandalous stories which people spread about Demetrius when he first lived in the Parthenon, that the memory of that relationship of the two deities was not renewed. Perhaps it was because the relations between Deme-trius and the Athenian State had changed since that earlier period; for after the second 'liberation' Demetrius was much more of a master, though still a benevolent one. In general, of course, it is the special characteristic of all syncretistic cults that the unions and identifications between different gods vary and fluctuate.

The song, both as a whole and in all its parts, expresses the mood of an age of transition — the more strikingly because it emanates from the world of the ordinary citizen. The religion of the Polis had broken down, but this did not merely lead to rationalism and individualism, scepticism and atheism. A new soil was being prepared in which the indigenous seed was soon to grow, together with alien and even artificial products. One of the latter kind was Sarapis, the creation of the first of the Ptolemies. The third century, realistic and matter-of-fact as it was, in many respects, yet had its religious needs and pious devotion. This is one of the new and creative forces which are revealed in our song. Another is the importance of the 'great man'. The powerful personality of a man like Demetrius found an expression at once religious and political in the worship of the ruler. The idea of the Polis was replaced by that of monarchy; the Greek civilization of the city-State grew into the Hellenistic civilization of the *oecumene*. And the divine kings were the chief agents in this historic move. Their ideal, derived from Alexander, became real for the first time in the fascinating personality of Demetrius Poliorcetes, and has been shaped into the famous statue of the *Museo dei Termi* in Rome, known as 'the Hellenistic Ruler', the statue of a man, naked like a mythical hero, of superhuman physical strength, triumphant as a conqueror and majestic as a god.

The song which the Athenians sang, and to the tune of which they danced, when they received Demetrius with incense and garlands and libations, is not great poetry, in spite of its liveliness and occasional fine phrases. Its unknown author is no great loss to literature. One could hear the song in the streets or at drinking parties, and the singers certainly were not conscious of those many associations and ideas that have been mentioned in our discussion. And yet, the fact that the writer, however tentatively and even unconsciously, does touch on such religious themes shows that it is not only an 'occasional' poem of a chance street-singer, nor, on the other hand, simply a traditional religious hymn. It expresses something more than the mood of the author, although it sprang from a definite historical moment. The prayer was the refuge to which the citizens of Athens turned in their distress, those citizens who once had been the teachers of Hellas, but were no longer prepared to face the essential task of defending home and State. The prayer was equally a proclamation of monarchy, both in its political and its religious aspects. Thus our song mirrors man's mind changing with the times. It is the witness to a new epoch of world history.

XIII

THE FORM OF RULE IN THE ROMAN EMPIRE

ACCORDING to the general verdict of history no more definite and autocratic type of monarchy has ever existed than the rule of the Roman emperors. Their 'Caesarism' has become a standard expression for autocracy, which may cover the despotism of the Ancient East as well as the absolutism of Louis Quatorze or Napoleon. But the man whom we call the first Roman emperor claimed to have restored the Republic, and later, when this claim could no longer be upheld, some of the emperors tried to avoid at least the appearance of autocracy, paid homage to the senate, and even shared the throne with a partner. These tendencies partly coincide with the popular distinction between the 'good' and the 'bad' emperors. But the true reasons lie deeper than in the personal characters of a few rulers. It is, after all, understandable that no one constitutional scheme covers the varying aspects of several centuries and particularly the fundamental change from the 'Principate' of the first century A.D. to the 'Dominate' of the third. Modern scholars have made great efforts to find out what the true foundations and characteristic features of the Roman monarchy actually were. No full agreement has been reached, and many intricate questions remain unanswered. Every genuine attempt to throw light upon the situation has met and will meet with particular interest.

A book by Professor E. Kornemann puts forward an entirely new theory.[1] Mommsen had coined the expression 'dyarchy' (or diarchy) for the Augustan combination of princeps and senate, that is of the monarchic and the republican principle. Professor Kornemann maintains that from Augustus onwards the Principate was a dyarchy but of a different kind. He asserts that the highest position in the empire was generally

---

[1] *Doppelprinzipat und Reichsteilung im Imperium Romanum.* By Ernst Kornemann. Leipsic and Berlin, 1930. The following review was published in a somewhat abridged version in the *Deutsche Literatur-Zeitung* (1931).

held by two persons simultaneously, and from the beginning it was considered to be a 'Dual Principate'. This form of rule, 'shaped as it was by Augustus as a co-regency (*Mitherrschaft*), by Marcus as a common rule (*Samtherrschaft*), was to be, if not the only, certainly the most important cause of the division of the empire'. 'It was only natural that the frequent repetition of a double-headed form of the supreme government eventually resulted in a double empire.' In the last paragraph of Kornemann's book a line is drawn right through history, stretching from Romulus and Remus through the strange dual office of republican dictatorship (*magister populi* and *magister equitum*) and 'the even stranger rule of the two consuls with their undivided *imperium*' to the Dual Principate and the divided empire. If this were accepted, a great and formative idea would for the first time have been realized in its supreme historical importance. At the same time, an answer would have been found — undoubtedly a surprising answer — to the much discussed question of the true nature of the Principate. Professor Kornemann has pleaded for his thesis with that combination of learned knowledge and new and attractive ideas in which he generally excels and which has made him one of the leading ancient historians. Still, this book will probably encounter serious opposition from many quarters, just as did for example his attempt to divide the *Monumentum Ancyranum* into various strata of composition. It is an important and very interesting book which deals lucidly and successfully with many minor questions, but its main thesis is not convincing. I cannot claim a knowledge of the sources of the period, comparable with the wide and deep knowledge of Kornemann. I shall make use of the material which the author so amply provides, but my opposition to many of his conclusions is based on general principles. In following this procedure I hope to do the fullest justice to the remarkable qualities of the book.

The difficulty of forming an unambiguous view of the legal and historical nature of the Augustan Principate has led some scholars to assert that it was no definite constitution at all — neither republic nor monarchy nor dyarchy, but the expression of a gradual process of change from republic to monarchy. This view, foreshadowed to some extent by J. Kromayer's well-known dissertation,[1] has recently found a defender in a jurist,

[1] *Die rechtliche Begründung des Prinzipats* (1888).

E. Schönbauer, in a very helpful article.[1] Historians have little reason to contradict the purely historical thesis of an author who as a jurist is professionally compelled to think on systematic rather than historical lines. They will be pleased to find confirmation for the view, already held by many historians, that the true nature of the Principate was monarchical, even though the legal form developed only gradually. An Italian jurist, P. de Francisci, has criticized Schönbauer in a paper[2] which Kornemann could not have seen. In spite of his criticism he comes to similar conclusions when he describes the act of 27 B.C. as 'a transformation, or rather a deformation, of the republican régime', which was followed by the final creation of the Principate in 23 B.C., 'the beginning of a true and genuine monarchy grafted upon republican institutions which were nominally preserved'. Kornemann approves of Schönbauer's article (p. 5, 2) and thus seems to accept his fundamental approach. He declares at the same time that we have to understand the Principate as one special and definite form of constitution. But he cannot have it both ways. The psychological explanation of his contradictory attitude is, I think, that in the pleasure which he naturally derived from the belief that he had discovered the clue to the mystery of the Principate, he approached the problem with the *a priori* notion of the Dual Principate fixed and ready in his mind. This I realized while working through the book, and I shall in this review point out some spectacular examples.

The fundamental facts are, according to Kornemann, the following:

25-23 B.C. Marcellus as Iulia's husband and 'crown-prince'. Tiberius in the position of a 'prince'. 'The beginning of arranging the succession under the scheme of "four eyes".'

23-17 B.C. Dual succession secured for Tiberius and Drusus; after 17 B.C. considered as a 'reinsurance'.

18-12 B.C. Co-regency of Agrippa (Dual Principate).

17 B.C.-A.D. 2. Dual succession of adopted sons C. and L. Caesar.

6-1 B.C. and A.D. 4-13. Co-regency of Tiberius, though effective only from A.D. 4 (Dual Principate).

[1] *Zeitschrift der Savigny-Stiftung, Romanist. Abteilung*, XLVII (1927).
[2] In *Studi in onore di P. Bonfante*, I (1930).

A.D. 4. Adoption of, and succession by, Tiberius and Agrippa Postumus. Further reinsurance through the grandsons Germanicus and Drusus.

A.D. 13-14. Tiberius a full colleague.

We may to some extent agree with the legal views on which this list is based, particularly with the view that any co-regency depended on the bestowal of the *tribunicia potestas*, and not of the *imperium proconsulare*.[1] But the list itself, with its obvious gaps, fluctuations, and forced statements, shows at a glance that Augustus never looked upon the Principate as a dual rule, and that his monarchy cannot be explained as such by us. Kornemann himself draws the opposite conclusion only when he speaks of the fundamental principle which he believes himself to have discovered. He admits that the principle was as yet only incompletely carried through, but does not admit that there is any discrepancy between legal form and historical reality. In other words, he does away with the discrepancy which is typical of all the other attempts to explain the Principate simply because it is largely typical of the Principate itself. Kornemann uses the expression 'Dual Principate' to cover all the various degrees of co-regency, and does not even distinguish as something different the dual succession, which was a mere safety-measure. Thus the author tries to dispense with the contrast between legal form and reality by bringing everything under a single preconceived and purely legal idea.

The policy of Augustus was, as Kornemann himself stresses, essentially a family, or rather a clan, policy. This is typically Roman, and in accordance with the character of the man who always emphasized his bonds with the old Republic. Perhaps Mommsen's verdict went too far when he said[2] of Augustus that 'the interest taken in the family always crossed and often superseded that taken in the State'. In his university lectures (as read in a student's notes from 1877-78 which are in my possession) he expressed the same thing less pointedly: 'The idea that his blood relations should be his successors' (note the plural!) 'was always in his mind and governed his political activities.' To explain, however, Augustus' family

---

[1] The latter was the view of Mommsen (*Staatsrecht*[3], II, 2, 1152f.).

[2] *Staatsrecht*, II, 2, 1168, 2. Cf. E. Groag, *Studien zur Kaisergeschichte* 42, 5; also Kornemann, 23.

policy merely by his interest in the succession, as is frequently done, is not correct, or at least it needs considerable qualification. Succession in this context is a matter of personal monarchy. But Augustus, for many years at least, pursued a true clan policy, a policy based on, and in favour of, the *gens*. Previously the political and social leadership of the State had been the business of the senate and the *principes* of the great clans which were built on kinship and clientele. Augustus, now *the* princeps, concentrated the leadership upon himself and his clan.[1] This peculiar position of Augustus, not so much as an individual but as the head of his *gens*, was made particularly manifest by the fact that the *nomen gentile* (Iulius) had been dropped and replaced by the name of Caesar. Thus a clear demarcation line was drawn against the rest of the Roman *gentes*.[2] It was the tragedy of Augustus that, by ill fate, the ruling family was decimated to such an extent that adoptions had to be repeated several times to preserve the continuity of the *gens*. This explains 'Augustus' anxieties'. His care for the succession was intended, above all, to secure the continuity of the family and thus, in fact, also of the Principate; the personal succession was of secondary importance. The position of Agrippa, on the other hand, shows that co-regency was at first entirely separate from the question of succession. It merely provided the necessary support in a task which was beyond the strength of one man, and a delicate man at that. It was in line with Augustus' general clan policy that later the co-regent had to drop his family name and became a member of the *gens* of the princeps. Even when, after the death of the two grandsons, Tiberius combined in his person co-regency and succession, the main idea was again to secure the future existence of the family; for the succession was not confined to Tiberius. Thus actually a new form of 'succession to the throne' had been created, and it remained effective. Nothing, however, shows that the dual succession necessarily involved any combination with the co-regency, or that this combination was in Augustus' mind. Even the equal position of the grandsons is fully explained by Augustus' wish to put the continuity of the family on

---

[1] These questions have meanwhile been fully discussed and illuminated from various points of view by A. von Premerstein, *Vom Wesen und Werden des Prinzipats* (1938) and R. Syme, *The Roman Revolution* (1939).

[2] Cf. Mommsen, II, 2, 766.

as broad a basis as possible, and it is significant that neither L. Caesar when he died, nor Agrippa Postumus when he was disinherited, found a successor   Although the number two was predominant in the arrangements for the succession, and only for the succession, it was never in itself a goal and purpose, but only a means.

It is therefore beside the point to say that 'the Principate time and again became a dyarchy', but retained 'an aristocratic element' in the 'preservation of a distance between the first and the second ruler'. Nor, on the other hand, is it likely that 'through the continuous endeavours to procure successors monarchy was automatically brought about'. The truth is that, on account of the strongly monarchic character of the Principate, which by inner necessity grew steadily stronger, the care for the continuity of the family, and the temporary nomination of co-regents, changed into a combined scheme of personal succession. Moreover, the minor regent stood on a definitely lower level than the princeps; as Tacitus (*Ann.*, III, 56) tells us, he had to display *modestia* while to the princeps belonged *magnitudo*. It was indeed a monarchy, and not a dyarchy, which emerged from the struggles and traditions of the Republic and the great families. The absurd idea that the dyarchy was a sort of approach on the part of the monarchy towards the republic does not appear in a passage of Mommsen's (II, 1, 624), as Kornemann asserts; that has quite a different meaning. There never were under Augustus two contemporary *principes*, nor was there any official or unofficial name for the co-regent. All these facts together make it sufficiently clear that the position of the 'second man' was of an accidental and supplementary nature.

The words of the famous section 34 of Augustus' *res gestae*, definitely restored as they are, prove that he did not himself consider the position of the princeps as an office, or even as an accumulation of offices — rather as its opposite, the outcome of a unique superiority in *auctoritas*. This was no legal expression, but one of personal and social potentiality. In reply to the objections which R. Heinze 'implicitly' expressed,[1] I should like to maintain the position which I had previously taken,[2] that *de facto*, though of course not *de iure*, the *auctoritas principis* had replaced the *auctoritas senatus*. In both cases it was

---

[1] *Hermes*, LX (1925), 348, 3; 355ff.
[2] *Klio*, XIX (1924), 206f.

auctoritas which provided the power for the actual rule of the State.[1] Here again is the state of affairs which is so significant of the nature of the Roman political structure — I mean the incongruity between legal constitution and political reality. Even anyone who does not share the view which I hold must object to the attempt to do away with the position of the one man, who *auctoritate praestitit omnibus*, on the assumption that this position was, in fact, an intended dyarchy. The most striking records we have of the princeps Augustus, apart from the *res gestae*, are some edicts recently discovered in Cyrene. Kornemann does not even mention them. They confirm and emphasize Augustus' monarchic position to an extent which we should not have expected in a senatorial province. Augustus uses phrases like 'for the sake of my own safety and the public weal' (45, cf. 48). Other passages are significant of the relations between the princeps and the senate. In 86 (cf. also 81) A. v. Premerstein[2] assumes that one of the usual expressions for the *princeps senatus* (πρῶτος, πρόκριτος) was purposely replaced by that for the leader of the State (ἡγεμών), and other scholars even believe[3] that the Latin original of this Greek edict spoke of *princeps noster*.

Never during the early Principate was a co-regent called princeps, and never did he receive the name of Augustus. If further evidence be still needed to disprove Kornemann's thesis, as far as Augustus' own reign is concerned, it is given, as I believe, in the bestowal through the last will of Augustus of the *cognomen* Augusta on Livia. In general, in accordance with a remark (though it is a very cautious remark) by Mommsen (II, 2, 821), which is carried much too far by Kornemann (p. 35 f.), this act of Augustus is considered as a sort of sanction of some kind of co-regency. But Livia was at the same time adopted, and she abandoned her *nomen gentile* for the original name of the imperial family; she became a Iulia. This seems to indicate that the whole affair was not so strange or such a breach of the traditional order as is usually assumed. Although she was adopted and called Augusta, Livia did not share the Principate as a co-regent, a position which she legally — that is

---

[1] Cf. also Heinze, *l.c.*, 357.

[2] *Zeitschrift der Savigny-Stiftung, Roman. Abt.*, XLVIII (1928), 480.

[3] G. Oliverio, *Notiz. Archaeol.*, IV (1927), 26, 55. L. Wenger, *Abhandl. d. Bayr. Akad.*, XXXIV (1928), 65.

to say, within the legal fiction which dominated the Principate — could never obtain. No woman ever had *potestas* or *imperium*, and Livia certainly had neither the *tribunicia potestas* nor the *proconsulare imperium*.[1] Although the name of Augusta was then bestowed for the first time, and thus was of greater significance than later when it became an honorary *cognomen* of most of the female members of the imperial family, it was an honorary name from the beginning — in fact, the counterpart of 'Augustus'. Livia was to be, not a co-regent, but the most exalted woman of Rome. In other words, she was to hold the position among women that Augustus had held among men. Moreover, the adoption confirmed the unity of the imperial house in the form of the Iulio-Claudian dynasty, continuing the original family of the Iulii but not admitting Livia among the Caesares. It may be that Augustus through the honours bestowed on Livia wished also to hurt his little-loved stepson; but it was Tiberius, when he checked his mother's political ambitions, who truly acted in the tradition of the first princeps.

When Tiberius made Drusus a co-regent (from A.D. 22, but Drusus died the next year) he was consciously continuing Augustus' policy, as he expressly stated in his letter to the senate (Tac. *Ann.*, III, 56); but he did not regard this as a Dual Principate any more than his own co-regency under Augustus. The dual succession, on the other hand, of the sons of Germanicus and later of Gaius and the younger Tiberius (A.D. 35-37) corresponds to that of Augustus' grandsons. The part played by Sejanus is, of course, of outstanding importance. But his amazing career and the fact that he was overthrown just before he succeeded in becoming a co-regent, show the dangerous possibilities involved, not in a supposed Dual Principate, but in a form of monarchy which was mainly founded on a clan basis rather than that of a dynasty. 'The dynastic idea and the tendency towards a real monarchy were undoubtedly strengthened during the years of Sejanus' machinations' (p. 46), but the monarchic principle prevailed against the republic, not against a dyarchy.

Kornemann (p. 48ff.) reminds us that Tiberius, when he succeeded Augustus, mentioned the possibility of a division

[1] Cf. F. Sandels, *Die Stellung der kaiserlichen Frauen aus dem iulisch-claudischen Hause* (Diss. Giessen, 1912), 22f., 75ff.

of power, and he well emphasizes that this is not to be taken as a prelude to the later division of the empire. He should, however, have made it clear that the proposed division was, in fact, one between princeps and senate (that is to say, a dyarchy in Mommsen's meaning), and not between the princeps and a co-regent. Kornemann, although he takes Dio Cassius' report as unhistorical, is still too much influenced by it. He then sums up the general constitutional aspect of the era of Augustus and Tiberius, and declares that the temporary co-regencies were never considered as interfering with the unity of the Principate: *unum esse rei publicae corpus atque unius animo regendum* (Tac. *Ann.*, I, 12). The co-regent had the position of an assistant (*Gehilfenstellung*), and as such was not only permissible but even necessary. I fully agree with these conclusions, but they are at variance with Kornemann's earlier arguments and even more with his later summing-up. For at the end of the book we find in a statistical table (p. 179) the periods of co-regency under Augustus mentioned as full examples of the Dual Principate, and in the conclusion of the book (p. 187) Augustus appears as its creator.

Even Kornemann realizes that the so-called system of Augustus was not continued under the Claudian emperors. The rule of the three successors of Tiberius actually brought about, although with differences and degrees, the importation of the Hellenistic idea of king and queen, of βασιλεύς and βασίλισσα. The combination of a ruling couple did not originate from Livia as Augusta, and even less from the Roman idea of a plurality of *principes*. When the typical form of Hellenistic kingdom began to influence the Roman Principate, this was wholly due to the orientalizing madness of Caligula and to the weakness of Claudius and the young Nero in the face of Agrippina's ambitions. It is remarkable that the dynastic monarchy developed so far, although neither men nor institutions were ready for it. When Nero killed his mother, the new form of government suffered a set-back and became impracticable for a very long time. The couple who ruled, in Caligula's case significantly a brother married to his sister,[1] were called Augustus and Augusta. Thus a new meaning was given to the parallelism of these names, first

[1] Cf. E. Kornemann, *Die Stellung der Frau in der vorgriechischen Mittelmeerwelt* (1927), 13ff.

introduced by Tiberius and Livia. The 'queen' even then had no official title, no *imperium* and no *tribunicia potestas*. She was co-regent, being, as Mommsen put it, 'a real partner in the Principate'; for she enjoyed the power, if not the legal position. The position of 'assistant', such as that of Agrippa and Tiberius had been, was out of question for the Augusta, but so was any position of a legal colleague, whether of equal or minor status. Mommsen[1] is not quite definite about this possibility, but his reluctant utterances should not be used to claim that there was a full status of equality. We may apply also to the 'Augusta' of the Claudian era Mommsen's phrase on the Principate in general (II, 2, p. VI); it was typical of it 'to create no names for the positions of power, and no powers for the names'. Despite all the attempts of the various ladies to co-operate in, or to interfere with, the government, there was no Dual Principate. It is hard to understand what Kornemann means when he first speaks of the Hellenistic monarchy as something that replaced 'the semi-office of the Roman Dual Principate', and afterwards expressly treats the same Hellenistic monarchy as a form of the Dual Principate.

The clan policy of Augustus found its true successor in the family policy of Vespasian. Again co-regency and dual succession were the means used in this policy, but again only the means. They did not exclude other forms which might even be predominant. The position of Vespasian's two sons, although from 69 to 71 they were both *principes iuventutis* like Augustus' grandsons, was so unequal that the whole idea of dual succession seems out of place. In 71 Titus became a co-regent, Domitian his presumptive successor. All three of them, on the other hand, are placed on an equal level in many honorary inscriptions. All this does not fit into the 'system', nor does Domitian's position under Titus, which wavered between that of successor and that of co-regent. There was again a dual succession of two boys when Domitian adopted his two great-nephews. On the whole these are simple actions, largely determined by expediency. But Kornemann, approaching them from the *a priori* standpoint of his prevailing theory, tells us that 'the old idea was turned into the new form of family rule', that 'then for the first time by the conception of the *gens* the Dual Principate was led along the lines of a dynastic

[1] *Staatsrecht*, II, 2, 788, 4; 821; 831.

family rule'. It seems possible to define the situation in almost opposite terms. The Flavian emperors, by laying decisive emphasis on the idea of the family,[1] brought about (in Kornemann's own words) 'the beginnings of the building-up of a Plural Principate (*Mehrprinzipat*)', which is thus distinct from the Dual Principate. Occasionally and exceptionally they used what Kornemann calls 'the system of four eyes', but only as an accidental effect of the dynastic idea which dominated their policy, as it had, in a sense, gained the throne for Vespasian.[2] I also doubt whether it was the more elevated position of the successor, as created 'by the strong personality of Domitian', that laid 'the foundations for the *Caesares* as co-regents during the second and third centuries'. Although Titus and Domitian bore the title *Caesar* during Vespasian's rule, the later institution of the *Caesares* was not based on family policy, but served the personal succession guaranteed by adoption.

The new form was used in the period from Nerva to Marcus. The princeps provided an heir by adoption, and the new son received successively the name of Caesar, the title of Imperator, and the *tribunicia potestas*. Thus created through his adoption successor to the throne, he gradually rose to co-regency. Kornemann (p. 73) regards this new system as another intrusion of Hellenistic ideas. It was a new feature, according to Kornemann (or originally to Professor Alföldi), that Hadrian's co-regent L. Aelius Caesar was allotted a part of the empire (Pannonia) which was no longer directly under the princeps. In Hellenistic States it was indeed fairly common to give a province of the realm to a member of the royal family to rule as an almost independent ruler. In the case of Hadrian, if we adopt this view, it would be the first sign, not to be repeated for a long time, of a disruption of the unity of the empire. But the ingenious conclusion rests on the *argumentum ex silentio* of a single type of Hadrian's coins, and it seems doubtful whether this evidence is sufficiently strong to justify such a far-reaching conclusion.[3]

More important, at any rate, is another point. The monarchic idea found its clearest realization in the reign of the

[1] As strikingly described by K., p. 67f. Cf. also J. Vogt, *Alexandrin. Münzen*, I, 43.

[2] Cf. Tac. *Hist.*, II, 77 (Mucianus' speech): *tuae domui triumphale nomen, duo iuvenes capax iam imperii alter*, etc.

[3] Mattingly writes: 'Presumably Aelius had some sort of *maius imperium* in Pannonia.' Cf. *B.M.C., Empire*, vol. III, p. clxxivf., clxxxv, 544.

optimus princeps Trajan, in the rule of the 'best man' and therefore also in the succession of the best man. Incidentally, this idea was already implicit in the restriction which Augustus imposed on possible successors by the words *si merebuntur*,[1] but it was then only a secondary consideration and remained in general a theoretical formula. Now came the transition from the dynastic idea to the adoption of 'the best'. According to Tac. *Hist.*, I, 15 Galba had already coined a striking phrase to distinguish the two methods: *Augustus in domo successorem quaesivit, ego in re publica.* What was Hellenistic in the new method? Certainly not the general principle; for the Hellenistic king saw the natural successor in his own flesh and blood. It was the Roman form of adoption, and the part it had played in Roman family policy for centuries, which alone made the new scheme workable. Also Roman was the form and substance of the government of the great Trajan. Only the idea that the 'best man', the ἄριστος ἀνήρ, is to be the ruler, is Hellenistic or even Greek. Its symbol in the Roman Empire is the emperor with the beard of a Greek philosopher — a fashion which started with Trajan's successor Hadrian. The successor was no longer taken 'from the family of the emperor which, after all, was closely bound to Rome by education. He was "the best", and he was selected according to philosophical and moral principles rather than political ideas and the interest of the State'.[2] This was clearly a process of Hellenization of the Principate, and at the same time a change which, at least in theory, was concerned exclusively with the personality of the individual princeps. The first phase of the Principate, characterized, as it was, by dynastic policy as well as the frequent appearance of a co-regent, ended in pure monarchy. Kornemann, once again, discloses his *a priori* point of view when, for this culminating point of a long and positive development, he finds no other description but the negative one of 'a decline of the Dual Principate'.

It has always been recognized that something new began with the year A.D. 161. Marcus, immediately after his accession to the throne, gave the title Augustus to Verus, his brother by adoption — that is to say, he made him a co-ruler of equal rights. Thus the later *vita Marci* (7, 6) can state: *tuncque*

[1] Cf. Kornemann, p. 19.
[2] R. Laqueur, *Probleme der Spätantike* (1930), 3.

primum Romanum imperium duos Augustos habere coepit. Since
Mommsen's day, scholars have been used to calling this form
of rule *Samtherrschaft* (common rule), but Kornemann, as I
mentioned before, combines it with the earlier *Mitherrschaft*
(co-regency) under the common name of Dual Principate.
We have seen that for the earlier period the new name cannot
be justified. To use, on the other hand, an identical expression
for the two forms would be justifiable and useful only if they
had more common than distinguishing features, or if the second
form had developed from the earlier. In my view neither is the
case. Kornemann believes emphatically that the real reason
why Marcus acted as he did was that he as a co-regent and
presumptive successor was called Caesar, but his wife as the
daughter of the ruling princeps was called Augusta. We may
find this remarkable, although 'Augusta' had become a name
without political importance. But it seems absurd to assume
that 'the unnaturalness embodied in the combination Caesar-
Augusta' caused a fundamental change in the legal foundations
of the Principate.[1] This seems specially inapplicable to an emperor who certainly did not care for the formal dignity of his
position. All these suggestions completely falsify the real situation. It was the very personality of Marcus, the simplicity and
self-criticism of the sage as well as the gentleness and humanity
of his heart, which were responsible for the introduction of the
real equality of the two Augusti. The only deviation from this
principle was that the elder brother alone was *pontifex maximus.*
But this was due to the indivisibility of that priesthood.[2] It
was impossible to remove this seeming inequality since the
position of the *pontifex maximus,* which involved one of the
most cherished titles of the emperors, had to be preserved in its
traditional sanctity, which allowed no arbitrary alterations. The
few exceptions in unofficial inscriptions, in which Verus
appears as *pontifex maximus,*[3] do not confound these facts.
They confirm, however, that the two Augusti had completely
equal rank.

Kornemann's general thesis largely depends on the assumption of a close connection between the new form of rule and

[1] Mattingly writes: 'I think Marcus *did*, by his immediate advancement of Verus,
silently criticize Antoninus Pius.' But even then Kornemann's conclusions go much
too far.

[2] Cf. Mommsen, II, 2, 1108.

[3] Dessau, 361, 367, 6965. Cf. Kornemann, 79, 3.

earlier forms. As far as I can see there is no evidence for any antecedents, apart from an occasional *Samtherrschaft* in Hellenistic monarchies. Marcus' action was in complete contrast to Antoninus Pius' last will, in which Marcus was selected as successor as being 'the best'. Nor does the double monarchy of 161 derive from the Flavian co-regency, either that of Vespasian and Titus or that of the two brothers. The idea of an imperial family, predominant as it was in the earlier rule, had no meaning for Marcus and his new order. The only fact we may perhaps admit is that the earlier examples of a 'second man' in power to some extent paved the way psychologically for the new dual rule. *Concordia* (ὁμόνοια) had been for a long time past a favourite inscription on the imperial coins; now, by the addition of legends like *concordia Augusta* or *concordia Augustorum*, by the symbol of two clasping hands or a picture of the two emperors joining hands, it became the expression of a new form of imperial rule.[1]

It is somewhat different with the question of succession. Here were indeed antecedents and examples. When Marcus in A.D. 166 made his small sons *Caesares* and thus destined them for the succession, he probably wished to secure the new form of dual rule. Consequently, by a strange irony of circumstance, it was Marcus, the philosopher-emperor, who had to abandon the idea of the succession of 'the best' and to accept the dynastic idea — later even to the extent of ruling in common with his son, whose lack of ability he must have realized in one way or another. Marcus' handling of the problem of succession followed partly the line of the dual succession of Augustan times, partly that of the nomination of a successor as Caesar, as it had been in use since Nerva. It can therefore be understood as a combination of earlier examples, but this combination itself, and even more the institution of the two Augusti, was something completely new. Kornemann quotes as an analogy the position under Tiberius and Claudius of 'Augustus and Augusta with two *Caesares*'. For two reasons this comparison is mistaken. Neither was the combination of Tiberius and Livia or that of Claudius and Agrippina a 'common rule', nor did the adopted sons receive the title Caesar which was then the family name. The new system of Marcus',

---

[1] Cf. J. Vogt, *Alexandrin. Münzen*, I, 137. Mattingly, *B.M.C., Empire*, vol. IV, p. 385ff.

on the other hand, as Kornemann well emphasizes, fore-shadows Diocletian's order, although the *Caesares* were only children and not co-regents. Yet whether Verus fought in the East or Marcus in the North, the unity of the empire remained unquestioned. The first common rule did not yet forebode a partition of power and a partition of the empire.

The premature death of the second Augustus and the second Caesar (A.D. 169) disrupted the system. Marcus then gave to his son, although he was only sixteen years of age, the position of Augustus. He thus demonstrated that he wanted a real and equal rule of two. After his death, however, Com-modus restored a strict monarchy. Under the Severi common rule, once again, was introduced; but I cannot accept the conclusion that, when Septimus Severus fought Pescennius Niger and Clodius Albinus, 'the actual partition of the empire' derived from the (alleged) fact of a Plural Principate. The temporary co-regency of Albinus, the governor of Britain, as Caesar was nothing but a weapon which Severus used. Albinus' nomination as Augustus, which alone would have created a common rule, was not the doing of Severus but the very opposite; it was the answer of the army in Britain to the challenge of Severus, who had declared Albinus a *hostis*. What Kornemann calls partition of the empire was therefore not the consequence of a Dual Principate, but of the struggle *for* the Principate, and also of the growing independence of the provinces. The leaders of the provincial armies, who were the masters of the parts of the empire, were anything but *consortes imperii*.

Severus and Caracalla, on the other hand, and later Severus and his two sons, shared in a 'common rule', in the latter case forming a triarchy, despite Kornemann's absurd argument (p. 88) that behind the appearance of three Augusti was actually a duumvirate 'as an anticipation of the situation after the death of the old emperor'. This surprising assumption is explained by the fact that Severus at that time was — suffering from gout. Once more the bias is revealed with which Korne-mann treats everything that comes within the reach of his Dual Principate.

The common rule of the two hostile brothers Caracalla and Geta lasted for only a year after their father's death. Then Geta was murdered. But the discord between them had the effect, rightly stressed by Kornemann (p. 89), that 'for the first time a partition of the empire was seriously considered'. Iulia Domna, the great mother of the two Augusti, killed this plan (Herodian. IV, 3, 4). But though the plan came to nothing it seems natural to suggest that these events prove a connection between dual rule and the partition of the empire. Actually, I believe, the opposite conclusion is right. Even the strongest possible enmity between the two Augusti did not eventually destroy the unity of the empire. When, later, partition came it was not mainly due to the enmity between some of the rulers.

During the reigns of Elagabalus and Severus Alexander women had a large share in the government. This has some-times been called co-regency, sometimes common rule. But whichever it was, there was no Dual Principate, quite apart from the fact that no form of imperial Roman government was ever in any way compatible with the rule of women. Even the position of Mammaea, the *mater Augusti et castrorum*, was never legally fixed. Moreover, there were sometimes two women standing beside the emperor, although they might differ in power and influence, and in their case it is even less possible to speak of a dual rule. Kornemann enumerates all later appearances of common rule, but only one is remarkable, the unusual and temporary rule of the two senatorial emperors of A.D. 238, Pupienus and Balbinus. Hitherto this has been regarded as a unique case. But Kornemann (p. 96f.) believes that this election of two Augusti was not exceptional but the example which proves him right. I doubt whether it is possible at all to take a senatorial election, by which two members of the *vigintiviri* were nominated,[1] as in any way typical of the Principate. Had the senate any reason not only to follow, but even to lay stress on, a principle which is alleged to have been that of the emperors, by doing the impossible and giving to each of the two *principes* the dignity of the *pontifex maximus*? Can we assume any fixed scheme when a Caesar was created without adoption (Gordian III), 'for the first and only time in the history of the Principate'? Whether the senate had in mind, as Mommsen believes, the two consuls of the republic, or whether it simply conformed with the accepted fashion of common rule, the election of 238 remains a special case. It is in principle unsound to make use of such an exceptional

---

[1] Cf. A. Stein, *Hermes*, LXV (1930), 228f.

event in support of a hypothesis which is supposed to explain the very nature of the Principate. Incidentally, the one senatorial emperor of A.D. 275, Tacitus, provides another argument against Kornemann.

On the whole, common rule became more and more frequent during the third century. The evidence as collected by Kornemann makes this manifest. But it is not sufficient to state the fact. We want to know why it happened that common rule increased as compared with mere co-regency, why Marcus' individual action had such a definite and lasting effect. Mommsen (II, 2, 1169) points out that by the later form the purpose of securing the succession was more completely achieved, and the special conformation by people and senate no longer needed. The form of common rule therefore 'conformed with a development which tended more and more towards an absolute and hereditary monarchy'. We may add that also 'the general depreciation of the titles of the emperors' (K., p. 91) played its part. According to an interpretation by Vogt[1] the name of Caesar Augustus was given to the son when at the moment of his father's proclamation as emperor he was made Caesar. Thus a new form was created which combined common rule and succession, but was usually applied to infants or boys. The surnames of the emperors had largely become stereotyped before; but by now even the most exclusive and ponderous names were used lightly and without restraint. The main reason for this was the endeavour, understandable in those restless days and in view of the increasing power of the Praetorian guards, to make the succession as safe as possible. The deeper explanation, however, is, I believe, not so much the uncertain fate of the emperors and their continuously renewed attempts to found a dynasty; this is a symptom rather than a reason. An important fact was that the imperial family with their African or Syrian origin had no roots either in the society of Rome or in the realm of Hellenistic thought. Still more important was the general situation of the empire. From within, the forces of dissolution were fostered by economic decay and religious particularism, which led to increasing barbarization and independence of the provincial armies, and to a far-reaching disappearance of the uniform Greco-Roman

---

[1] *Alexandrin. Münzen*, I, 174; Kornemann, p. 92, accepts this view. But, as Mattingly points out to me, this Alexandrian usage was never shared by the Roman mint.

basis of civilization. From without, the empire was threatened at almost every frontier. The military and political tasks set to the government of the empire grew in number, variety, and danger. Each province threatened to become the basis for the rise of its governor. Even Aurelian, the restorer of the decay-ing empire (*restitutor orbis*), had first to accept the king of Palmyra as a partner in the rule of the empire. When this barbarian and his famous mother Zenobia eventually pro-claimed themselves as Augustus and Augusta, the Eastern half of the empire had, at least for a short interval, gained independence. No clearer proof is needed to confirm that it was not the fact of a dual rule that caused disruption, but disruption that caused the duplication of the ruler.

Ranke in his *Weltgeschichte* (III, 471) calls it 'perhaps the strongest inner contradiction' of the constitutional aspect of the empire 'that the emperor, who was and remained the corner-stone of the inner order of the empire, had at the same time to face war from outside'. Only by multiplying the holders of the highest office could a chance be given to master the ever increasing difficulties. The mere fact that it was less simple to kill several emperors than one might be helpful. Moreover, when two men decided on a common action, frequently a potential enemy was eliminated. The words by which J. Burckhardt[1] characterizes the Diocletian system are true even for an earlier period. By the nomination of successors and co-regents alone 'were the ambitious aims and intentions of usurpers foiled, and the success of camp revolts made difficult indeed'.

Thus it was that for some time past, because of the general situation, more than one ruler in power and a partition of the empire were urgently asked for. Modern scholars have realized that Diocletian's new order brought existing forces into shape and that the result was not completely new. Korne-mann's book has made it even more obvious that the system of the two *Augusti* and the two *Caesares* had its precedents. But this does not mean, as I hope this review has made clear, that Diocletian only continued and developed a form of rule which had been a dyarchy all the time. The common rule of two Augusti was nothing new, although they seemed now as Iovius and Herculius to be even more strictly differentiated

[1] *Die Zeit Konstantins*, 38.

than before. It had also happened sometimes during the third century that the *Caesares* as the heirs to the throne became co-regents. But as in the case of Marcus' order so now, by the combination of earlier forms, a system was created which as a whole was novel. Through the various 'grades' accorded to the partners in the rule an 'artificial family' was created, in which the predominant principle was no longer that of inheritance, but that of the selection of the best, which had been the idea of the great emperors of the second century. The artificial *gentes* of the Iovii and Herculii in particular bear witness to the 'replacement of a dynasty which was formed by natural descendency, by a line built up through selection and adoption' (p. 116). The principle of the succession of the best found its complement in the magnificent idea of the voluntary resignation of the ruling Augusti, by which the succession was finally to be secured.

It seems very doubtful whether the connections with the past justify the assumption of a really continuous development. This assumption becomes, in fact, meaningless, as Kornemann himself emphasizes, so far as the territorial demarcation of the parts of the empire is concerned. And this is after all, despite the manifest centralizing tendencies, the characteristic feature of the new order, and the real antecedent of the final partition. 'Henceforth plural rule and the idea of partition become inseparable'; but this is so, not because the latter was the consequence of the former, but because each as well as the combination of the two originated in the general situation of the empire. This is also expressed in the fact that the centre of gravity travelled eastwards.

It is hardly necessary to deal in equal detail with the development of Diocletian's order under his successors, particularly under Constantine. As far as Kornemann discusses other than well-known facts, all his statements are based, naturally enough, on his conclusions for the earlier periods, the essential features of which have been questioned in this review. Diocletian's artificial order of succession soon broke down, but the distinction between *Augusti* and *Caesares* remained. A number of new features, all of which are described by Kornemann in detail — such as tetrarchies of four Augusti, the independence of the parts of the empire, sometimes triarchies and temporary • tripartition — reveal the

P

importance and mutual influence of plural rule and partition. They were overcome by some of the great emperors, such as Constantine and later (in spite of Theodora) Justinian. But it is equally certain that the dual principle was never decisive or even predominant. No Romano-Hellenistic tradition prescribed the Dual Principate. This is confirmed, once again, by the rule of Julian, who has been characterized as a man 'whose fundamental tendency was to look back'.[1] In a very modest letter (17 b, Bidez) he informed the ruling Constantius of his acclamation as Augustus, asking to be acknowledged as younger Augustus, as the 'second'; but later on he carried through a pure and complete monarchy.

The exaggerated emphasis on the dual and plural rule fails also to take into account that the later emperors, according to both the Christian and the pagan view, ruled *Dei* (or *deorum*) *gratia*.[2] I cannot imagine that divine grace singled out more than one ruler at a time. There was only one really important 'duality', and that was the great historical contrast within the empire between East and West. When partition was accomplished, dual and plural rules still occurred in the Western as well as the Eastern empire. This proves, once again, that they were not the cause of the partition. On the other hand, they were generally quite unimportant, since they were no longer exponents of living historical forces. They had become a traditional form used for 'the process of handing on the crown without friction' (p. 156). In mediaeval Byzantium also, as is shown in a contribution by Dr. G. Ostrogorsky, the frequent co-regency was nothing but a form of succession.

Kornemann (p. 179ff.) sums up his results first in a section of 'Statistics of the years of Dual Principate'. As against statistics in general it can be objected that it is possible to prove almost anything with the help of numbers; for numbers — and this is often not realized — can be indefinite, when not, or not sufficiently, qualified. Thus Kornemann counts not quite a third of the first period (27 B.C.-A.D. 161) as years of Dual Principate, taking the most different kinds of co-regency (or what he calls by this name) as the same thing, such as for example the combination of Agrippa or Tiberius with Augustus, that of Agrippina with Claudius or Nero, that of Vespasian

---

[1] E. Stein, *Geschichte des spätrömischen Reichs*, I, 261.
[2] Cf. R. Laqueur, *Probleme der Spätantike*, 13ff.

and Titus, and that of Antoninus and Marcus. Equally doubtful are the 'Statistics of the victims of the idea of the Dual
Principate'. The 'victims of the dual succession', which
Kornemann mentions first, were not in truth victims of the
dyarchy; they were killed for the very principle of monarchy,
very much as in the East the princes excluded from succession
were frequently executed.[1] If Kornemann were quite consistent he would have to take all the Eastern monarchies as
potential dyarchies. Of all the co-regents, on the other hand,
who were put to death during the three centuries before
Diocletian, none but Geta can be regarded as a victim of
common rule, which in his case simply failed to be realized.
But it seems absurd to mention under the same heading
Agrippina, the pretender Clodius Albinus, Sallustius Macrinus
who was the father-in-law of Alexander Severus, and even the
two senatorial emperors of A.D. 238. Kornemann then enumerates twenty-three victims of the later period, but they died
as victims of the disruption of the empire, in the struggle
between its hostile parts. None of them died either for the
idea of the dual rule or as a result of it.

The concluding remarks (p. 187ff.) provide a historical
survey in which the following sentence goes perhaps beyond
the rest of the book. Kornemann tells us that 'the creators,
defenders and builders of the Dual Principate were those
principes who were most conscious of the responsibility which
the government of the empire laid upon them, and who
therefore believed that they needed assistance'. This statement confirms the view that the Dual Principate was never a
great and creative idea, much less the basic idea on which the
Principate rested. Whatever its particular manifestation, it
was merely the practical outcome of the fact that the task of
the emperor was too heavy. The notion, on the other hand,
which is at the core of Kornemann's thesis, that the partition
of the empire chiefly derived from the frequent appearance of a
'second man' who shared the rule of the empire, is, at best,
superficial. The connection between the two phenomena was
but a secondary consequence of greater historical facts.
Neither the witnesses of the past (Romulus and Remus, and
the dictators and consuls of the Republic), nor the co-regents
of the first two centuries A.D., started a development which

[1] Cf. K. J. Beloch, *Griechische Geschichte*, IV, 1, 378, quoted by K. himself (p. 181, 1).

was to affect the unity of the State or the empire. Monarchy became dyarchy or even triarchy, because the emperors could no longer master their tasks; and it provided the help they needed. The pretenders, on the other hand, resulted from the dissolution within the empire and the dangers from without, not from an artificial legal idea.

This review, I hope, has shown that Professor Kornemann's theory is mistaken from beginning to end. But his book has stimulated a detailed discussion of the constitutional aspects of the Roman Empire, which at least for the present writer has clarified a number of points. Kornemann's book is bold and partly superficial, but it is also informative and suggestive. We must never forget that scholarship learns just as much from its mistakes as from its correct conclusions.

XIV

EDUARD MEYER

THE expression of what is due to the memory of a great man is a task not accomplished by the praise of the ordinary obituary notices nor, on the other hand, by a more or less complete enumeration and description of all his achievements. An attempt must be made to clarify one's own attitude towards the personality and work of the deceased, and to give some account of his nature and importance inside the framework of his age and environment. We therefore have the right, or rather the duty, to pass judgment, and probably no one would have admitted this more readily than the man to whose memory these pages are dedicated.[1] These remarks, I hope, will make it clear that I am aware of the difficulty of my task in what follows, and fully conscious that this first attempt to describe the essential features of such a man as Eduard Meyer is bound to be in many ways inadequate. But it may be hoped that no-body will regard as daring, or even presumptuous, something which derives from a kind of inner compulsion, based on an acquaintance which was both near and distant, and which included personal relationship besides a common interest in the subjects and methods of scholarship.

E. Meyer was born in Hamburg on January 25th, 1855. His father was an assistant master of the *Johanneum*, and he as well as other members of the staff of this ancient Grammar School introduced the boy at an early age to the methods of scholarly thinking. While still at school he had decided to become a historian, and he was no more than seventeen and at the beginning of his university studies, when it became clear to him that he was to be an ancient historian, and that for this purpose he must learn Oriental languages. To them therefore he gave almost all his time during his years as a student at Bonn and Leipsic. It was then still possible to some extent to take the languages of the Ancient East as a whole; no more than the foundations had been laid in the study of the different branches,

[1] This appreciation of the great historian was written shortly after his death and published in the *Historische Zeitschrift*, vol. 143 (1931).

and the extant sources were still of moderate compass. As early as 1875 Meyer graduated with a thesis for the Ph.D. on the Egyptian god Seth. He then became a tutor in the house of the British Consul-general at Constantinople, thus getting first-hand knowledge of the modern East. In 1879 he became a *Privatdozent* in Leipsic, and in 1884 the first volume of the *Geschichte des Altertums (G.d.A.)* was published. In the following year he was appointed to the chair of ancient history at the University of Breslau; in 1889 he went to Halle, and in 1902 from Halle to Berlin. Since 1923 he had been Professor Emeritus. On August 31st, 1930, he died peacefully, from heart-failure; he had begun, but not finished, re-writing volume II, 2 of the *G.d.A.*

It is rarely so justifiable as it is with Eduard Meyer to follow the custom of calling a man's chief work his life-work. The idea of a general history of antiquity filled Meyer's mind when he was young, and the work was his companion throughout his whole life. It was not in itself revolutionary for a historian to conceive all his work as illustrating the unity of antiquity. What was new was that the whole history of antiquity should be subjected to full and independent investigation by one historian; it was new and without parallel that a man should show himself capable — naturally to an increasing extent as his work proceeded — of setting forth with the help of a synchronistic method the unity of the whole, and the great outlines of its interconnections. This unity is limited by the fact that in early times the history of every country was isolated. But by coordinating what was contemporary, it was possible to discover even in those early times bridges and transitions between the isolated parts, and thus to reveal the unity behind them, or the tendencies towards unity.

The *History of Antiquity* is not a history like other histories. The difference is perhaps best suggested by an image. It is not an elaborate building with pillars and columns, gables and towers, but a kind of Cyclopean fortress, gigantic, without joint and without art, piled-up and shaped by the magnificent will-power of a dominating mind. It seems fitting that the work remained incomplete. The last volume ends about the middle of the fourth century B.C., and in the new edition, even when the unfinished volume has been published, there will be a large gap of several centuries before 500 B.C. This is, of course, regrettable, and a number of smaller books and articles on Hellenistic and Roman history do not really make up for the missing parts of the *G.d.A.* It is, however, more important that for once a history of the various peoples and countries of antiquity has not dealt with them in isolation. For once there has been shown the inner unity of that immense section of universal history which stretches from Menes and Hammurabi, from Moses and Homer, to Diocletian and Justinian; and at the same time the geographical unity of the world of the Near East and the Mediterranean, throughout all the periods of this epoch, has been made plain. The same goal which thus was approached by the amazing breadth of one mind, has since been the aim of collaborating scholars in several countries. It is natural that they have achieved a higher degree of completeness; but their work is necessarily lacking in that close unity of spirit which can spring only from the impress of a single great personality.

There can be no doubt that the course of contemporary scholarship favoured Meyer's own development and work. Without the simultaneous growth of a young branch of scholarship not even he would have become the first universal historian among ancient historians. The situation is now so changed that perhaps he will be not only the first, but also the last.

It is well known that between 1884 and 1930 a great change occurred in our knowledge of the history of the Ancient East. Eduard Meyer, when he was working in 1908 on the new edition of the first volume, himself described this change during the twenty-five years between the two editions. As late as 1895 nothing was known of Egyptian history earlier than the fourth dynasty. It was much disputed whether there was an early people in Mesopotamia, called the Sumerians. No one had any idea that the Babylonian civilization of the third and second millennia was to be distinguished from the Assyrian and Chaldaean cuneiform civilizations which flourished in the first millennium. As late as 1900 the first evidence of an early Cretan civilization became known. It was only by degrees that historical treatment of the Old Testament became possible, and it was not until 1911 that an event as late as the creation of real Judaism by Ezra and Nehemiah was illuminated by the Papyrus of Elephantine. In this last case Meyer's own earlier research was strikingly confirmed. We must realize that his work was continuously tested by new knowledge acquired by excavation. Meyer never hesitated to learn and to unlearn when necessary; his untiring energy was never stopped or checked, even though some of the results of his research were superseded. Frequently new evidence confirmed his views on the most important points. There could be no more impressive proof of the soundness of his methods and the correctness of his vision of the world of history.

Greek history, too, was in a special, though entirely different, position. When Meyer began his work, two men were out-standing in forming what that age believed to be the true picture of the Greeks: George Grote and Ernst Curtius. Their names connote political liberalism and aesthetic classicism, and Eduard Meyer — and with him a whole generation of scholars, notably K. J. Beloch — was opposed to both. To Meyer as a 'pure' historian, politics was unquestionably the heart of history. He therefore put an end to the pale picture of the Greeks as mere paragons of beauty and harmony, and set himself to under-stand their real nature as it found expression in their political, social and economic life. On the other hand, he opposed the idealization of Athens by nineteenth-century Liberals. It was only thereby that Sparta and Macedon came into their own within the framework of Greek history. The road away from the idealization of Demosthenes in his fight against Philip had already been shown by J. G. Droysen, whose genius had grasped the fact, nowadays almost self-evident, that Hellenistic history has a value and a character of its own, apart from earlier Greek history. It was only natural that the pendulum swung too far to the other side. But at least, much-treated questions were dis-cussed again from new points of view, and constructive criticism was applied to all the old material. Some exaggeration and distortion is undeniable, but so too is the gain.

In one respect, however, the new critical school of ancient historians fell into an error which in itself was at variance with their critical attitude. They expected to be able to find in antiquity much in common with their own time. In this the young historians of the 'eighties resembled Theodor Mommsen who, though respected and revered by them as the great leader in Roman history, was none the less looked upon with critical reserve. The interpretation of ancient history in modern terms became particularly manifest in the field of economic history,

to which Meyer contributed an excellent general survey under
the title *Die wirtschaftliche Entwicklung des Altertums*. But the
same tendency could be seen everywhere, and many examples
show how far these historians had lost their feeling for historical perspective. In the understandable endeavour to turn the
Greeks from ideal figures into real human beings it was found
easiest to turn them into one's equals. It is here in particular
that a younger generation has started a counter-movement.
But they know not only that they will make their own mistakes
of a different kind, but also that it was the work of that earlier
generation of great scholars which accomplished the much
more difficult task of paving the way.

Eduard Meyer's untiring research in the fields of both
Oriental and Greek history resulted in a considerable number
of books and papers which were published while he was working at the *G.d.A.* They alone, in their number and importance,
considerably surpass what may be called the average of even a
good and productive scholar's labours. There is no need here
for a lengthy list, but a few works may be mentioned, more or
less at random, which will bear witness to Meyer's amazingly
wide range. His *Entstehung des Judentums* (1896) has already
been referred to. In this book the critical historian opposed the
hyper-criticism of certain theologians. He naturally shared
with them the fundamental position of biblical criticism, but
from this ground he refuted over-hasty scepticism, and confirmed the truth of our evidence for the age of Ezra and
Nehemiah, by interpreting that evidence within the historical
framework of the Persian Empire. Meyer's placing of the
chronology of ancient Egypt on a new foundation in 1904 was
no less important. Apart from a few corrections and in spite
of at least one strong attack, in all essentials it has been generally accepted as final. On the other hand, the theory that
Theopompus is the author of the historical book which was
discovered among the Oxyrhynchus Papyri has been much
disputed and is to-day denied by almost all scholars. Nevertheless Meyer's book (*Theopomps Hellenika*, 1909) is still the most
important contribution to the subject, both in linguistic interpretation and historical evaluation. These three examples
suffice to show that Meyer was an expert in Egyptology, Old
Testament, Greek language and chronology; in other works he
excels, for instance, as an archaeologist or an Assyriologist. But

he was not a polyhistor of eighteenth-century stamp. He overcame specialization by being a specialist in every separate field
of research concerned with the ancient world.

Apart from these and many other works which all served to
provide the foundations for, as well as additions to, the main
building of the *G.d.A.*, there are other books and articles which
lie outside the framework of the main structure so far as it was
finished. Meyer had, for instance, something essential to say
on the nature of the monarchy of Alexander. He also made
important contributions to Roman history, the most outstanding example being the book *Caesars Monarchie und das Prinzipat
des Pompeius*, which was written during the war (1918). The
continuation of the *G.d.A.* had been interrupted by the stress
and anxieties of the immediate present, but the historian,
anxious to deal with questions less detached from his own inten-
sive political activities, found a more congenial subject in the
confused times of the Roman civil wars and the political
activities of the men of that age, of which we know chiefly from
Cicero's speeches and letters. The great value of the book is
its power to make the reader hear the throbbing heart of political life. By this inherent vitality it will outlive its questionable
main thesis which is that Pompey consciously aimed at, and
actually held, the position of the *princeps*, and was thus the true
predecessor of Augustus.

The history of the Roman Empire remained, on the whole,
outside Meyer's range. So he has not described the last great
period and the end of ancient history, of which he realized and
brought out the unity as no other scholar has done. This
deficiency is due to the general position of the study of that
period. Even Mommsen did not think the time had come for
a comprehensive history of the Roman Empire, although he
had completely mastered the material which already in his lifetime had become immense. It could hardly be different a
generation later when the material was still steadily increasing,
and Meyer certainly did not know it as well as, for example, the
material for the history of the Ancient East. Nevertheless, he
took up the matter in one particular, and indeed essential,
aspect. Ever since his dissertation, Meyer had shown a special
interest in the phenomenon of religion. He was himself irrelig-
ious and a sober rationalist; but he tried time and again to
study what, after all, was apart from the State the most powerful

factor in human history. He never realized when he studied
religious questions that there was a discrepancy between subject
and object. After the war and before resuming his work on the
G.d.A., he attacked the greatest problem in the history of
religion, which is also the greatest problem in ancient history.
During the years 1920-1923 the three volumes of *Ursprung
und Anfänge des Christentums* were published, and met with
severe criticism from theologians. Their chief objection was
that Meyer had almost completely neglected the most recent
and important research on the New Testament, and thus had
put forth views which either were well known or had been
rejected. This was a criticism which in principle Meyer himself would have admitted to be just. It was for the same reason
that he considered works like Ranke's *Weltgeschichte* and Burckhardt's *Griechische Kulturgeschichte* to be without scientific value.
But just as he was mistaken about those earlier works, so were
his opponents mistaken about this work of his. Great creative
work cannot be affected by an objection which may be appropriate in criticizing minute scholarly investigations. There are
large sections in Meyer's book which should be differently
judged — his elaborate description, for instance, of Judaism
during the Hellenistic Age, particularly of its position in the
history of religion, shaped as it was by its own traditions as well
as by Iranian and Hellenistic influences; or, on the other hand,
his picture of the gradual change of Christianity from a Jewish
sect to the Catholic Church — a change which altered and
determined the course of the history of the world. Chapters
like these, and, in fact, the work as a whole, do not, of course,
reflect a religious mind, but they give wide and magnificent
perspectives of universal history. This remains true even
though Meyer's criticism of the Gospels may be obsolete and
even though it becomes plain now and then that his mind was
not capable of coping with a subject that cannot be understood
and mastered by the reason alone.

I have said that Meyer did not realize how alien the subject
of the rise of Christianity was to his inner self. This should not
be explained by a deficiency in self-criticism, but rather by the
whole character of his mental outlook. He always emphasized
that within the sum-total of historical scholarship political
history held the first place, but he would never have admitted
that any subject demanded a special spiritual attitude or quality

on the part of the historian. Nothing was needed, he thought, but full mastery of sources and methods, and familiarity with the results of earlier research. This standpoint is generally called 'positivist'. This is not the place for criticism or refutation of positivism as a principle. But it seems necessary to describe the position which Meyer held within the intellectual history of his time by more than this single word. This is the more desirable because positivism has become a term of abuse which is sometimes applied to things which are very much alive and creative. It is true that we can no longer believe in the idea that scholarship is something absolute and objective, free from presuppositions and values. We see the limits of purely positivist research, and we do not share the confidence of some scholars that science and scholarship are progressing steadily and will lead to 'final' results. But we should not forget that in all 'positivism' there lives something really magnificent and impressive, a truly fanatical search for truth, which over and over again has opposed fashionable idols like the delusions of racial doctrine. Historians have recently spoken of the 'invasion of subjectivism'. But historical scholarship, if it is to remain scholarship at all, must never discard the absolute will to aim at the truth together with all the obligations which that will involves. It must, however, be admitted that 'absolute objectivity', usually attributed to Ranke and postulated as an ideal by the generation of historians of about 1900, became an idol, at least to the most typical of its worshippers, because it was not what it was supposed to be. No one shows better than Ranke that scholarship cannot last without something that is beyond scholarship.

This is also the main reason for the fact that Meyer wrote in rather a poor style. He is the only one among the great German historians to whom it was not given to clothe his material in a form worthy of it. He displayed neither the nobility and transparency of Ranke's style, nor the passionate fire of Mommsen, neither the shining marble of Burckhardt's nor the boisterous beauty of Treitschke's language. Meyer's style is sober and impersonal, a language fit for exact research into particular and narrow problems, but inadequate for the creative writing of universal history. Even this, however, is less a personal deficiency than a consequence of his age and its positivist and naturalistic character. An inability to write in a good style almost amounted to an unwillingness to do so. This fault threatened indeed the very life of historical scholarship and the writing of history. For it is because of its very nature, and not for any 'aesthetic' reasons, that history, second only to poetry, is called upon to serve language and to create through language.

Meyer frequently stressed the fact — the last time in the autobiographical sketch which he wrote to return thanks for the congratulations on his seventieth birthday — that from his earliest years he considered the main purpose of all historical scholarship was 'to achieve a clear and firm *Weltanschauung* on a historical basis'. This is what has lately been called *Historismus*. The clear will and determination are wholly admirable; but what are the real contents of his philosophy of life? Meyer gave an answer to this question in the introduction to his main work (vol. I, 1) which he called *Elements of Anthropology*, expressly rejecting the 'misused expression' of philosophy of history. In this introduction he tries to display 'the general forms of human development', but this merely amounts to a sociology of prehistory with, as an appendix, a methodology of history. Many of the views expressed here are open to strong objection. But that makes it all the more desirable to emphasize the fact that it has been up to now a rare, if not a unique, thing among ancient historians to attempt any general examination of their own methods and principles. His attempt in itself deserves the highest admiration. The results, however, are disappointing. Meyer tries to solve fundamental questions in a wholly factual manner, simply by inquiring into our historical evidence. But it is impossible to arrive at fundamental principles without using fundamental categories, even though history is neither a philosophy nor a science. Meyer is fully justified, though his polemic is no longer topical, in opposing those historians who thought they could preserve the scientific character of history only by finding historical laws. But his own definition of 'historical' as 'effective' (beyond the time of the event) does not go very far. He has to admit himself that a strong element of subjectivism is left. Moreover there will have been many 'effects' which no longer existed at the time when a particular historian wrote, nor even in the period which he selected as his subject, while others may well have made their appearance at a later time when that historian was already dead. Meyer would be mistaken even if there were a platform from

which it could generally be decided which historical phenomena were to be called 'effective' — that is to say, important
as a cause of following events. Max Weber, in a detailed
discussion of Meyer's theory, has pointed out that there are
historical events, men, institutions, deeds, which are historical
not because of their actual effects, but on account of their
intrinsic value, or even simply of their value as an element con-
tributing to our knowledge.

Meyer regarded his *Elements of Anthropology*, though also as
an attempt to investigate the methods of history, chiefly as an
expression of his *Weltanschauung*. In approaching this claim we
enter a region beyond the competence of the historian. But it is
the historian in particular who will thank Meyer for having felt
compelled to inquire into the fundamental aspects of history at a
time when the average scholar entirely excluded such questions
from the field of his activities. Meyer was no positivist as far as
the purpose of his thoughts was concerned; but his philosophy
was pure positivism. It may perhaps be admitted that the postulate of the omnipotence of the State is a logical deduction from
the theory, first expressed by Aristotle, that the State is earlier
than Man. But the danger of this kind of reasoning becomes
manifest when Meyer says that religion can be understood only
through the knowledge that it has grown from magic, and that
in all religions we have to distinguish between gods and spirits.
This shows to what consequences a *Historismus* leads which is
nourished on nothing but empirical knowledge. If Meyer's
philosophy is *Historismus* — and it was not meant to be anything
else — it is as remote from Hegel as it is from Dilthey; with
the latter Meyer has in common only the negation of meta-
physics. In fact Meyer's theories have their place outside all
philosophy as an expression of belief in the omnipotence of
rationalist scholarship. Its only analogy, and indeed its contemporary, is the monistic belief in the omnipotence of natural
science.

It is not accidental that Meyer largely agreed with Oswald
Spengler, whose so very successful book is a pure expression of
Historismus and at the same time of a strong belief in human
reason. He called Meyer the greatest German historian since
Ranke, obviously intending to exclude Mommsen and Treit-
schke. Meyer, on the other hand, pleaded vigorously for
Spengler's work, which he compared, in its importance as a

creative stimulus, even with Herder's *Ideen zur Philosophie der Geschichte der Menschheit*. He apparently did not accept as the essential part of Spengler's construction of world history the law of the identical course which all civilizations are supposed to take. Against this theory Meyer would rely on his deeper knowledge of universal history. But he did agree with Spenglers' idea that all historical life has to follow a scheme of destiny, and it was this fateful scheme which turned the so-called 'morphology of world history' into a philosophy. It is enough to allude to these connections between the two men, which prove the superiority and width of Meyer's outlook, even though they also confirm the limitations of his mind. He certainly never shared in the petty *Besserwisserei* which was displayed in the criticism of Spengler by men who were prominent in their own line of work.

Meyer was great even in his limitations. It is impossible to do him justice without taking the man as a whole and always remembering the living human being behind his *Weltanschauung*, which I have possibly treated too much as something abstract and detached. The man who with striking unconcern defended the principle of 'scholarship for its own sake' saw no problem whatever in the relations between scholarship and life; to him and in him they were one. In every way he took a full share in the life that went on around him. He worked untiringly for organizations to help scholars and scholarship, or to improve the social conditions of undergraduates. He took an active part in political work. To this side of his activities belong the books and pamphlets on England and America which he wrote during and after the war. They prove the sincerity of his views, rigid and one-sided as they were, but they do not add anything of importance to the picture of the historian. He was a politician, like many German scholars, honest and idealistic in spite of the *Realpolitik* which he professed, a fervent patriot, typical in his merits and limitations. Instead of expressing my own judgment I should like to quote the words which Meyer wrote in an obituary of Mommsen, and which seem surprisingly appropriate now to himself: 'Many may have regretted that the man whom they looked upon with deep reverence identified himself so completely with a view which to them seemed to belong to the past and no longer to provide an adequate standard for judging the present and its great tasks.' But even as a politician Meyer remained human, and in order to describe him, perhaps I may be forgiven for mentioning my own experience. I had been Meyer's pupil for only one *Semester* when war broke out. During the whole of the war and while I was at the front, he wrote me frequent letters in which he expounded his political views, although I never concealed from him that my own opinions differed widely from his.

One of the great impressionists, Lovis Corinth, has painted a portrait of Eduard Meyer which reveals much of the man. The tall stature and serious face reflect the greatness and straightforwardness of his mind; they also show that he was not given to posing. His eyes show his warm and strong feelings. He was capable of sincere attachment, though also of sincere hatred. Countless people were grateful to him for kindness and help. The number of his personal pupils was never large. This was partly due to the fact that Meyer was not a naturally gifted teacher. His influence, if compared with that of Mommsen, was in a higher degree due to his books, although these books were much less fascinating than Mommsen's *Roman Public Law*, and still less than his *History of Rome*. But comparison with Mommsen teaches us something more. Meyer was no organizer of scholarship. Unlike Mommsen, he was never in a position to use his pupils and colleagues in the framework of a mighty scientific organization. It is doubtful whether this should be regarded as a shortcoming. Certainly the wholesale organization of co-operative works like the *Corpus Inscriptionum Latinarum* is something that is both necessary and admirable. But, in Meyer's own words, 'with his ability, attained by intellectual training, to produce and create work of his own, man counts for more than all organization'.

This postulate always gave Meyer's judgment a truly ethical sincerity. This, above all, I believe, is his personal legacy. In his work, in the planning and the execution of a *History of Antiquity*, he will probably find no successor in the near future. But the framework of universal history, in which all ancient history has to be seen, will never again be lost sight of. It is true that the ambiguous position of the ancient historian thus becomes a problem; for his subject belongs to History as well as to the Classics. Meyer refused to acknowledge the latter bond, and accepted it only for reasons of practical expediency. But to everyone who sees in the heritage

of antiquity not only a subject of historical research, but also
a humanistic debt, the twofold bond exists as a problem and
an obligation. Perhaps for the time being this is a German
rather than an international question. In fact, the work of
Mommsen as well as of Meyer was typically German, in spite
of their naturally high international reputations and in spite
also of their necessarily numerous international connections.
Just as Mommsen all his life remained the old democrat of
1848, so Eduard Meyer remained a citizen of the Second
Reich. The succeeding generation has to stand on its own feet,
but it must attempt to continue the work of the former generation with true reverence.

'Men come and go, but scholarship remains.' This saying of
Mommsen's is true even of the greatest among scholars. But
it is equally true if it is put the other way round. Scholarship is
always changing, but the work of great scholars remains as a
lasting challenge.

XV

THE ANCIENT WORLD AND EUROPE

WHAT IS EUROPE?

IT can be asserted, I hope, that most of the preceding essays, while dealing with one or another aspect of the ancient world, have also referred, sometimes openly and sometimes implicitly, to the importance of that ancient world for the history and the spirit of modern Europe. But it may be worth while to attempt briefly to outline the problem from the European point of view rather than that of antiquity.

I am writing this a few weeks after VE-Day: Victory in Europe. There has rarely been in history a victory so complete, never a collapse of the defeated on so large a scale. A very great task has been accomplished — and yet, how far away is still the fruit of victory: peace! Will there be peace in Europe? Is there still a Europe?

European cities are in ruins. Misery is threatening those who brought it to so many others. In the heart of Europe the dead bodies and living corpses of many thousands of starved and tortured human beings have been discovered in the hell of the concentration camps. Millions of others have been murdered. The Satanic masters of Nazi Germany have brought doom and disaster even to their own people. All the nations of Europe are bound to realize that the denial of everything we used to call the European tradition has led to a denial of humanity itself. Nazism, let us hope, is dead for ever, but the evil sources from which it sprang cannot be removed so quickly. The disease which devastated the body and mind of the German people has infected, in one way or another, the whole of Europe. The world is out of joint, and Europe with all she stood for is stricken down.

It will be difficult enough to rebuild the cities of Europe and to feed her people. But what an easy task, compared with that of rebuilding and restoring the mind and soul of Europe!

It is only natural that many take the fatalistic and pessimistic view, and proclaim the end, or at least the beginning of the end, of European civilization. Other civilizations have perished before — why not ours? Spengler's seed, nourished and brought to full growth by the labours of others,[1] is bearing fruit. The view that the whole pattern of history is just a bundle of different and independent civilizations provides such a neat and persuasive solution of the great riddle of the story of mankind, and in particular of that of our own times. Expressed in the terms of the fashionable science of biology, the theory of the birth, growth and death of each civilization has impressed even those who as a rule are not inclined to be deluded by fashions of any kind. The historian who still believes in the dominating continuity of human history, or at least of the history of our Western world, sees the very foundations of his belief questioned and challenged, not only by new theories but also by his own tragic experience of contemporary events.

The question whether there will be a future for Europe and European civilization cannot be answered by historical knowledge alone. But if it can be answered at all we must have some idea of what Europe was. The story is told that Bismarck once asked: 'What is Europe?' and that a British diplomat answered: 'Many great nations.' I do not think that this answer is quite satisfactory. It is right as far as it goes, but that is not very far. Against Bismarck's scepticism it was appropriate to state that Europe is more than a geographical conception. This, I believe, everyone to-day feels very strongly, even though often unconsciously, unless he is wrapped up in his own nationalistic ideas. But to claim as the content of the conception of Europe nothing but the sum total of her national sections does not leave her with any content of her own. No one can deny that for many centuries past the history and the civilization of each nation have made, and are still making, a far stronger impact upon human imagination than the forces of supra- or international ideas. But that is just the main reason why we ought to realize what it is that provides for the national histories and civilizations, to say the least, a common background. I believe that it is much more than a background. I believe that the

[1] I think, of course, in particular of Dr. A. J. Toynbee's impressive and learned work, *A Study of History*.

236 ASPECTS OF THE ANCIENT WORLD

ground itself in which they grow is common, and·that this is Europe.

We must not expect to find the common soil of the European nations of one kind only. History is never simple, and the greater the issue the more complex are its foundations. It is a commonplace to say that Europe is based on the twofold heritage of the ancient world, the Judaeo-Christian and the Greco-Roman traditions. Commonplaces, however hackneyed, often contain the truth, or at least an essential part of it. I am convinced that this is so with the European legacy of antiquity. This in itself is not a simple but a very complex answer to our question, and it is open to a great many different interpretations. Moreover, it may not contain the whole truth. At least one different answer has been given in recent times. That is that the real foundations either of Europe as a whole or of the European nations individually were laid by prehistory. Let us consider this answer first.

THE CLAIM OF PREHISTORY

Prehistory has become, during the last half century or so, a legitimate branch of historical scholarship. But frequently it claims to be more. 'Aided by archaeology, history with its prelude prehistory becomes a continuation of natural history.'[1] I do not wish to enlarge on the claim, implied in this sentence, that archaeological methods are likely to supersede, or at least essentially to correct and improve, the methods of historical research. I should like to concentrate on the last words of the sentence. If prehistory, and even history, is a continuation of natural science, it must be of the same kind as natural science. In some aspects, as far as the history of the earth is involved, or the earliest development of man, prehistory is indeed part of natural science. Geology and geophysics, biology and biochemistry, are only some of the sciences towards which prehistory has to build bridges. All this is, of course, completely outside our scope. Prehistory as natural science, including psychological research, can outline the origin and early development of man, but it has nothing whatever to do with the conceptions of history or historical geography. 'Europe' is no part of this kind of prehistory. In fact, biology and psychology

[1] V. Gordon Childe, *What Happened in History*, 7.

are in their very essence non-historical and almost anti-historical.
Neither animals nor souls have a history; only men have, being
both of these and something more. This is one of the reasons
why any racial theory, even a more subtle one than those
usually encountered, does almost nothing to explain history.
Eventually all attempts to write history on a biological or
psychological basis lead to some kind of myth—whether it is
Marxist or Nazi, Freudian or the product of some other
modern-ism. All that may sound old-fashioned and reactionary,
but I am firmly convinced that none of these ways, whatever
else their merits, will lead us to true historical insight.

In the borderland between history and science, prehistory
meets other approaches to the knowledge of early man, and
partly shares their methods and results. Prehistory becomes
related to anthropology and ethnology. Nourished by fruitful
investigation into the world of primitive thoughts and beliefs,
what in J. J. Bachofen and other mystagogues had been
intuition became the rational sport of numerous scholars, and
eventually, through the leadership of a true genius, Sir James
Frazer, an influential branch of real scholarship. The brilliance,
however, of *The Golden Bough*, which for some time outshone
most other lights, has by now been slightly dimmed, and the
number of attempts to explain history, and not only its obscure
antecedents, through the growing knowledge of Primitive Man
has decreased. But many people still believe that the measuring of
skulls or the study of the customs of Australian or African abori-
gines—in themselves completely justified sections of scholarship—can teach us something essential about the nature of the
great civilizations. It is a delusion to think that 'experimenting'
with the so-called primitives of yesterday and to-day provides
scientific material for prehistory and history. It is certainly
possible to discover certain aspects of the primitive mind as
distinguished from the psychical and intellectual life of historical man. But that is a limited subject, and those prehistorians
and anthropologists who are not satisfied with remaining within
its limits tread on dangerous soil. Even where the results of
this kind of research come nearest to true history, they remain
a mixture of rationalist pleading and fanciful story-telling, a
'rationalized myth'. This was taken for history once before,
when the writing of history was still in its infancy, by Herodotus, and even more clearly by his predecessor Hecataeus of

Miletus, whom we may call the grandfather of history. Bacho-fen's mystical fantasies about the working of the masculine and the feminine principle, not only in the structure of primitive society, but also in the very essence of human history, are just as far from historical understanding as the rationalistic fantasies of some of the modern anthropologists.

It is indeed surprising how near in this kind of research the materialist comes to the mystic. But G. K. Chesterton knew that 'the materialist is always a mystic and often a mystagogue.' The former tends to explain primitive man by the standards of modern psychology or economics, and thus to bridge the gulf which separates prehistory from history. He believes that in explaining the primitive world — and 'primitive' frequently becomes identical with 'prehistoric' — he has found the Open Sesame to the very secrets of history. Jane Harrison's famous utterance: 'I knew Zeus was only that old snake!' is just as significant and just as absurd as, say, the Marxist explanation of the origin of Christianity as a Communist revolt of the underdog.

There is yet another kind of prehistory which I would call nationalistic archaeology. It is another rationalized myth, the myth of the prehistoric foundations of the nations of to-day. We find examples of it even in the books of sober and sound historians. To Dr. Toynbee we owe the knowledge of an outstanding example.[1] The great historian of early Gaul, Camille Jullian, succeeded, almost unconsciously, 'in the twinkling of an eye', in discovering the unity and central position of modern France in the primitive and unpolitical world of prehistoric Gallic tribes. The madness of Nazism has led to worse blunders, against which some sensible men among German prehistorians protested in vain. I once saw a text-book of Germanic history which contained a chronological table of 'accurate' dates back to 200,000 B.C. Popular patriotism, usually of the parochial kind, but recently often enough on a far larger scale and therefore much more dangerous, is responsible for much misreading of prehistory.

But now, after having done with all these aberrations from historical scholarship, it is only fair to say something of that kind of archaeology which is an established and increasingly important part of man's investigation into his early past. It is a

[1] *A Study of History*, vol. I, 11f.

fascinating story, but the trouble is that it is never the same in the accounts of different writers. All the rich evidence of archaeological excavations cannot tell us anything definite about the facts of history, unless it is controlled by some sort of dated or written evidence. Even outstanding events, such as the migrations of peoples, the mixture of races, the destruction of settlements, remain very often hypothetical assumptions, though they may be proclaimed as historical facts. While it is possible to outline the main stages of the development of prehistoric man in their general character and to draw increasingly accurate pictures of them, it is man in general who is the centre of this story, and not any particular kind of man, not the European man nor even the white man. There were throughout the early ages many different civilizations or societies of a more or less primitive character, but all of them conformed to a slowly progressive general standard. There was no continuity of one or another individual trend, only that of the general trend.

At least one bold and very learned attempt, however, has been made to show the unity of Europe as a product of prehistory and then naturally as the ancestor of historical Europe — by Mr. C. F. C. Hawkes in his book *The Prehistoric Foundations of Europe* (1940). The book provides difficult reading for the non-specialist, but if I am not mistaken, Mr. Hawkes' picture, with all its disturbing multitude of effects, influences, mixtures, local developments, and so on, does not prove any really unifying force within Europe — except the facts of nature. It is, of course, certain that the geographical position and the climate of Europe exerted a certain unifying influence on every group of men, every kind of settlement, every expression of civilization, within her area. Nevertheless, the prehistory of Europe is not the story of a European civilization and has, in fact, no unity. Even from Mr. Hawkes' book it becomes clear that the 'European' development rested essentially on the prehistory of the Near East and the Mediterranean. Ancient Greece was European, but she was not Europe. European civilization began with the Greeks or their Minoan predecessors, but it was long indeed before it deserved its name. There was no European unity of any kind before the Roman Empire. I am glad to see that Professor Gordon Childe[1]

[1] *l.c.*, 21.

emphatically stresses the fact that there was only one main stream of cultural tradition, and that is the one 'that flows from Mesopotamia and Egypt through Greece and Rome, Byzantium and Islam to Atlantic Europe and America'.

I do not pretend to have discussed all the relevant aspects of such a vast subject as prehistory. But I feel justified in assuming that neither the sound archaeological research of some prehistorians nor the scientific or fantastic mythology of others establishes anything like a common European ancestry. Historical man is naturally the offspring of his prehistoric ancestors. But that is equally true of any man to whatever civilization he belongs. Those things that made Europe what she was, and determined the course of the history of our civilization, were not embodied in any part of prehistory. In earlier passages of this book I maintained that the separation of history from prehistory — more or less out of fashion to-day — is justifiable and even necessary. It is equally to the point to say that Europe — for us the very centre of history — is not a child of prehistory.

THE LEGACY OF THE ANCIENT WORLD

It is a historical fact that European civilization received its chief content and strongest impulses from the ancient world. It is another historical fact that the most important legacies of the ancient world are those usually described as the Judaeo-Christian and the Greco-Roman traditions. It is also a historical fact, although perhaps not recognized as such to quite the same extent as the two above-mentioned, that only by the combination of the two trends — a combination which greatly varied in character throughout the ages — was the continuity of European civilization guaranteed. Whatever section of its history we may try to investigate, we shall always find evidence of the heritage of Moses and the Prophets, and Jesus and the Christian Church on the one hand, and, on the other, of Greek and Roman life, thought and belief, literature and art. In a general way the first line of development belongs essentially to the ancient East, the second one to the West. The conclusion is that Europe at all times was and is a union between East and West.

This, though true, is a statement of such a general character that it does not lead us very far. A first and very important

distinction to be made derives from the consideration that
each of the two aspects of the ancient world is itself divided
into East and West. When the ancient world found its last
political form in the Roman Empire, it was a unity, ruled by
one government and administered by one type of man, the Roman
citizen. But, even in the centuries in which this unity was at its
strongest, there was always the division between a Greek East
and a Latin West. After the East had been united in Alexander's empire, it broke up into a number of States which yet
were bound together by one, the Hellenistic, civilization. A
century later, Rome had subdued most of the Western
Mediterranean and began steadily, though reluctantly, the
conquest of the East. The empire grew together from two
different parts, but it was to be a single empire. Roman
soldiers, magistrates and traders brought the Latin language
and Western habits to the East, while Greek teachers and
Oriental priests taught the West the language and the thoughts
of the Greeks and the worship of Eastern deities. This mutual
intercourse in a way strengthened the unity of the empire,
although it also weakened the true forces of unification — the
traditions of Rome the ruler, and the purity of a Greco-Roman
civilization. The unity of the Roman Empire was not based
on an attempt at *Gleichschaltung*. Within a community and a
civilization of world-wide extent, the local and regional communities and civilizations survived. Eventually, however, the
absolute rule of the Empire, though often wise and moderate,
turned into a strict system of absolute theocracy and absolute
bureaucracy. This suited the East far better than the West,
and this is one, though only one, of the reasons why, despite
all unifying forces of the empire, the division between East
and West grew wider and wider, until at last the empire broke
up into its Eastern and Western halves.

The same happened to Christianity. When the Jewish sect
became 'Greek' and thus, in fact, Christian — in other words,
a universal religion, eventually recognized by the Roman
emperor — full unity seemed achieved. But a division of the
Church had clearly grown up along with the growth of the
Church as a whole. Political and spiritual issues soon worked
together in destroying the common unity, and the triumphant
Church surpassed the secular power in this as in other things.
The Roman Church separated from the Greek Church, to

outlive the shorter lifetime of the Western Empire. The conflicts between the various Churches and the ever renewed attempts at restoring unity went on for centuries. But the Roman Church emerged eventually as the true heir to the empire, the spiritual lord of the larger part of Europe, the guardian first, but soon also the rival, of a new 'Holy Roman Empire'. In the East the Church, though very powerful, remained the spiritual upholder of the Byzantine emperors, and no Patriarch ever gained the worldly power of the Pope. This is one reason among many why the East knew no Reformation. Christianity in the West and in the East went different ways, and the later political creations followed suit. Thus the East lived remote from the general development of Europe, and only since the seventeenth century — in a full sense not before the nineteenth — has a mutual *rapprochement* been taking place. It had, and still has, to overcome the most formidable obstacles, and it is as yet too early to say whether, when and how the East and West of Europe will come together again.

Still, the original heritage was derived from the same Roman Empire and its civilization. It is a mistake to think of the Orthodox Church, of the Slavs or the Balkans, as lying outside Europe. We have to realize that there is more than one trend of European history, and the partial separation of the East from the body of Europe finds a parallel, although one of a less definite kind, in the partial separation of Britain from the same body. I remember how shocked I was when in Athens — of all places — I heard the train which connected Greece with Belgrade and Budapest being called the train to Europe. And it was only recently that I heard a man talking on the B.B.C. of the retreat from Dunkirk as the moment 'when the British left Europe'. This may be, in both cases, a loose way of speaking, but it is a significant one. The histories of Eastern Europe and of Britain were less closely bound up with the common history of Europe than, say, those of France, Germany and Italy.

This is another historical fact which can teach us something. We may doubt whether the Classical tradition in Eastern Europe, after the Byzantine scholars had left and brought the ancient authors to 'Europe', was of a strength comparable to that in the West; and we may take this as one of the reasons for the difference between spiritual developments in the East and in the West. Even after Russia had admitted the ideas of the West, she had not lost her own soul. The bridge which connects the world of, say, Goethe, Dickens and Flaubert with that of Tolstoy, Dostoevsky and Chekhov is very narrow indeed. 'I will go to Europe', says Ivan Karamazow to his brother Aljosha; but he is the 'Westerner' who meets his fate, and Aljosha is the true Russian who survives.

The position of England is, of course, quite different. It is difficult to deny that both the Classical and the Christian traditions have permeated British life far more deeply than that of any other country. No other section of Christianity, I believe, — certainly of Protestant Christianity — is so sure, as the Anglican Church is, of the necessity of counting the Greeks among its ancestors, and no Humanism was ever so Christian as the English one. It may be that these traditions have become to-day to some extent a matter of routine and have lost much of their inner vitality. If so, it would only prove that they have to fight again for their future — and that may be a good thing. It certainly does not disprove their strength in the past, a past which reached, if I am not mistaken, down to a very recent time. If the history of the British Isles took a slightly different course from the European in general, this was not due to a lack of either Classical or Christian heritage; it was due to the mere fact that it was an island history.

It is well known and yet often not sufficiently stressed that England was the victim of many invasions from the early Stone Age down to the Danish and Norman invasions, but never again after 1066. 'The battle of Hastings was not only a great English but a great European event.'[1] With that year began the history of the English nation as well as that of the English language. While the Normans brought all the legacy of Latin Europe to the barbarian island, there began the rise of a people which, after the Hundred Years' War, retreated from the continent, and eventually were prepared to repudiate the Roman Church, to become a nation and to rule the seas. England no longer belonged to Europe, or it is perhaps safer to say, while still being part of Europe she lived a distinct life of her own. This, too, rested on the European heritage and, in fact, added to it in the most spectacular way. What would

[1] G. M. Trevelyan, *History of England,* 102.

Europe be without England's creation of free political institutions and without the poetry and drama of the Elizabethans?
And yet, the Channel separated England from Europe.

The examples of the countries farthest in the East and West
of Europe, Russia and the Slavs on the one hand, Britain on
the other, do not refute the fact that everything European
depends on the ancient heritage. Certainly, its influence
varied, but variety is the necessary expression of a living entity.
Only when what is inherited has become a dead letter, does it
cease to change and to influence the world. To give proof of
the immense influence of the ancient world on Europe is a
task undertaken by so many, competent in the various branches
of history, that the only embarrassing thing about it is its
abundance. I shall not add to it. Whoever knows anything
of the history of European art or literature or philosophy,
whoever knows anything of his own language or of the law and
administration of his own country, whoever aims at higher
moral standards for the individual or the community — one
and all cannot escape from the legacy of the ancient world.
Monsieur Jourdain did not know that he had spoken prose all
his life. But how many people are aware that they are speaking
and thinking in terms of 'Greek', 'Roman', 'Jewish', or
'Christian'?

EUROPE

We saw that Britain and Russia were, in a sense, remote
from Europe. This did not result from a weakening of the
ancient heritage; it was due to the impact of other forces. To
trace and describe them would be beyond my task and far
beyond my power. Only this can be said: Europe, throughout
the ages, was the battlefield on which East and West met. In
an earlier passage of this book I spoke of Europe as lying
between East and West, between Asia and America. She also
lies between Russia and Britain, both of whom were and are
creative partners in that inner tension between East and West
which was typical of Europe from her beginnings. This
tension is expressed in innumerable events and issues of
European history, and it is only natural that it is strongest in
the centre and weakest on the wings. Thus, Britain and Russia
are less European than the nations nearer the centre, because

they did not share the experience of some of the outstanding events of European history.

The experience of common history is another essential factor in the formative process of Europe. The Middle Ages were conscious of this in the unity of a Christian Europe. The disruption of Christian unity and the growth of the European nations destroyed that unity, but did not destroy the continuity of common experience. Although history now tended to break up into its national units, it still embraced them all. Unity was followed by variety, but the colours of the rainbow are parts of the same sunlight. Europe broke up, but it was still Europe. New vigour filled the Classical heritage, and the Humanist came into his own. Christianity went through the terrible dissensions and wars of the sixteenth and seventeenth centuries. All this was common history, and also common heritage. The distribution of the ancient legacy varied; there were stronger and weaker impacts on this or that nation or age. There was also a change of emphasis on this or that part of the heritage. This, to some minds, is actually the main issue. They realize the contrasts within the heritage rather than the common front against the danger from without. I shall say a few words about this later. First, I want to point out certain limitations of the debt which Europe owes to the whole heritage of the ancient world. But while we try to avoid too sweeping statements and to set limits, we can do so only because of the overwhelming grandeur and richness of that heritage. In all the variety the unity, I believe, remains unmistakable. There is a peculiar affinity between figures as different in character, time and surroundings as, say, Lorenzo the Magnificent, Henry VIII, and Peter the Great, or, on the other hand, Ignatius Loyola, Cromwell, and Robespierre. It may not be easy to define those affinities, but I do not think we can deny them.

The experience of common history means the sharing of contemporary events and of essential aspects of life. The latter are, we believe, largely shaped by a common heritage. But this heritage goes beyond the conscious and obvious debt we owe to Christianity and the Classical world. There may be something that is found to be essential in the pattern of the European mind, even though it may be difficult or impossible to trace the moment or even the nature of its influence. What exactly, for example, was and is the part played by Chinese art and thought, or Indian philosophy, in the development of the European mind? What difference did it make to Europe that the art and music of the negroes became the fashion of the early twentieth century? Is it mainly the strangeness of exotic civilizations that at certain times makes them dear to Europe, or is it not perhaps some kind of secret affinity and kinship that suddenly finds its expression?

I consider it sufficient to put such questions, and shall not try to answer them. But I should like to point out one example of a similar and yet different kind, of an affinity to Europe at a time when no Europe and even none of her known ancestry yet existed. Is it mere chance that the most perfect illustration of the ideal of female beauty as cherished by our own times dates from the fourteenth century b.c.? Nefretete (Plate IV) was the young wife of the 'heretic' Pharaoh Amenhotep IV or Ikhnaton, whose ugly and nervous face gives the same impression of 'modernity' as the beauty of his queen. The man who founded a new monotheistic religion and was able to express himself in a language which at once reminds us of some of the Psalms, had a truly revolutionary mind in a weak and decadent body. The god of his creed, the sun, was not a mythological god. His symbol was the disk of the sun with its rays, as everyone saw it, radiating life and energy to all nature — men, animals and plants alike. This symbol reveals a truly philosophical, if not scientific, view of the universe. Ikhnaton's new city (El-Amarna), dedicated to the service of the new god, was planned as a pleasant place with green gardens, and a palace full of naturalistic paintings of plants and animals, surrounded by stables and other agricultural buildings — the dream of a man, refined and even surfeited with civilization, who tried to create artificially a life close to nature and to the god to whom nature owed its life. This artificial creation sprang from a genuine source, and the deeply personal and human touch in Ikhnaton's poetry and the intimate pictures of his family life are as unique as they are touching. Little is left of the traditional pomp and solemnity of a Pharaoh. A brother's voice speaks to us over many centuries, a soul struggling for truth and beauty. Here in Egypt, a thousand years before Socrates, lived a European who deserved the name if ever one did.

The essence of Europe is a matter of the mind, and it has been called 'a condition of thought'.[1] This is true, if only we make our conception of 'thought' wide enough. Generally, when we try to point out the essential features of a historical epoch, we turn first to its expression in politics. But politics result from the impact of temporary forces on general and eternal ideas. It is in the particular form which in a certain age is given to these ideas that we learn to understand the spirit of that age. Therefore, we must ultimately take account of its beliefs and thoughts. They are partly, but by no means completely, found in literature. A Greek temple, a Gothic cathedral, a Holbein portrait, express just as much the spirit of their ages as the constitution of a State, the structure of its society, or, on the other hand, the treatise of a great philosopher, or a great poem. We speak of the age of Absolutism or the age of the National State. But we also speak of the age of the Reformation and the age of Enlightenment. We speak of the Periclean or the Augustan age, but we could also speak of the age of the *Divina Commedia* or Michelangelo's Moses or *The Marriage of Figaro*, or, on the other hand, of the age of Plato's *Republic*, or Thomas Aquinas' *Summa Theologica*, or Kant's 'Categorical Imperative'. All this is part of 'Europe', her great and common tradition, the common 'condition of thought'.

Let me try to expound one or two of these examples. When we look at Michelangelo's Moses, we naturally admire the statue as a great masterpiece of art. We see the result of the labour of a genius who mastered the stone and filled it with life and vigour and beauty. The movement of the body, the expression of the face, the fall of the garment — everything is perfect because it is subject to aesthetic laws which ruled the sculptor's mind and hand. It is also possible to compare the statue with other works of art, whether Michelangelo's own or those of others, whether Italian or Roman or Greek; in other words, the work is an event in the history of art. But then there is quite a different approach. The artist, both consciously and unconsciously, expressed certain ideas, certain beliefs and thoughts. The old wonderful story of the great lawgiver of Israel, of his closeness to God, of his love for his people and his wrath over its sins, has come to life again. The legacy

[1] Charles Morgan, *Reflections in a Mirror*, 35.

was there, and filled the artist's mind. But he created a Moses who was *his* Moses, the great man of his own age, a man with the titanic strength and self-reliance of the epoch of the Renaissance. Intended to adorn the tomb of a Pope, the statue was 'Christian'. But we realize that it is the Christianity of the Renaissance Church — just as in the figure of Christ in the *Last Judgment* in the Sistine Chapel: Hercules rather than Christ. There is all the greatness of Renaissance Man, but also his lack of humility. One glance back to Giotto's frescoes or a Byzantine mosaic, and we feel how the spirit of the age burns in every one of these great works of art, and how every age stands in the great European tradition.

Kant discovered the 'Categorical Imperative' as the ultimate moral law: 'Act only on that maxim whereby thou canst at the same time will that it should become a universal law.' This is, as far as one pronouncement can be, the quintessence of European ethics, and its earliest ancestors are, I believe, the 'Know thyself' at the temple of Delphi and 'Love thy neighbour as thyself'. Kant's law implies the whole tradition of humanistic individualism as well as the belief in a universal law, whether natural or divine. If later philosophers have challenged Kant's ethics in one aspect or another, this only shows that his work, too, is a product of his own age, while at the same time the result of many centuries of the history of the European mind.

The conceptions of Christianity and Humanism cover what are essentially two aspects of the same European standards, by which man is recognized as an individual with an immortal soul. But, as I said before, there was and is an open and sometimes violent conflict between those who believe, above all, in the freedom and greatness of man, and those who see in man mainly God's creature. The pride of the humanistic view appears a deadly sin to many Christians, and Christian humility a contemptible weakness, if not hypocrisy, to many humanists. The nineteenth century saw much of the latter attitude, recent times more of the former. It has become a widespread view that Humanism has had its day and used it badly enough. Monsieur Maritain writes:[1] 'La raison a été mise en péril par l'adoration de la raison, l'humanisme par l'humanisme anthropocentrique, par l'humanisme manqué.'

[1] Jacques Maritain, *Le Crépuscule de la Civilization*, 20.

And Protestant voices join with the Catholic one. Mr. G. O. Griffith, for instance, in his important book *Interpreters of Man* (1943) speaks of the end of the Renaissance view of man. The 'failure' of the nineteenth century has become a failure of Man as made in the image of God, as 'man being essentially divine'. The historian will shrink from the idea that five centuries of human history, however brilliant, were one complete mistake, and he may even doubt the utter futility of the much-blamed nineteenth century. We have just begun to emerge — at least we hope so — from a terrible trough between the waves, but I cannot believe that the new crest will be a new mediaevalism. Quite apart from the fact that science will play a decisive part in the shaping of the future and in particular of its humanism, the great torchlights of human ideas which lit the way from the 'dark ages' and found their popular and effective, though superficial, expression in the slogans of the French Revolution, have been dimmed but are not extinguished. Liberty more than ever stirs the mind and heart of men, but it is no longer the merely political freedom of the citizen, it is the freedom of man as a social and spiritual being. Equality, much misused and therefore abused, still stands as a signpost, in fact as the same signpost which for two thousand years has pointed towards the Kingdom of God. It is the equality of men, not in society where equality is but a bad dream, but before God. And Fraternity, brotherliness — does it not stand before us as the same ideal that appeared in the days when Greeks and Jews for the first time thought of the brotherhood of mankind? This ideal is not only unfulfilled as an ideal must be, but has hardly even been approached and is therefore the ideal of which the world is most in need.

Whatever the future may bring, we must pray that nothing essential will be lost of the great and common heritage. Europe cannot live without the Bible nor without Homer and Plato. If anything has been wrong in the development of Humanism, it has been, on the one hand, its alliance with materialism, and on the other the fact that man made God in his own image. The first fact led to an overwhelming preponderance of the materialistic point of view in what probably is the most urgent task of our times, the adjustment of the social position of the 'common man'. The other, a real offspring of the anthropomorphism of the Greeks and, in fact, of the

R

Christian Church, led to the replacement of God by the Superman.

This, of course, brings us to Nietzsche, who more than anyone else claimed to be a 'good European'. He had a right to say this, even in his fight against Christianity. Nietzsche was not only the prophet of Dionysus, but also the greatest moralist of the nineteenth century, and Christianity needs its heretic moralists as well as its priests and prophets. But there is an Anti-Christ who is also Anti-Man. The nihilism of Nazi Germany raged against Christian and Classical standards and education alike. Hitler gave Mussolini Nietzsche's works as a present. Poor Nietzsche, who hated nothing more than the nationalism and anti-semitism of the *petit bourgeois*! What would he have said of the nationalism and the right of self-determination of every people, large and small? What of the attempts at shaping the world according to the desires of the masses instead of leading the masses into a world built on eternal principles? Europe and her nations will live only if these nations acknowledge the overruling power of the moral values, expressed in the Decalogue and the Sermon on the Mount, and accept the intellectual heritage of Greece and Rome.

Europe to-day is in mortal danger, in body and mind. In the midst of our fears and hopes we naturally look to America. Will it really be the 'New World'? Some people think that the exodus of hundreds of great scientists and scholars from Europe to America will be a repetition of the story of A.D. 1453 when the Greek scholars fled from Constantinople. Have the last few years set up the signal for an American Renaissance? It is a hope, but a hope born of despair. The American contribution to our civilization has been great and will grow even greater in times to come. And yet, we may ask whether American civilization has the foundations necessary for a task like that performed by Italy and Europe in the fifteenth century. I do not know the answer. The only thing I do know is that Europe is in danger of losing her heritage and her future.

There is still hope that the danger may be overcome. But that can happen only if and when the common and twofold heritage of Christianity and Humanism survives, so that it will shape, and be shaped by, the common experiences of future history. If Christianity and Humanism keep fully alive, this will mean that they are prepared for eternal change and eternal re-birth. Neither the Christianity nor the Humanism of the future will be that of the present and the past, but it is in their repeated union rather than in the victory of one over the other that Europe will prevail. Europe can say with Nietzsche: '*Nur wer sich wandelt, ist mit mir verwandt.*' But as long as she is able to change her true traditions, and yet, through every new experience of her common history, to preserve them, she will survive.

I should like to end this essay, and thus the book, with a short essay not from my own pen. I do not fully agree with its historical interpretations, but I do believe that it expresses something of that union of religion and humanism for which we are hoping in the future.[1]

VIRTUE IS KNOWLEDGE

The wise men of ancient Greece set out in search of the Supreme Good, which, in the Greek fashion, they called Virtue. The ascent was attempted by various means, and there were various ways in which the goal was defined. But the wisest of them had an answer which, in the true spirit of philosophy, seemed to settle the question. He said that Virtue is Knowledge.

Knowledge, thus linked with Virtue, cannot have the vague meaning of general knowledge. It can only mean the definite knowledge of what is good and what is evil. It must, consequently, mean that man, having such knowledge, chooses the right and rejects the evil. Only thus, but thus clearly, can Virtue be Knowledge.

It follows that the Supreme Good, as defined by Socrates, is not Faith, nor Hope, nor Charity, nor can it be achieved by good works. It is gained by the force of the human spirit or, to be more precise, of the human intellect. Virtue is the outcome of reason as bound up with Man.

It sounds proud, almost overbearing. It is reminiscent of the maxim of Protagoras that 'Man is the measure of all things'. Such was the philosophical creed in the fifth century B.C., when men devoted their lives to the finding of Truth, Happiness, and, above all, of Virtue. They were themselves representatives of the highest development of human reason, and they believed in Virtue as the highest goal of the human

[1] The essay was written by my wife without any thought of having it printed.

mind. It is only logical that Socrates, the wisest of the wise, defined Virtue as Knowledge.

But it was the same Socrates who said of himself that the only thing he knew for certain was that he knew nothing. Does not this saying contradict his other maxim, and does it not in its supreme humility, separate Socrates from the over-confidence of his fellow-philosophers? Only in putting together the two verdicts as two halves which make up one whole can we understand what Socrates meant. It is true, he believed that there is nothing more sublime than the human intellect, and that therefore the most sublime good cannot be achieved by any other means. But the conclusions which he drew for himself are as moving as they are illuminating. On the lips of the man who, though in wisdom surpassing all mortals, confessed to knowing nothing, the sentence that Virtue is Knowledge sounds proud no more; it is a statement no longer; it either expresses resignation or becomes at best a postulate. Socrates was neither triumphant nor optimistic; he was sceptical, he was pessimistic, he was a Greek.

This becomes even clearer when his words are compared with the words of the Bible: 'And the Lord God commanded Man, saying: Of every tree of the garden thou mayest eat freely, but of the tree of the knowledge of good and evil, thou shalt not eat of it.' Because Man had put forth his hand to take of that tree, he was driven out of Paradise. For it is not for Man to 'become as one of us, to know good and evil'. Virtue is Knowledge, said the Greek. Knowledge is Crime, says the Lord. Man shall not know what is right or wrong, what is Good and what is Evil.

Here is the difference between the wisdom of the Greeks and the religion of Israel. The gods of Olympus had none of the severity of the God of the Old Testament. Neither were they ethically superior to men. Hence the wise were led to believe in the Human Spirit as the revelation of the Supreme Good. Here also is the difference between freedom of thought and obedience to the commandments of God. But one man overcame the difference. It was the same voice that spoke to Socrates and to the children of Israel, to them from without, to him from within — the voice that speaks throughout the ages, telling mankind that Virtue is the knowledge that we know nothing.

INDEX

(Numbers in brackets refer to notes)

253

INDEX

Cleisthenes, 90, 92, 112-14, 125, 129f., 140, 143
cleruchy, 116-43
Clodius Albinus, D., 213, 219
coins, 105-15, 118, 123f., 137, 185f., 190, 192, 196, 209, 212
colonization, 43-5, 116-43
Commodus, 212f.
Constantine, 217f.
Corcyra, 36, 182, 185
Corinth, 10, 40f., 44, 47, 72
Crete, 7f., 10-12, 16, 24, 31, 36, 46f., 93 (2), 223. See Minoan
Crithote, 126, 137
Curtius, E., 54, 224

DARIUS (CODOMANNES), 170, 172, 174
Deianeira, 145, 148-54
deification, 73, 76f., 175, 183-97
Delian League, see Athenian League
Delphi, 32, 112, 129, 182f., 184, 187, 248
Demeter, 179, 182-5, 191f., 194, 196
Demetrius of Phaleron, 183, 193
Demetrius Poliorcetes, 179-98
democracy, 65, 89-93, 94f., 97, 103, 113f., 183, 194
Demosthenes, 68, 140, 168, 224
Dike, 70-7, 79, 82, 84, 86, 92
Diocletian, 213, 216f., 219, 223
Dionysus, 146, 190-3, 195f.
Doloncians, 120, 123, 126f., 143
Domitian, 208f., 212
Dorians, 9, 16f., 24, 26, 47, 96, 99, 134
Dostoevsky, 20, 243
Draco, 107
Drusus, 201, 206
Dual Principate, 200-19
Duris, 180f., 195
dyarchy, 199f., 204, 206f., 216, 219f.
dysnomia, 84f., 88

ECBATANA, 172
economics, 23, 39, 41, 56f., 64f., 100f., 102, 106f., 127, 224f.
Egypt, 7f., 14-16, 23, 26, 30, 32, 94, 170f., 173, 176f., 196, 223, 225, 240, 246
Eirene, 70-3, 77, 86, 92f.
Elaeus, 122, 126, 129, 137
Elagabalus, 214
Eleusis, 182, 184f., 192
Elgin, Lord, 69
Empedocles, 187
England, 242-4
ephors, 80, 91, 95, 97f., 101
Ephorus, 121, 138

Epicurus, 162, 188
Eros, 57, 99
Eteobutadae, 108f., 113
Etruscans, 18, 22-8
Euboea, 9, 37, 107, 116, 134
Eucleia, 73f., 92
Euhemerism, 189
Eunomia, 70-93
Euripides, 65, 146f., 152, 158-66, 168
Europe, 4-6, 8, 17f., 20f., 30-5, 54, 58, 175, 178, 234-51
Eurystheus, 160f.
Ezra, 223, 225

FRANCE, 238, 242

GAIUS (CALIGULA), 206f.
Galba, 210
Germany, 5, 13, 24, 234, 242
Gerusia, 78, 97
Geta, 213, 219
Goethe, 4, 29, 243
Gomme, A. W., 63-9
Gordian III, 214
Greece, 7, 9, 23, 29-52, 69, 179, 181, 239f., 242
Greek religion, 11, 16, 49, 59f., 70-3, 148-57, 161f., 175, 180f., 183-98
Greek State, see Polis
Grote, G., 180, 224

HADRIAN, 209f.
Harrison, Jane, 238
Hasebroek, J., 65, 127
Hawkes, C. F. C., 239
Hecataeus of Miletus, 32, 123, 237f.
Hegel, 59, 230
Helios, 195f.
Hellenistic, 46, 49, 93, 167, 176f., 180-98, 207-10, 212, 215, 224, 227, 241
helots, 50, 96f., 98, 100, 102
Hephaestia, 128, 133
Hera, 144, 158, 160-2
Heracles, 99f., 144-66, 169, 191
Heraclitus, 17
Herculius, 216f.
Herodotus, 24, 32, 79, 91 (3), 92, 111, 113, 117-41, 237
Hesiod, 16, 36, 70-7, 79, 82, 84-6, 188
Hestiaea, 134f.
Hipparchus, 89
Hippias, 89, 112f., 118
Hitler, 167, 178, 250
Hittites, 7, 9, 13, 15f., 23f., 26, 196
Homer, 4-6, 10, 14f., 17, 25, 29, 48f., 74-6, 90 (2), 99, 110, 144, 187f., 192, 223, 249

GREEK HISTORY

AN ARNO PRESS COLLECTION

Aeschinis. **Aeschinis Orationes.** E Codicibus Partim Nunc Primum Excussis, Edidit Scholia ex Parte Inedita, Adicoit Ferdinandus Schultz. 1865.

Athonian Studies; Presented to William Scott Ferguson (*Harvard Studies in Classical Philology*, Supplement Vol. I). 1040.

Austin, R[eginald] P. **The Stoichedon Style in Greek Inscriptions.** 1938.

Berve, Helmut. **Das Alexanderreich:** Auf Prosopographischer Grundlage. Ersterband: Darstellung; Zweiterband: Prosopoghaphie. 1926. 2 volumes in one.

Croiset, Maurice. **Aristophanes and the Political Parties at Athens.** Translated by James Loeb. 1909.

Day, John. **An Economic History of Athens Under Roman Domination.** 1942.

Demosthenes. **Demosthenes,** Volumina VIII et IX: Scholia Graeca ex Codicibus Aucta et Emendata, ex recensione Gulielmi Dindorfii. 2 volumes. 1851.

Ehrenberg, Victor. **Aspects of the Ancient World:** Essays and Reviews. 1946.

Finley, Moses I. **Studies in Land and Credit in Ancient Athens, 500-200 B.C.:** The Horos Inscriptions. 1952.

Glotz, Gustave. **La Solidarité de la Famille dans le Droit Criminel en Grèce.** 1904.

Graindor, Paul, **Athènes Sous Hadrien.** 1934.

Grosmann, Gustav. **Politische Schlagwörter aus der Zeit des Peloponnesischen Krieges.** 1950.

Henderson, Bernard W. **The Great War Between Athens and Sparta.** 1927.

Herodotus. **Herodotus: The Fourth, Fifth, and Sixth Books.** With Introduction, Notes, Appendices, Indices, Maps by Reginald Walter Macan. 1895. 2 volumes in one.

Herodotus. **Herodotus: The Seventh, Eighth, and Ninth Books.** With Introduction, Text, Apparatus, Commentary, Appendices, Indices, Maps by Reginald Walter Macan. 1908. 3 volumes in two.

Jacoby, Felix. **Apollodors Chronik.** Eine Sammlung der Fragmente (*Philologische Untersuchungen,* Herausgegeben von A. Kiessling und U. v. Wilamowitz-Moellendorff. Sechzehntes Heft). 1902.

Jacoby, Felix. **Atthis:** The Local Chronicles of Ancient Athens. 1949.

Ledl, Artur. **Studien zur Alteren Athenischen Verfassungsgeschichte.** 1914.

Lesky, Albin. **Thalatta:** Der Weg der Griechen Zum Meer. 1947.

Ollier, Francois. **Le Mirage Spartiate.** Etude sur l'idéalisation de Sparte dans l'antiquité Greque de l'origine Jusqu'aux Cyniques and Etude sur l'idéalisation de Sparte dans l'antiquité Greque du Début de l'école Cynique Jusqu'à la Fin de la Cité. 1933/1934. 2 volumes in one.

Ryffel, Heinrich. ΜΕΤΑΒΟΛΗ ΠΟΛΙΤΕΙΩΝ Der Wandel der Staatsverfassungen (*Noctes Romanae.* Forschungen Uber die Kultur der Antike, Herausgegeben von Walter Wili, #2). 1949.

Thucydides. **Scholia in Thucydidem:** Ad Optimos Codices Collata, edidit Carolus Hude. 1927.

Toepffer, Iohannes. **Attische Genealogie.** 1889.

Tscherikower, V. **Die Hellenistischen Städtegründungen von Alexander dem Grossen bis auf die Römerzeit** (*Philologus,* Zeitschrift fur das Klassische Alterum, Herausgegeben von Albert Rehm. Supplementband XIX, Heft 1). 1927.

West, Allen Brown. **The History of the Chalcidic League** (*Bulletin of the University of Wisconsin,* No. 969, History Series, Vol. 4, No. 2). 1918.

Woodhouse, William J. **Aetolia:** Its Geography, Topography, and Antiquities. 1897.

Wüst, Fritz R. **Philipp II. von Makedonien und Griechenland in den Jahren von 346 bis 338** (*Münchener Historische Abhandlungen.* Erste Reihe: Allgemeine und Politische Geschichte, Herausgegeben von H. Günter, A. O. Meyer und K. A. v. Müller. 14, Heft). 1938.